TWO–TIER COMPENSATION STRUCTURES

Their Impact On UNIONS EMPLOYERS and EMPLOYEES

James E. Martin

in collaboration with
Thomas D. Heetderks

1990

W. E. UPJOHN INSTITUTE for Employment Research
Kalamazoo, Michigan

Library of Congress Cataloging-in-Publication Data

Martin, James. 1943–
    Two-tier compensation structures : their impact on unions,
employer, and employees / James E. Martin, in collaboration with
Thomas D. Heetderks.
        p.   cm.
    Includes bibliographical references.
    ISBN 0-88099-087-2. — ISBN 0-88099-088-0 (pbk.)
    1. Two-tier wage payment systems—United States.   I. Heetderks.
Thomas D.   II. Title.
HD4928.T932U65   1990
331.2'16—dc20   ∞   89-48881
                                                           CIP

PREFACE

The basis for this monograph grew from my efforts to explore employee attitudes toward new labor-management issues. As a result of those efforts over the past few years, I became increasingly aware of both the controversy surrounding tiered compensation systems and the relationship between tiers and employee attitudes. Given the plethora of articles concerning tiers and the differing opinions expressed, I saw a need for a comprehensive treatment such as this to summarize what others have stated and to assess the long-term impact of tiers at one company.

The project was made possible by the primary financial sponsorship of the W.E. Upjohn Institute for Employment Research. Also, substantial support was received from my ANR Pipeline Company Business Administration Fellowship. The following units within Wayne State University provided additional support: the Master of Arts in Industrial Relations program, the School of Business Administration, and the College of Urban, Labor, and Metropolitan Affairs. Administrative assistance was received from a number of units on campus, but particularly from the Center for Urban Studies and from my department, the Department of Management and Organization Sciences, whose able secretary, Dawn Havard, coordinated the typing of numerous drafts of the chapters and complex tables.

Although only two names appear on the cover of this book, in reality this project represents the efforts of many people. I would like to take this space to thank those individuals who were instrumental in the completion of the project.

First, I would like to thank the many employees, union leaders, managers, and neutrals who were interviewed, as well as those employees who completed the survey. While the individuals in these groups must remain anonymous, I must express my gratitude for their cooperation and support.

Second, students from Wayne State University assisted in all phases of the project. The following School of Business Administration students were involved in the research as part of their course work: William Barnes, Pasquale Cassasanta, Lawrence Cellini, and William Sturgeon. In addition, the following Industrial/Organizational Psychology doctoral students who served as research assistants were heavily involved in this project: Nannette Black, Ruth Berthiaume, John Gilbert, Raymond Lee, and Melanie Peterson.

Third, I would like to thank the staff of the Upjohn Institute, particularly Timothy Hunt and H. Allan Hunt, for their considerable support throughout the completion of this project, and Judith Gentry, who copy edited the manuscript.

Fourth, every research project of this magnitude certainly benefits from one who contributes tremendously to all phases of the project. As this project progressed, that role was taken by Thomas Heetderks, a doctoral candidate in industrial/organizational psychology. His extensive theoretical and empirical contributions to this monograph were indispensable and led to the resultant collaboration.

Finally, I must thank my family, who bore the brunt of the many weekends and long nights associated with my work on this project. I appreciate their tolerance and support.

James E. Martin
Detroit, MI
November 1989

THE AUTHORS

James E. Martin is Professor of Management and Industrial Relations in the School of Business Administration, Wayne State University, where he has been since 1976. He received his Ph.D. and M.B.A. degrees from Washington University, St. Louis, Missouri. He has served as consultant on preparation for collective bargaining, coordination of human resource policies, and union-management cooperation to various business, labor, and government agencies. Dr. Martin has published widely in the areas of commitment, union-management cooperation, and concession bargaining. He is co-author of *Readings and Cases in Labor Relations and Collective Bargaining* (Addison-Wesley, 1985). His published articles have appeared in journals such as *Personnel Administrator, Journal of Management, Academy of Management Journal, Monthly Labor Review, Industrial and Labor Relations Review,* and *Journal of Labor Research.*

Thomas D. Heetderks is a Ph.D. candidate in industrial/organizational psychology at Wayne State University. He received an M.A. degree in psychology from Wayne State University. His research interests are in the areas of compensation decisionmaking, job evaluation, and benefits.

CONTENTS

1 An Introduction to Tiered Compensation Structures 1
   Definition and Classification of Tiers 2
   A Framework of Labor-Management Relations 9
   Views of Tiered Compensation Structures 11
   Plan of the Book 15
   Notes 18

2 Tiered Compensation Structures in Practice 21
   Characteristics and Frequency of Tiers 21
   Sector Differences in Relation to Strategy and Wage Changes ... 26
   Industry Groups in which Tiers are Prominent............... 32
   Potential Benefits of Tiers 39
   Potential Problems and Concerns Associated with Tiers 43
   The Incidence of Tiers 53
   Notes 61

3 Labor-Management Relations in the Retail Food Industry 63
   History of the Retail Food Industry Through the 1960s 64
   Market Saturation and Increased Competition................ 69
   Changes in Bargaining Process and Outcomes 72
   Conclusions 78
   Notes 79

4 Tiers and the Mayway Food Market Company 81
   Historical Development of Mayway's
      Union-Management Relations 81
   State-Level Environment 87
   State Bargaining Developments 94
   Summary... 103
   Notes 104

5 Sample Characteristics, Research Design, and Data Analysis 107
   Area Descriptions 107
   Characteristics of the Surveyed Stores...................... 114
   Survey Development 118
   Survey Administration and Response....................... 119
   Tier Forms at Mayway 121
   Data Analysis 126
   Summary... 128
   Notes 129

6 Research Questions Concerning Tiers 133
  Research Question Development 134
  Results and Discussion 136
  Concluding Comments. 168
  Notes 168

7 Hypotheses Concerning Tiers 171
  Hypothesis Framework Based on Equity Theory 171
  Hypothesis Development 180
  Results and Discussion 187
  Summary. 200
  Notes 201

8 Summary and Conclusions 203
  Propositions 204
  Costs and Benefits of Tiers at Mayway. 208
  Generalizability of the Mayway Experience with Tiers 210
  Limitations of the Study and Additional Areas for Research 212
  The Future for Tiers 213
  Note 215

Appendix A – Survey items and Response Formats 217
Appendix B – Scales. 227
Appendix C – Tiers and Store Productivity 229

References 237

Index 247

LIST OF TABLES

2.1 Cross-Tabulation of Average Pay Difference Between
    Tiers by Experience with Plan 23
2.2 Two-Tier Wage Settlements, by Industry, 1983–88 24
2.3 First-Year Median Wage Changes in the Manufacturing and
    Service Sectors and Overall Inflation Rate, 1983–1988 28
2.4 Comparison of First-Year Median Wage Increases in All
    Contracts and Two-Tier Contracts by Industry, 1983–84 30

3.1 Overall Inflation Rate and Estimated Negotiated First-Year
    Wage Increases in the Retail Food Industry 74

4.1 Characteristics of the Major Unionized Chains in the State
    in the Mid-1970s and 1986 89
4.2 Top Pay Rates Paid at the End of Selected Years 93

5.1 Selected Characteristics of the Urban Counties Where the
    Surveyed Employees Worked 109
5.2 Selected Characteristics of the Rural Counties Where the
    Surveyed Employees Worked 112
5.3 Selected Economic and Employment Characteristics
    of Urban Area Stores in 1986........................... 115
5.4 Selected Economic and Employment Characteristics
    of Rural Area Stores in 1986 117
5.5 Means of Selected Characteristics of Old and New Stores 118
5.6 Demographic Profile Comparison of Survey
    Respondents and Population 120
5.7 Cross-Tabulation of the Wage-Tier Form with the
    Low and High Levels of the Other Tier Forms 124
5.8 Correlation Matrix of the Tier Forms, Pay Rate,
    and Seniority... 125

6.1 Perceived Possible Reasons for the Original Negotiation of the
    Two-Tier Wage Structure Related to Research Question 1 138
6.2 Perceptions of How Much Various Groups Have Benefited
    from the Two-Tier Wage Structure Related to
    Research Question 2 141
6.3 Perceived Effects of the Two-Tier Wage Structure on
    Employment-Related Outcomes Related to Research
    Question 3... 142

6.4   Analysis of Scales Related to the First Set
of Research Question 146
6.5   Predicted Outcomes of Future Bargaining Over the Two-Tier
Wage Structure Related to Research Question 4 150
6.6   Attitudes Toward Selected Changes in the Tiered Wage
Structure and the Potential Related Outcomes Related
to Research Question 5 154
6.7   Attitudes Toward the Establishment of a Third Wage Tier
and the Potential Related Outcomes Related to
Research Question 5 156
6.8   Attitudes Toward Selected Statements Concerning Two-Tier
Wage Structures Related to Research Question 6 158
6.9   Analyses of Scales Related to the Second Set of
Research Questions 160
6.10 Significant Scale Differences by Area Related to
Research Question 7 164
6.11 Equal Employment Opportunity Items Related to
Research Question 8 167

7.1   Relevant Referents for Employees in Each Tier Group 176
7.2   Behaviors to Restore Equity Variables Testing Hypothesis 1 ... 188
7.3   Behaviors to Restore Equity Variables Testing Hypothesis 2 ... 189
7.4   Work-Related Outcome Variables Testing Hypothesis 3 190
7.5   Perceived Promotion and Employment Opportunity
Variables Testing Hypothesis 4 191
7.6   Commitment and Job Satisfaction Variables Testing
Hypothesis 5 192

C.1   Summary of Mayway Store Characteristics 232

LIST OF FIGURES

1.1   Permanent Tiers 3
1.2   Temporary Tiers 4
1.3   Rates of General Merchandise Clerks on Different Tiers
Hired at Different Times 8

4.1   Time Chart of Major Events Surrounding the
Bargaining Rounds 92

1
An Introduction to Tiered Compensation Structures

The purpose of this monograph is to examine the impact of tiered compensation structures on unions, employers, and employees. Several methods were used to accomplish this goal. First, an extensive review of the literature was conducted for the purpose of summarizing what others have found concerning tiers. A detailed study was conducted at one large company where various forms of tiers had been in existence for many years, making it possible to assess the long-term impact of tiers. As part of that case study, rank-and-file employees were surveyed as to their attitudes concerning tiers and topics related to tiered compensation structures. Survey items were derived from the literature and from additional information obtained in interviews. The survey was designed to explore eight research questions related to tiers and to test five hypotheses. These will be discussed in more detail at the end of this chapter.

Chapter 1 provides an introduction to tiered compensation structures. Tiered compensation structures are defined and a means for classifying tiers is introduced. In addition, a framework of the labor-management relations process is presented, focusing on the influences that may affect the development of tiers. Finally, two views of the role tiers play within the industrial relations system are presented. The chapter closes with a section that briefly outlines the organization of the monograph. Chapter 2 completes the introduction to tiers by examining the characteristics and relative frequencies of tiers, how they have functioned in practice, and trends associated with the number of existing tiered compensation structures.

Definition and Classification of Tiers

Tiers are defined as the result of a compensation system change that adds lower compensation levels for workers who either change positions or begin employment after a certain date, usually the date when the union-management contract becomes effective.[1] These employees perform the same or equivalent duties as workers employed prior to that date, but they receive less compensation. This definition extends the concept of tiers beyond two-tiered wage structures, upon which most writers have focused, to other forms of tiers directly affecting compensation.

Types of Tiered Compensation Structures

Tiered compensation structures can be classified into two categories: permanent or temporary (Jacoby and Mitchell 1986; Ross 1985). Under a "permanent" plan, the "new" or low-tier employees are compensated on a separate and lower scale than the high-tier employees.

Figure 1.1, adapted from the work of Cappelli and Sherer (1987), illustrates for permanent tiers the compensation levels of employees on each tier with differing levels of seniority. The compensation of the high- and low-tier employees is represented by segments AB and CD respectively. For a high-tier employee, point A represents a compensation level which exists at the time of the implementation of tiers. For a low-tier employee, point C represents a starting compensation level existing at any time after the implementation of tiers. Employees on the separate tiers do not have identical seniority at the same time. For example, one year after tiers are implemented, all high-tier employees have seniority of one year or more, while all low-tier employees have seniority of less than one year. Examined cross-sectionally, it can be seen that the compensation level of the low-tier employees, represented by line CD, will never equal that of the high-tier employees, represented by line AB, regardless of how long the low-tier employees remain with the company, unless the labor contract is changed. With permanent tiers, when the contract is negotiated there is no understanding by the parties that the tiers will merge at some date in the future.

Figure 1.1
Permanent Tiers

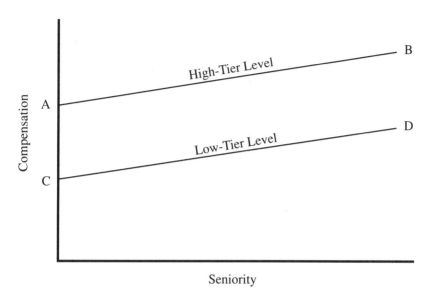

In figure 1.2, also adapted from the work of Cappelli and Sherer (1987), the compensation level for the new employees on the low tier under a "temporary" tiered compensation structure is represented by segment CD. If these employees remain with the company for a given period of time, their compensation level will eventually merge with the higher-compensation level of the high-tier employees (represented by segment AD) as a result of progression adjustments (at point D). Previous "high-" and "low-" tier employees would then be on the same compensation scale, which is represented by segment DB. At that time, there would no longer be two separate tiers. The entry-level compensation for all employees would then be at point C, and all employees would be on the compensation scale represented by line CDB.

It should be noted that the concept that underlies temporary tiers is not a new one. For example, in many industries there are often wage progressions of varying length through which employees pass before they attain the top pay rate for their job class. Apprentices in the construction trades are an example of traditional wage progressions. Although the concepts underlying temporary tiers and the traditional wage progressions are similar, their usage differs in two respects. With temporary tiers, for employees hired after a certain date, some portion of the wage scale is lowered below that which existed for employees hired prior to that date. In addition, the time it takes low-tier employees to reach the top rate may be lengthened, therefore slowing down the rate of increase in compensation relative to that of the high-tier employees. For temporary plans, the length of time prior to the merger with the high-tier rates is predetermined.

Figure 1.2
Temporary Tiers

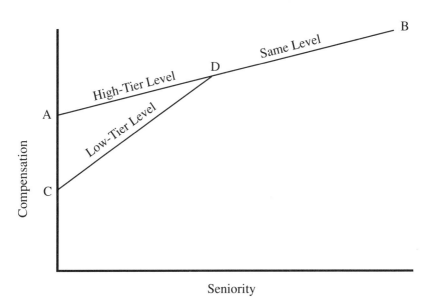

While permanent and temporary wage tiers are distinguished in theory, in practice the demarcation between them can become blurred (Jacoby and Mitchell 1986). All tiers are subject to the collective bargaining process[2] and thus may be altered or removed from the contract in any future bargaining settlement. Further, temporary tiered agreements where the low-tier scale merges into the high-tier scale during the term of the contract in which they were implemented have different implications from those that do not merge within that time period. Ross (1985) noted that temporary plans with such a ''long progression to parity that the delay may seem eternal,'' (p. 82) represent a third classification of tiered structures. Jacoby and Mitchell stated that if the period for merger is sufficiently long, few employees are likely to work long enough to reach the high-tier rates. They also noted that if the merger date is set after the contract expires, the date may be postponed, perhaps indefinitely, in future bargaining.[3]

Forms of Tiered Compensation Structures

In addition to being classified as temporary or permanent, tiered compensation may also be classified into several forms. Tier forms manifest themselves when lower compensation is implemented for employees hired after a certain date, for example, (1) affecting either wages or benefits within the same job classification, (2) affecting new job classifications with the same or very similar duties as already existing job classifications, or (3) affecting part-time positions compared to full-time positions in the same job classification. It should be noted that in employment settings where more than one tier form exists, employees may be concurrently on multiple tier forms, and within each tier form, an employee may be compensated at either a high or low level.[4]

Wage Tiers

Tiers with different wage scales for employees in the same job classification are the most prevalent form of tiers and are generally what is referred to by the term ''two-tier wage structures.'' With wage tiers, workers employed after a certain date are placed on a lower wage scale than previously hired employees. Data from both Essick (1987) and Thomas (1988) suggest that for a company or contract, the most common average pay difference between the high- and low-wage tiers (as a percentage of the high-tier wage) is in the range of 20 to 29 percent.[5]

Benefit Tiers

Tiers also have been applied to employee benefits, with new employees receiving fewer benefits than high-tier workers. Such benefits may include compensation given to employees in the form of health care, life insurance, holidays, or vacations. A distinction should be made here in benefit compensation between a tiered-employment situation and a straight seniority system. In a tiered-employment situation, the differences in benefits between high- and low-tier employees are based on whether the employee was hired prior to or after the date when the benefit tier was implemented, as opposed to basing benefits only on seniority as under a straight seniority system. Under a benefit tier, an employer could give workers with approximately the same seniority but on different tiers different amounts of vacation time. Thus, a benefit tier takes into account both the fixed date when the tier was established and the employee's seniority level. Under a straight seniority system, all employees receive the given amount of vacation time as specified in their contract for their level of seniority, irrespective of their hire date.

Other Tier Forms

Tiered compensation plans may be classified into other forms, but these forms appear to be far more restricted in their applicability to particular industries than wage and benefit tiers. For example, job-duty tiers arise where new job classifications are created for at least some new employees. The new job classifications generally contain job duties that are similar to job classifications already existing but introduce lower compensation. The most prevalent application of the job-duty tier appears to be in the retail food industry. Here, nonfood clerks and food clerks perform the same tasks with different products, yet the nonfood clerks are paid considerably less (Jacoby and Mitchell 1986; Ross 1985; Wessel 1985). Ross (1985) argues that such employees who do similar tasks in new and "nonconventional" jobs while receiving a new lower rate constitute a "third tier."[6]

Another form of tier exists where new employees are paid less under the same contract while performing the same duties at newly established work locations within the same general geographic region. This tier form, which will be referred to as the location tier, does not appear to be very common, although it does exist in the retail food industry where new locations are established to directly compete with nonunion operations. Manufacturing firms have also implemented location tiers (Wessel 1985).

A tier form that manifests itself through the division of employees into part- or full-time employment groups will be referred to as the "employment status tier." This tier form has the widest application within service-sector industries such as retail foods and airlines where companies frequently have extended hours of operation and often hire part-time employees to assist in servicing regular peak workloads occurring within the workweek. Employment status tiers may arise in several different ways. For example, in some service-sector companies where a progression from part- to full-time status comes only as vacancies occur, new restrictions may be placed on the movement of new employees from part time to full time. Also, the wage progressions may be lengthened for the part-time positions, and/or the previously separate part- and full-time wage progressions may be combined for low-wage tier employees with the newly established wage progression equal to or lower than that of the previous part-time, high-wage tier schedule. Thus, employees would no longer receive an increase when moving from part- to full-time status. Salpukas (1984) states that a new contract could allow the employer to hire part-time employees where none were previously permitted.[7]

An Example of Tiered Wage Rates

Figure 1.3 provides a specific example of the wage rates for one job classification from the company involved in the case study. The figure shows wage rates over time for the general merchandise clerk job classification and illustrates how the wage tier and employment status tier forms (implemented in 1978) may function together in an employment setting. The figure shows that the high-wage tier rates for both the part- and full-time employees were at the same rate ($3.13) in 1978. Note that the two scales diverged in 1980 as the wage progression for the high-wage tier, part-time employees was 24 months versus 36 months for the full-time employees on the high-wage tier.

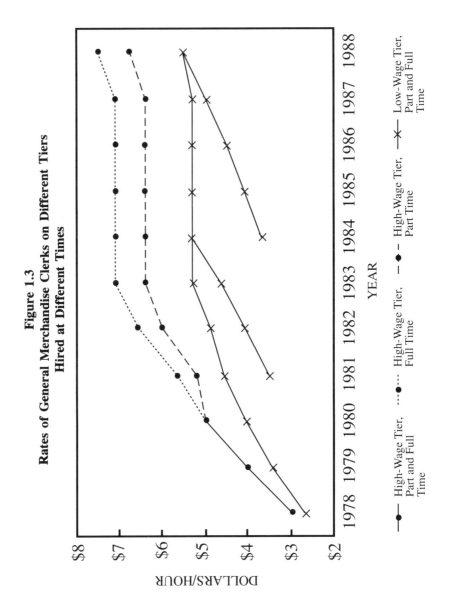

Figure 1.3
Rates of General Merchandise Clerks on Different Tiers
Hired at Different Times

The figure indicates that the part- and full-time low-wage tier employee scales that were implemented in 1978 are identical, with the result that after 1978, it was no longer possible for low-wage tier, part-time general merchandise clerks to receive additional hourly wage increases upon becoming a full-time employee. Also, one can see in figure 1.3 the lengthening of the wage progression, and thus the length of time it took to reach the top rate within the low-wage tier. After the 1984 contract negotiations lengthened the general merchandise pay progressions, new general merchandise clerks took four years to reach the top rate; the general merchandise clerks hired in 1981 took three years. While not evident in the figure, a part-time, high-wage tier employee moving to full-time status would not receive the full-time, high-wage rates that would have been received prior to the implementation of these tier forms.

A Framework of Labor-Management Relations

A brief examination of the labor-management process should assist in understanding the historical and environmental influences on the development of tiers. The following framework is based on the conceptualization of labor-management relations developed by Holley and Jennings (1988). Their framework is comprised of three primary elements. The first element includes the principal participants in the process—employees, union leaders, and management. The second element includes all of the potential influences and pressures that may affect the labor relations process. The third element in the framework is the focal point of the labor relations process—work rules. According to Holley and Jennings, work rules include the rules governing compensation, such as tiers, and the rules that specify obligations and job rights of the employees and employers. The description of work rules provided by Holley and Jennings has been expanded here to include all the union-management agreements, both those written in the labor agreement or contract, and those referred to as implicit or informal. The next two sections will examine three of the principal participants and look at some of the external influences in the process.

Principal Participants

Holley and Jennings noted that since the employees' desires may influence the existence and content of particular work rules, employees should be considered as a principal participant in the labor relations process. They contend that employees may represent the most significant participant category, since they often determine whether a union is even present. Employees also determine whether a negotiated labor agreement is accepted or rejected and whether a threatened strike is actually carried through. Certainly, a goal of employees is to partake in the rewards and successes of their organizations; the goal is specifically directed at increased job security and improved work rules, such as compensation.

Union officials are the second major participant in the labor relations process. One goal of union officials involves keeping job security for the union members, although this goal often becomes more important to the union when management asks for labor cost concessions (Cappelli 1985b). In bargaining, particularly when concessions are granted, this goal may be translated into preserving or increasing the number of jobs available in the bargaining unit. Another goal of the union leadership is to satisfy sufficiently the needs of the different membership groups so as to strengthen the leadership's political position. Instrumental to obtaining this goal is the negotiation of a contract that will be ratified by the membership by a wide margin. Given that the initial negotiation of a tiered compensation structure does not decrease the compensation of the previously hired union members, a contract that implements tiers is usually more easily ratified than a contract involving an across-the-board cut. The simultaneous achievement of these two union goals may not always be possible. For example, to obtain the wages desired by the membership may result in layoffs later on.

A third major participant in the process identified by Holley and Jennings is the management officials who negotiate and administer the labor agreements. The negotiated work rules involve managers at many different organizational levels and functions. The labor relations objectives are developed and coordinated at the corporate and divisional levels to ensure that a particular work rule, such as compensation for a specific job classification, does not adversely influence conditions elsewhere.

While greatly simplified, the goal of the management officials is to satisfy the owners and other managers, mainly by increasing profits.

Obviously, the differences between the participants' goals may result in conflict. For example, Holley and Jennings note that conflict may occur between the members and officers over the specific tactics to be used in accomplishing shared bargaining objectives. Also, factions may develop within an employee group if different goals and work rule preferences are present among the employees. As a result of these member differences, the union leaders may not represent a consensual grouping given the different viewpoints among the membership. Different labor relations priorities may exist between locals within the same international union and between a local union and the international union with which it is affiliated. Thus, the resulting contract represents a compromise among the different participant goals with the parties settling for satisfactory goal attainment concerning work rule agreements.

External Influences

The second element in the Holley and Jennings framework includes the external influences or constraints that affect the labor relations process. Holley and Jennings discuss several external influences, such as international factors, the product market, and technology, which can influence the process. Their discussion of the external influences also included the state of the economy, which impacts on the union and management negotiators and administrators, and the competitors, who impact directly on management officials. The latter two influences will be shown to be the most relevant to the implementation of tiers. Such external influences may affect the goals of the participants, the means by which participants attempt to attain them, and thus the subsequent compromises reached.

Views of Tiered Compensation Structures

Kochan, Katz, and McKersie (1986) attempt to add a more dynamic component to industrial relations theory by developing the concept of strategy, or strategic choice. They indicate ways in which the framework for viewing industrial relations could be expanded and discuss the role of strategic choice within a more complex paradigm. In their discussion of the prevailing paradigm, they outline some of the unexpected developments that exposed the apparent inadequacy of the current theoretical approaches. It does appear that the concept of strategic choice adds a more dynamic component to industrial relations theory, and in the first part of the following section we examine tiered compensation structures in the context of a business strategy.

Two predominant views of tiers have been expressed in the literature: (1) as part of a firm's business strategy, and (2) as an outcome associated with concession bargaining.[8] The discussion of tiers as part of a firm's business strategy will include both business strategies associated with expansion/investment and strategies associated with economic survival. Given the relative newness of tiers, most of the discussion will focus on the initial negotiation of tiers as it relates to a firm's business strategy, although a firm's strategy may be modified over time due to changes in the external influences that operate on the union-management relationship. Also, there will be a separate discussion of tiers as an outcome associated with concession bargaining. We recognize, however, that a firm's business strategy for economic survival often incorporates concession bargaining.

Tiers as Part of a Business Strategy

The economic environment of the 1980s has persuaded many firms to adjust their human resource management and business strategies. As the human resource management strategies were altered in the past decade, firms reexamined their compensation systems. With our inconstant economy along with the pressures for cost reduction and productivity increases, many firms have sought new compensation policies and new business operating strategies (Bureau of National Affairs, Inc. [BNA] 1988; Katz and Milkovich 1986; O'Dell and McAdams 1986). Attaining competitive advantage[9] through human resources requires that these activities be conducted from a strategic perspective (Lengnick-Hall and Lengnick-Hall 1988). Tiered pay plans are one means for coping with the increased competitive pressures that have led to the revisions in business strategies.[10]

Katz and Milkovich (1986) state that a causal flow appears to run from the economic environment through business strategies and then on to human resource management strategies, i.e., compensation policies. Lengnick-Hall and Lengnick-Hall (1988) suggest there is a reciprocal interdependence between a firm's business strategy and its human resources strategy. Researchers in industrial relations have recently begun to investigate the relationship between business strategies[11] and such bargaining outcomes as tiers (e.g., Cappelli 1985a; Kochan, Katz, and McKersie 1986). Such an investigation would be useful in understanding the role of tiers in the American industrial relations system.

The BNA (1988) and Katz and Milkovich (1986) view tiers as part of a changed compensation policy in response to a new, more competitive economic environment and a revised business strategy. They argue that deregulation, increased competition, technological change, and other competitive pressures have forced companies to change their operating strategies. These changes have resulted in compensation policies that include tiered compensation plans, lump-sum payments, gain sharing, profit sharing, stock ownership plans, and knowledge-based pay being made an explicit part of a new business operating strategy. They state that compensation plans and other personnel policies that were adequate in a stable growth environment would not work well in a frequently changing environment.

It appears that the different business strategies selected in response to competitive pressures, through their impact on the collective bargaining environment, have a large impact on the labor relations outcomes (Kochan, Katz, and McKersie 1986). We propose the following process models of how tiers relate to business strategy, focusing on two different strategic choices in response to external pressures: (1) the implementation of tiers as part of a strategy associated with expansion and investment, or (2) the implementation of tiers as a strategy for economic survival.[12]

Strategy for Expansion/Investment

Tiers negotiated as part of a strategy for expansion/investment[13] can be understood in terms of the causal flow provided by Katz and Milkovich (1986), which runs from the economic environment through business strategies and then on to compensation policies such as tiers. When tiers are negotiated according to an organization's strategy for expansion, it appears that firms take a proactive position based on the anticipation of possible future economic difficulties or to gain a competitive advantage. That is, the firms appear to have implemented tiers for the purpose of reducing costs associated with expansion; such expansion becomes a part of their long-term strategic objective. Two-tier plans are an especially attractive cost control device in such a situation, because as expansion takes place, all additional employees will be on the low tier. To gain union and employee approval for this long-term strategic objective, however, management often provides monetary and/or other forms of incentives in the new contract to the employees who would be on the high tier (Cappelli 1985a; Harris 1983a).

Strategy for Economic Survival

While the negotiation of tiers for the purpose of expansion can be understood in terms of the causal flow provided by Katz and Milkovich (1986), the causal flow for the strategy for economic survival appears to run from the economic environment directly to concessions. Businesses that negotiate tiers for economic survival usually are under great pressure from the competition. The increased external pressure forces the employees, union, and management to share in the responsibilities of cutting costs during contract negotiations (Cappelli 1983; Kassalow 1983; Mitchell 1983).

In short, businesses that negotiate tiers as part of a strategy for survival believe that the new pay plan or some other cost cutting device is necessary if their operations are to continue without exacerbating the effects of the existing economic pressures. Employees who ratify such plans also generally feel that they have to approve the two-tier plan or some of them could lose their jobs (e.g., Cappelli 1985a). Thus, if tiers are negotiated by management as a strategy for economic survival, they are usually accompanied in the contract by other concessions; current employees' wages and/or benefits are often adversely affected, i.e., decreased or frozen. In contrast to the proactive stance taken by firms negotiating tiers for the purpose of expansion, it appears that firms take a reactive position if tiers are negotiated according to a strategy for economic survival. Miles et al. (1978) contend that if the firm permits the environment to dictate its strategic choices in a reactive manner, the opportunities of long-term survival are reduced.

Tiers as an Outcome of Concession Bargaining

Since tiers are generally negotiated in response to a proposal by management (Jacoby and Mitchell 1986), tiers are viewed by the union and employees as a concession (e.g., Balliet 1984; Craft, Abboushi, and Labovitz 1985). Many have labeled two-tier wage structures as an outcome which is associated with concession bargaining (Balliet 1984; Craft, Abboushi, and Labovitz 1985; Jacoby and Mitchell 1986; Mitchell 1983). Most concessions generally affect the wages, benefits, or working conditions of those workers already employed (e.g., Ploscowe 1986). Although the implementation of tiers alone typically affects only those employees not yet hired, we contend that tiers are a concession bargaining outcome resulting in potentially lower labor costs than would have existed otherwise. Thus tiers meet the definition of a concession.[14]

Plan of the Book

In this chapter, tiered compensation structures were defined, classified according to type and form, and discussed in terms of their role in the industrial relations system. Chapter 2 examines the characteristics of tiers and the trends in their incidence. The different roles tiers appear to play in the manufacturing and service sectors will also be discussed. An explanation will be provided for why tiers are more likely to exist in certain types of industries than in others. Also, chapter 2 discusses the potential benefits and problems associated with tiers and concludes with a discussion of the conditions affecting the incidence of tiers and their future. Chapter 3 is a detailed discussion of labor-management relations in one of the industries that has implemented many tiers, the retail food industry. The chapter describes how the competitive pressures surrounding that industry changed and led to the subsequent implementation of tiers.

Chapter 4 presents the historical and environmental factors that influenced the development and maintenance of tiers in a retail food company whose employees were surveyed. The chapter also shows how tiers affected the company and the union representing its employees. Chapter 5 discusses the sample characteristics, research design, survey development, and data analysis used to survey the rank-and-file employees. Chapter 6 contains survey results in response to several research questions. The following three interrelated research questions focus on the employee views of why the two-tier wage plan at the surveyed employees' company was originally negotiated, how much various groups have benefited from its implementation, and the perceived effects of the plan on employment-related outcomes.

(1) What goals of the negotiating parties do employees believe the plan was negotiated to meet?

(2) To what extent do employees perceive that the various groups have benefited from the implementation of the plan?

(3) What employment-related effects do employees believe have resulted from the plan?

A second set of research questions focuses on the employee views of the predicted outcomes of future bargaining over the wage structure, attitudes toward selected changes in the compensation system and the potential related outcomes, and general employee attitudes toward tiers.

(4) What changes related to the plan do employees believe are likely to occur?

(5) What are the employee attitudes toward selected changes in the plan and the potential related outcomes?

(6) What are the employee attitudes about the company and union expectations, problems relating to the plan, and the relationship of tiers to the duty of fair representation?

The next research question examines whether differences exist for the first six research questions among the different geographic areas.

(7) What are the differences in the employee attitudes examined in the first six research questions among the geographic areas of operation?

The final research question focuses on equal employment opportunity, which may be of concern if the low-tier groups contain a disproportionate number of members from protected classes.

(8) Are the low-tier groups disproportionately comprised of women and minorities?

Chapter 7 also focuses on the survey results and develops and tests five hypotheses based on equity theory. The hypotheses focus on the relationship of employee behaviors and attitudes to tiers. Equity theory provides a particularly useful framework within which to generate hypotheses concerning attitudes and behaviors of employees in tiered compensation structures. Equity theory suggests that perceptions of equitable pay have an important role in defining employment-related attitudes and behaviors as individuals attempt to equate their ratios of outcomes to inputs with the ratios of relevant others (Adams 1965; Mowday 1983). The five hypotheses are:

(1) The employees in the low-tier groups will have a higher absenteeism rate and report less effort expended on the job than will the employees in high-tier groups.

(2) The employees in the low-tier groups will participate less in union activities, and be more likely to (a) vote against ratifying union contracts which maintain tiers, and (b) vote against incumbent union officers than will the employees in the high-tier groups.

(3) Compared to the employees in the high-tier groups, the employees in the low-tier groups will have: (a) perceptions of less pay fairness and lower union instrumentality in obtaining fair pay; and (b) lower satisfaction with their pay, the two-tier plan, and the number of hours they work.

(4) The employees in the low-tier groups will perceive greater promotional opportunity and greater opportunity for external employment than will the employees in the high-tier groups.

(5) The low-tier groups will have higher company and union commitment, and job satisfaction than will the high-tier groups.

Chapter 8 summarizes the key points and findings of this study and presents the conclusions.

NOTES

1. There is little mention in the literature concerning the effect of tiered compensation structures on employees who change positions; therefore, the discussion of tiers will use the terms "low-tier employees" and "new employees." While it is recognized that the phrase, "employees who change positions" could be substituted for these terms in some examples, the use of these two phrases simplifies the discussion.

2. Tiered compensation structures also may exist for employees not represented by unions. For example, Ruben (1987) noted that Delta Airlines had instituted tiers for that portion of its rank-and-file employees who were not unionized. The company in which the case study was conducted had instituted tiers for its managers. Further, the survey results of Essick (1987) indicated that 11 percent of all the companies that reported having two-tier wage structures were nonunion. Given that most of the interest and concern expressed in the literature has centered on tiered compensation structures for unionized employers, the focus of this study is limited to that sector.

3. A noted example of where temporary tiers were modified before any employee on the low-tier wage scale had moved onto the high-tier scale occurred at Northwest Airlines in 1988. A temporary low-wage tier that was supposed to merge in five years was implemented for Northwest's flight attendants in 1984 (Bureau of National Affairs, Inc. [BNA], June 17, 1985). After a threatened strike, partially because management wanted to lengthen the time of merger to nine years, a settlement was reached in which the two tiers would be merged in eight years (BNA, March 29, 1988).

4. It should be noted that an increasing number of contracts provide for more than two levels of tiers of compensation (BNA, February 26, 1987). For example, Sichenze's (1989) analysis of all retail food contracts covering 1,000 or more workers found that over half contained three or more tiers. Thus instead of being two-tiered agreements, many contracts are actually multi-tiered agreements.

5. Tiered wage structures generally affect multiple job classifications and within any contract there may be variation in the percentage pay difference between the two wage tiers across job classes. Thus, the *average* pay difference is the one that is reported.

6. Ross's "first tier" would be the high-wage tier for employees doing similar tasks in old and conventional jobs. His "second tier" would be the low-wage tier for those same jobs. Comparing his first and second tiers with his third tier is the same as comparing the high and low levels of a job-duty tier.

7. Sichenze (1988, 1989) identifies another tier form that is common in the retail food industry, the work-rule tier. Her investigation reveals that more than 61 percent of the retail food contracts contained modifications of work rules based on the date of hire. Sichenze notes that the work rules governing the standard workday and job security were most commonly affected.

Typically, work-rule tiers only affect compensation indirectly. For example, altering the standard workday to schedule new hires during peak hours eliminates the overtime pay opportunities for new employees. Other work-rule tier forms, i.e., job security in the form of no job guarantees for new hires, have no direct effect on compensation. Thus, this form is not discussed in the text.

8. There has been discussion in the literature that wage tiers initially were implemented to correct the internal pay structure problem of wage compression (Bowers and Roderick 1987; Jacoby and Mitchell 1986). While not viewing it as a pervasive influence, Jacoby and Mitchell conclude that wage compression may have been an explanatory factor in some instances. We believe that the implementation of wage tiers would do little to correct the problem of wage compression. Employees

at different compensation levels on the high-wage tier in a situation where wage compression exists would still have internal pay inequities. Other methods exist to correct for such a problem, such as giving the higher-paid employees raises and the lower-paid employees (the ones who are causing the wage compression problem) lump-sum payments. Thus, the text will not discuss wage compression as a primary reason for implementing tiers.

9. "Competitive advantage" refers to those capabilities, resources, relationships, and decisions that permit a company to capitalize on opportunities and evade threats within its industry (Hofer and Schendel 1978).

10. In this monograph, the term "business strategy" will be used broadly to describe those decisions taken by companies to address the competitive pressures operating in the environment. The term will apply to decisions that alter the company's role or its relationship with other parties, thus eliminating minor decisions not changing goals.

11. Much of the research on business strategies has focused on management, given that management has made most of the important strategic decisions (Kochan, Katz and McKersie 1986). The history of tiered compensation structures suggests that the initiative for such plans comes from management (Jacoby and Mitchell 1986). It is management that selects both the initial and subsequent role of tiers in a firm's industrial relations and business operating strategies. It should be emphasized here that the suggestion that a company's goals in the product market help shape its goals and priorities in collective bargaining needs to be understood within the framework that collective bargaining is a bilateral process. Thus, it is not certain how much impact a change in one side's negotiating position might have on the final outcome (Cappelli 1985a). Cappelli states that, at best, management's negotiating strategies influence contract outcomes by changing the relative importance it attaches to different items considered in negotiation. He notes that

in practice, however, business strategies have a much stronger and more direct effect through their influence on the bargaining environment. In bargaining, the wage/employment trade-off that helps shape union preferences is firm-specific and is determined largely by management's business decisions. (p. 320)

12. It is assumed that "strategic decisions" can only occur where the parties have discretion over their decisions—in other words, where environmental constraints do not severely limit the parties' selection of options (e.g., Kochan, Katz, and McKersie 1986). Thus, in instances involving a severe curtailment of alternatives, the term "strategy for economic survival" may be a misnomer.

13. Based on a review of the literature, it appears that the majority of proactive strategies involve business expansion. While it is recognized that a strategy for expansion is typically accompanied by investment, it will be referred to only as a "strategy for expansion."

14. Cappelli (1983) notes that while in theory it was easy to define concessions, determining which settlements or outcomes are concessions could be difficult in practice. He defined concessions as the outcome of a process involving an explicit exchange of labor cost moderation for improvements in job security. Cappelli (1985b) concluded "that unions may moderate labor costs through concession bargaining if jobs are threatened and if such moderation is likely to generate a clear improvement in employment security." (p. 91)

2
Tiered Compensation Structures in Practice

In chapter 1, tiers were defined, classified according to type and form, and discussed in terms of their strategic role in the United States industrial relations system. This chapter presents the characteristics and relative frequencies of tiered compensation structures. Differences between the manufacturing and service sectors are discussed in relation to wage changes and the use of tiers as part of a business strategy. The chapter examines the pressures that resulted in the implementation of tiers in certain industry groups, along with examples of the roles tiers have played in those industries. The chapter also examines the potential benefits and problems that may result from maintaining tiers, and concludes with a discussion of the factors affecting the present and future incidence of tiers.

Characteristics and Frequency of Tiers

The most comprehensive source of information about two-tier settlements has been the Bureau of National Affairs. The BNA (March 1, 1988) reported that of the 82 two-tier wage plans in its representative sample of contracts negotiated or modified in 1987, 41 percent were temporary, 11 percent were permanent, and for 48 percent the BNA could not determine whether the plans were temporary or permanent. Similarly, the BNA (February 23, 1989) reported for its 1988 sample that of the 45 two-tier wage plans that were newly negotiated or modified, 44 percent were temporary, 2 percent were permanent, and for 53 percent, they could not determine what type of plan was negotiated. Nine percent of the settlements in each year contained tiers for both wages and benefits. Fourteen additional settlements in 1987 and five in 1988 established tiers for benefits only, but the BNA did not include these in its subsequent analyses.

Other sources providing information on the types of tiers found have not been as detailed or as representative as the BNA's reports. For example, Jacoby and Mitchell (1986) received data from the BNA for 35 contracts with two-tier wage plans as of late 1984. Of these, 43 percent of the contracts involved permanent tiers, and the rest of the settlements established temporary tiers. Jacoby and Mitchell's data from a sample of private-sector personnel and industrial relations managers in the Los Angeles area showed that for the employers with two-tier wage plans, 30 percent had permanent plans, 51 percent temporary, and 19 percent had both types. While these data sources showed considerable variation in the types of tiers,[1] it may be concluded that temporary tiers are more prevalent than permanent tiers.

A characteristic of temporary tiers is the progression schedule, the period of time it takes for a low-tier employee's compensation to merge with that of the high-tier employees. Thomas (1988) analyzed the BNA's sample of contract settlements in 1985 and 1986 and found roughly equal percentages of merging tiers in one, two, three, and five years. An additional 17 percent of the contracts merged the tiers after a longer period of time. Essick (1987), in a survey of a large number of personnel administrators from 123 companies with two-tier wage structures, found that the temporary tiers of most companies merged the low-tier scale with the high-tier scale within one to three years, but 20 percent of the companies waited three to five years.

Table 2.1 summarizes Essick's (1987) findings that cross tabulate the years of experience a company has had with tiers and the average pay difference between the two wage tiers, which include temporary and permanent tiers. There is a wide range of pay differences between the high and low tiers, as can be seen in the table. The most common average pay difference between the tiers was from 20 to 29 percent. When the data are grouped into ranges encompassing 10 percentage points, it can be seen that the firms with the least experience with tiers tended to have the largest average differences between the tiers.

Table 2.2 shows the incidence of two-tier wage settlements by industry group based on the BNA sample of representative non-construction bargaining units that included between 1,211 to 907

Table 2.1
Cross-Tabulation of Average Pay Difference Between Tiers by Experience with Plan

Years of experience with two-tier plan	Number of responses	Average pay difference between the two tiers (as percent of upper tier)						Total
		Less than 5%	5-9%	10-14%	15-19%	20-29%	30% or more	
1 or less	39	5.1	7.7	30.8	12.8	28.2	15.4	100
2-5	55	5.5	14.6	20.0	23.5	27.3	9.1	100
Over 6[a]	23	13.0	13.0	21.7	21.7	13.0	17.4	100

SOURCE: Essick (1987).

a. 83 percent of responses in this category had more than 10 years experience with the plan.

Table 2.2
Two-Tier Wage Settlements, by Industry, 1983-88
(Frequency Expressed as Percentage of Industry Contracts)

	1983	1984	1985	1986	1987	1988
All industries, excluding construction	5	8	11	10	9	5
Manufacturing sector	2	4	6	6	7	2
Chemicals	1	1	0	2	5	0
Electrical machinery	0	5	16	3	3	0
Fabricated metals	0	15	0	10	0	0
Food processing	5	4	17	4	24	14
Furniture	0	0	0	6	0	0
Instruments	0	13	0	0	8	0
Lumber	0	0	20	19	0	0
Machinery, except electrical	3	11	10	5	8	3
Miscellaneous manufacturing	0	10	0	0	33	11
Paper	2	2	8	6	4	1
Petroleum	0	4	0	4	25	0
Printing	1	0	0	5	8	2
Stone, clay and glass	0	0	14	10	7	8
Textiles	0	5	0	0	0	0
Transportation equipment	13	16	20	24	11	10

Service sector	9	17	18	16	12	9
Airlines	8	35	62	70	20	33
Communications	0	7	0	2	0	0
Health services	0	9	7	12	5	3
Insurance and finance	0	5	0	27	14	0
Motor transportation	5	17	16	20	10	6
Postal	0	0	100	0	100	0
Rail	0	0	100	50	44	0
Services, except health	3	11	5	22	4	5
Utilities	4	14	0	2	13	11
Wholesale and retail	28	32	37	25	20	20
Number of contract settlements analyzed	1,211	1,145	1,053	1,054	907	904

SOURCE: BNA, February 23, 1989.

settlements annually. The BNA began counting two-tier settlements in 1983; the BNA counted as tiered contracts only those plans that specified lower rates of pay for new employees or those settlements that modified previous wage tiers. Because contracts in its sample that were renewed with no modification to already preexisting two-tier contracts may not have been counted, the BNA noted that its data likely underrepresent the incidence of tiers (BNA, March 1, 1988). Also, the BNA data do not include any tiers based on location, job duty, or employment status. Furthermore, except for temporary plans, the BNA analyses do not distinguish between newly negotiated tiers and those already existing plans that were modified from a prior contract. Thus, it is difficult to determine the prevalence of tiers in American industry and almost impossible to assess the number of employees currently on the low levels.

Sector Differences in Relation
to Strategy and Wage Changes

In this section, we examine the differences between the service and manufacturing sectors in strategies and wage changes when tiers are negotiated. The strategies employed by the sectors have been largely influenced by their economic development since World War II and differences in product market characteristics; most of the service sector industries have experienced considerable economic growth, while most of the manufacturing sector industries (with the notable exception of the defense industries) have experienced a decline in growth. Bell (1973) notes this trend and suggested that this pattern would continue into the next century. Figures from the Bureau of Labor Statistics (1988) show that, in 1950, 60 percent of the workforce was in the service sector and 40 percent in manufacturing. From 1950 to 1988, service sector employment increased 290 percent, while manufacturing employment increased 35 percent. Such a change in growth in the service sector is indicative of an ever increasing need for services and has been recognized as affecting union-management relations by industrial relations scholars in the 1980s (Kassalow 1983).

The product market in the manufacturing industries had been essentially sheltered through the late 1970s and had experienced little foreign competition (Block, Kleiner, Roomkin, and Salsburg 1987), although foreign products began to obtain a larger market share around that time. Industries in the service sector operate in a product market where the notion of imports is not relevant (Cappelli 1983), as services are delivered where they are produced. Thus, not only was there much greater growth in the service sector than in the manufacturing sector, but the former was protected from foreign competition (though not from lower-cost domestic competition). Certainly, these differences have influenced the strategies used in each sector.

To meet the increasing market demands, management within the service sector industries has sought to expand current operations or to invest in other similar markets. Management has looked for new ways, such as the implementation of tiers, to reduce the costs of expansion plans. In contrast, many manufacturing firms have had difficulty competing successfully with foreign firms and have had to reduce their expenses in order to remain competitive. Some of these firms have sought to contain labor costs by obtaining such concessions from their unions as two-tier plans.

Two-tier plans appear to have been initially negotiated for very different reasons in the two sectors. BNA data presented in tables 2.3 and 2.4 suggest that for most of the service sector, the initial negotiation of tiers often includes significant wage increases for current employees. There are some examples that suggest this is an incentive for contract ratification (e.g., Harris 1983a). In most of the manufacturing sector, the BNA data suggest that the initial negotiation of tiers was accompanied by a small wage increase or none at all for the then-current employees. Hence, we assume that when management views the implementation of wage tiers primarily as part of a business strategy for expansion, the wage increases given to the high-tier employees will be much greater than when management views tiers primarily as part of a strategy for economic survival.[2]

Table 2.3 shows the first-year median hourly wage changes in all contracts (including two-tier contracts) and in the two-tier contracts from 1983 through 1988 based on BNA samples for the manufacturing and

Table 2.3
First-Year Median Wage Changes in the Manufacturing and Service Sectors and Overall Inflation Rate, 1983–1988

	Sector and contracts								Inflation rate[b]
	Manufacturing				Service				
	All contracts[a]		Two-tier		All contracts[a]		Two-tier		
Year	$/hour	%	$/hour	%	$/hour	%	$/hour	%	
1983	.40	4.7	0.0	0.0	.50	5.5	.35	3.5	3.8
1984	.40	4.7	0.0	0.0	.35	4.0	.33	4.0	4.0
1985	.35	3.9	0.0	0.0	.35	4.0	.30	2.7	3.8
1986	.15	1.7	0.0	0.0	.27	3.0	.08	0.7	1.1
1987	.18	2.0	0.0	0.0	.30	3.2	.05	1.5	4.4
1988	.29	2.2	.25	2.0	.35	3.5	.30	2.4	4.4

SOURCE: *Economic Report of the President*, U.S. Government Printing Office, Washington, DC, various years, and BNA, February 20, 1985; February 26, 1987; March 1, 1988; January 25, 1989; February 23, 1989.

a. Includes two-tier contracts.

b. Changes from December to December in Consumer Price Index.

service sectors. The table also shows the inflation rates for these years. The table illustrates different patterns of median wage changes between the two sectors. In the manufacturing sector, for every year (except 1988) the median change for first-year wage settlements in two-tier contracts was zero, indicating a wage freeze.[3] For all manufacturing contracts from 1983 to 1985, the median increase was between 35 and 40 cents. On the other hand, in the service sector, two-tier settlements had median wage increases well above zero, between 1983 and 1985, and in contrast to the manufacturing sector, much closer to the median for all service sector settlements.

As seen in table 2.4, BNA (February 20, 1985) data from 1983 and 1984 show median wage changes greater than zero in only two of the six manufacturing industries that implemented tiers in 1983, and in eight of the twelve that instituted them in 1984. In addition, the BNA data indicate that none of the manufacturing industries that implemented tiers in 1983, and only two that implemented them in 1984, had larger first-year median wage changes than in all contract settlements for those industries in the same years. This same data show that all but one service sector industry with two-tier contract settlements had a positive median wage change in 1983 and all had positive median wage changes in 1984. Further, in three of the five service sector industries that implemented tiers in 1983, and five of the eight that implemented them in 1984, the median first-year wage change was greater than in all settlements.

These data support the previous discussion that viewed tiers as being instituted primarily as either part of a firm's strategy for expansion or as part of a strategy for economic survival. The data in tables 2.3 and 2.4 suggest that, initially, tiers were more likely to be used in relation to a firm's strategy for survival in the manufacturing sector and in relation to a firm's strategy for expansion in the service sector. Ballagh's (1985) conclusions, also drawn from the BNA data, are consonant with the above interpretation. He argues that the greater prevalence of tiers in the service sector was due to the facilitation of expansion of unionized employers into new markets where the employer would be competitive with nonunion companies. He noted that in the manufacturing sector, where tiers were less prevalent, rapid expansion of companies into new markets was less practical.

Table 2.4
Comparison of First-Year Median Wage Increases in All Contracts and Two-Tier Contracts by Industry, 1983-84

Sector and Industry	1983				1984			
	All contracts		Two-tier		All contracts		Two-tier	
	$/hour	%	$/hour	%	$/hour	%	$/hour	%
Manufacturing								
Chemicals	.49	5	.25	3	.47	5	.00	0
Electrical machinery	--	--	--	--	.31	4	.20	2
Fabricated metals	--	--	--	--	.20	2	.00	0
Food processing	.42	5	-1.64	-17	.28	3	.07	1
Instruments	--	--	--	--	.38	4	.06	1
Macinery, except electrical	.00	0	.00	0	.20	2	.00	0
Miscellaneous manufacturing	--	--	--	--	.33	4	.50	4
Paper	.51	6	.38	4	.51	6	.45	5
Petroleum	--	--	--	--	.20	2	.20	2
Printing	.62	6	.00	0	.55	6	.34	4
Textiles	--	--	--	--	.34	6	.37	6
Transportation equipment	.25	3	.00	0	.07	1	.00	0

Service sector							
Airlines	58	6	2.40	11	.00	0	.37	3
Communications	--	--	--	--	.54	5	.52	5
Health services	--	--	--	--	.41	5	.45	5
Insurance & finance	--	--	--	--	.40	5	.33	4
Services, except health	.43	6	.26	5	.31	5	.08	3
Motor transportation	.28	4	-.19	-1	.34	4	.60	5
Utilities	.65	6	.81	7	.58	5	.67	6
Wholesale & retail	.30	4	.35	3	.05	0	.23	2

SOURCE: BNA, February 20, 1985.

NOTE: Ordinarily the BNA does not publish industry medians where there are fewer than 10 settlements; an exception was made in this case due to the comparatively small number of two-tier contracts. Contracts in industries other than those listed are included in the manufacturing and service medians in table 2.3. They are not listed separately because settlements in them did not mention two-tier provisions.

-- No data for comparison.

Table 2.3 shows lower overall median first-year wage changes in 1986 and 1987 for each sector when compared to the earlier years, which suggests that in both sectors at that time tiers were used primarily in relation to a strategy for economic survival.[4] The changes were much lower in the manufacturing sector for all contracts and for two-tier contracts in the service sector; the changes for all contracts in the service sector were also somewhat lower. While those declines were likely affected by the low rate of inflation in 1986, the BNA (January 20, 1987) attributes the lower level of median changes in part to an increase in the percentage of settlements containing lump-sum payments.[5] These are counted as wage freezes when they are accompanied by no first-year raise because they are not included in the base pay rate. As they moderate labor costs over general wage increases, they fit the definition of a concession.

Industry Groups in which Tiers are Prominent

This section focuses on the experiences of selected industries shown in table 2.2 or particular companies within those industries. The examples used have been cited frequently in the literature and/or involve situations where many employees have been placed on a low tier. The industries are divided into four major groups,[6] based on the major force operating in the industry that led to the implementation of tiers: (1) manufacturing industries subject to competition from imports and/or nonunion companies; (2) industries affected by pressure from the government to cut costs; (3) service sector industries affected by deregulation; and (4) other service sector industries subject to competitive pressures.

Hall (1980) found that firms within the same industries addressed the increasingly competitive markets through widely varying business strategies. Cappelli (1985a) found that business strategies varied within a specific industry according to the competitive pressures, the company's current situation (product market, plant and equipment, finances, etc.), and the view of the future held by management. He further argued that the business strategy adopted played an important role in shaping a variety of labor relations outcomes. Although it is assumed that the major force leading to the implementation of tiers is the same within each of the four groups, the discussion will show that the strategy within the groups varied considerably. Further, it needs to be emphasized that these strategies and their associated outcomes may change over time and may even vary between service sector companies (such as the retail food industry) operating in several different geographic markets.

The discussion in this section also examines the factors that accompanied the implementation of specific tiers. Thus, this section will help us draw generalizations about the factors that may affect the incidence of tiers.

Manufacturing Industries Affected by Imports
and Nonunion Competition

Nearly all of the industries in this group are in a decentralized bargaining structure. The best examples of tiered employers in this grouping are the divisions of the automobile companies that make electrical components and are unionized by the International Union of Electrical Workers (IUE). Leaders of the IUE have argued that their auto industry members, who make small parts that can be easily purchased or manufactured elsewhere, are more threatened by low-wage competition than the United Auto Workers (UAW) members who assemble cars or make large parts (*Wall Street Journal,* October 14, 1985).

An example of where tiers have been implemented in a manufacturing industry affected by imports and nonunion competition is the General Motors Delco Products plant in Rochester, New York. There had been no hirings at the plant since 1979, and by 1982 the employment there had decreased sharply. The union approached management about increasing employment at the manufacturing plant. While not making any guarantees, General Motors suggested that lower labor costs were likely to attract new business. A tiered-agreement implemented in 1983 reduced health care benefits and days off for new employees. The top rate of the low-tier employees was set at $9.68 per hour (compared to $13 for those previously hired) and in the following two years, employment increased from 2,220 to 3,550 persons. Management stated that 25 percent of the increased employment was related to new business it would not have received had the two-tier contract not been negotiated (*Wall Street Journal,* October 14, 1985). This represents an example where tiers were used as part of an expansion strategy.

Another example, which was described by Hoerr and Cook (1984), was at the General Motors Packard Electric Division, where prior to a two-tier contract, total labor costs (wages and fringe benefits) for employees were $22 per hour. In contrast, similar manufacturing work was being performed for a total cost of less than $3 per hour in the Packard Electric plant in Mexico and for as little as $7 per hour at other U.S. companies. In 1984 an agreement was reached with the Packard Electric Division which guaranteed jobs to all employees hired before January 1, 1982, with full pay and benefits until they retired. In exchange, as a result of decreases in the wage and benefit package, the total labor costs for new employees would be only $8.99 per hour. The new low-tier wage scale will merge with that of the prior employees after ten years. This example represents the use of tiers as part of a firm's strategy for survival.

Government-Pressured Industry

Firms that make up the aerospace industry, a part of the transportation equipment industry, were among the first manufacturing firms to implement two-tier wage plans. The reason behind their implementation of such plans, which separates this industry from the other industry groups discussed, was the pressure from the government to cut labor costs. Aerospace industry firms had little nonunion competition. A spokesman for the aerospace industry noted that some executives had received letters from military and other government officials warning that excessive cost increases, especially for labor, would affect a contractor's ability to compete for government programs. Thus, it appears that the implementation of tiers in this industry was primarily based on management's desire to continue receiving government contracts, and therefore related to a business strategy for expansion. The government campaign to decrease costs began in 1982. Prior to the beginning of collective bargaining in 1983, Air Force officials and aerospace companies together examined options for holding down labor costs (Harris

1983b). The government attempted to show that aerospace labor rates were significantly higher than average manufacturing rates and cited several job classifications for which pay under union contracts appeared to be higher than in other industries.

The contracts between the Machinists union, the UAW, and Boeing, Lockheed, and McDonnell-Douglas expired in late 1983. Boeing was the first of these firms to propose a two-tier wage plan to the two unions. The company executives said the reason for implementing tiers was to save Boeing millions of dollars by attacking the problem of high wages without adversely affecting the wages of the current workforce. The unions stated that the company's objective was to reduce pressures from the government to cut labor costs. Boeing helped to increase the acceptance of the two-tier plan by offering the current employees a wage increase of at least 6 percent (Harris 1983a).

Company executives stated that under the new contract, Boeing could pay newly hired, less skilled workers up to 41 percent less than it would have paid under the prior contract. Lockheed reported that the introduction of tiers and the hiring of 2,800 employees on the low tier in Georgia had lowered its average labor costs by 81 cents per hour. Ross (1985) calculates that the tiers at Lockheed would save almost $19 million in labor costs during 1985. Ross, however, does not take into account some of the potential costs (to be discussed later in this chapter) that may accompany the implementation of tiers, such as increased turnover and recruitment costs.

Industries Affected by Deregulation

The deregulation of the transportation industry, followed by the development of nonunion firms with substantially lower labor costs than the union firms, was the principal force behind the implementation and spread of tiered compensation structures in this service sector industry. Deregulation has had its most visible impact on the airline industry. D. Walsh (1988) notes that two-tier plans were virtually nonexistent in the U.S. airline industry in 1982, but by 1986 were an established industry practice.

The airline industry was among the most heavily regulated in the United States until 1978. This regulation resulted in limitations on the number of carriers assigned to any route and the absence of price competition between the airlines. Thus, during the 1970s, the bargaining power of the unions increased relative to that of an unregulated market as a result of such factors as increased air travel and higher employment levels. That situation changed when the Airline Deregulation Act of 1978 took effect, and competition between the airlines intensified (Cappelli 1985a). New airlines established lower fares to compete with the trunk carriers on heavily traveled routes between major cities. The new airlines were primarily nonunion and therefore paid substantially lower wages than the established carriers paid to employees in equivalent positions.

Cappelli's (1985a) data on the four major airline craft groups at different airlines, categorized by him according to their business strategies since deregulation, revealed a relationship between the number of two-tier wage plans and the airlines' business strategy. Airlines that operated in markets with relatively little competition had two-tier plans in only 32 percent of their contracts.[7] Each of the other two groups of airlines for which he presented data, the carriers near bankruptcy and the strong carriers, had tiers in 82 percent of their contracts. Cappelli argues that those in the "near bankruptcy" group used concessions and tiers to avoid going bankrupt, and thus appeared to follow a strategy for economic survival. Also, he states that the strong carriers, those with sufficient financial resources to restructure their operations, used concessions (including tiers) to grow. In exchange, their employees received increased job security. For example, when American Airlines negotiated wage tiers, virtually all of its employees received lifetime employment guarantees. After the tiers were negotiated at American, they became a key element in its expansion strategy (Harris 1983c; Salpukas 1984). Ross (1985) calculates that through employee turnover and hiring, American Airlines' two-tier plans implemented in 1983 saved the airline $100 million in labor costs during 1984.

Two-tier structures also appear to have had a role in the method by which American Airlines decided to expand its operations. Brown and

Agins (1987) describe the role that two-tier plans may have had at American Airlines in its decision not to merge with Pan American World Airlines in 1987. Given that Pan Am's workforce had many employees on the high-wage tier, American Airlines expressed a preference to grow internally rather than by merger. Brown and Agins (1987) note that American preferred to buy routes from Pan Am, which it could then staff with its own pilots and other personnel. Thus, American could reduce average labor costs by increasing the percentage of employees on the low tier.

Airline deregulation and the subsequent increased competition among the airlines also led to the negotiation of tiers in the intercity bus transportation industry. The company most affected by such competition was Greyhound Lines, Inc. Greyhound had lost 45 percent of its New York-Buffalo business, mostly to companies such as the People Express Airline, Inc., which charged one-half of Greyhound's fare. Similarly, Southwest Airlines flew from Phoenix to Denver for $65 versus $99 by Greyhound (*Business Week,* November 21, 1983). Labor costs were also less at Greyhound's major bus competitor, Trailways Corporation (*Fortune,* January 9, 1984).

As a result of the increased competition, Greyhound turned to labor concessions and two-tier contracts as part of a survival strategy. In 1983 Greyhound Lines asked its employees for a 28 percent cut in wages and benefits, as well as work-rule changes (*Fortune,* January 9, 1984). One of the major work-rule changes proposed would have allowed Greyhound to hire an unlimited number of part-time employees at 80 percent of the full-time employee pay with no benefits. The Amalgamated Transit Union rejected the company's demands and struck. After a bitter two-month strike, during which the company started replacing the strikers and attempted to operate, a settlement was reached. On the average, salaries and benefits were cut 14 percent for prior employees and 19 percent for new employees.

Compared to the airline industry, table 2.2 shows that the incidence of two-tier contracts was much lower in intercity trucking (motor transportation) and came later in the railroad industry. Cappelli (1985a) argues that the industrywide bargaining structures in the trucking and railroad industries provided better protection for their unions from bargaining concessions and two-tier plans than the decentralized structure in the airline industry. For example, a permanent two-tier plan, which would have modified the 1982 major industrywide trucking agreement (National Master Freight Agreement) (Lublin 1983), was overwhelmingly rejected by members of the International Brotherhood of Teamsters in 1983, thus keeping tiers out of almost the entire industry. The Teamsters' president had supported the agreement and argued that the unionized trucking industry needed help to compete with the nonunion trucking companies that had arisen since deregulation. In the 1985 renegotiation of that contract, a temporary two-tier plan, which appeared to be part of a strategy for survival, was approved with the two wage scales merging in 1989 (the year after that contract expired). Jacoby and Mitchell (1986) report that employee skepticism about whether the tiers would actually merge led to a close ratification vote.

In the railroad industry, a national advisory study commission recommended major changes in its labor agreements to allow railroads to compete with trucking after the deregulation of the transportation industries (Arouca 1985). Arouca notes that railroad employment and business had steeply declined over the past three decades. Further, many railroads were threatened with collapse. In the case of the Consolidated Rail Corporation, which represented about 20 percent of the rail industry, survival was only possible with federal financial assistance. Therefore, in the 1985 negotiations, railroad management sought labor concessions in their labor agreements. The concessions that were obtained included wage tiers (Apcar 1985), which appear to have been part of a strategy for economic survival.

Service Sector Industry Affected by Nonunion Competition

The major example of an industry in the service sector affected by nonunion competition not related to deregulation or government pressure is the retail food industry (wholesale and retail), the focus of chapter 3. The BNA data indicate that the greatest number of tiered plans are in this service sector industry. There appear to be four factors that had a major impact on the penetration of two-tier settlements in the retail food industry. First, the employee turnover in this industry has always been high—30 or 40 percent per year is common (Ross 1985)—thus leading to more immediate savings to the employer from tiers than in some other industries. Second, as with all of the industries discussed, the retail food industry was subjected to pressure to reduce costs. Third, the retail food industry faced very strong nonunion competition in most of the markets it served. And fourth, since the retail food industry has operated in many different geographic markets and economic environments, there have been no nationwide contracts protecting its unions from bargaining tiers or concessions.

Sichenze (1989) completed a content analysis of all tiered contracts in the retail food industry covering 1,000 or more workers and also interviewed managers, union leaders, attorneys, and others involved in the industry. Her sources were unanimous "that two-tier labor contracts have helped management to be more competitive, and more profitable. Union jobs have been saved and some expansion has been fueled by these economic outcomes" (p. 493).

Chapter 3 shows that tiers of various forms were initially implemented in this industry on a widespread basis before they were in other industries. Many of the early wage tiers in the retail food industry were accompanied by large wage increases for current employees, suggesting that initially tiers were used primarily to help carry out strategic business plans for expansion. More recently, however, the changes to already existing tiers, along with the negotiation of new tiers, appears to be primarily part of a strategy for economic survival, as those tiers were generally accompanied by other concessions.

Potential Benefits of Tiers

The following sections will examine the potential benefits of tiers for employees, unions, and employers, based on the discussion in the literature and on what has actually occurred when tiers were implemented. It should be recognized that an outcome benefiting one of the labor relations participants also may be beneficial for the other groups. For example, the facilitation of an employer's expansion may increase a union's membership and improve employees' job security.

Thus, both Ploscowe (1986) and Ruben (1987) note that tiers, while enabling employers to compete more effectively, may reduce labor costs without increasing unemployment. Much of the following discussion of the potential benefits and the subsequent examination of the potential problems and concerns associated with tiers served as a source for the research questions and hypotheses.

Potential Benefits for Employees

Certainly, any discussion of the potential benefits for employees from tiered structures should examine benefits for both those in the low- and high-tier positions. For the low-tier employees, the literature identifies one major benefit, simply the creation of their jobs (Flax 1984; Ross 1985). For high-tier employees, the negotiation of a two-tier plan results in no immediate costs; they do not share in the concessions that will be made by the yet-to-be-hired, low-tier employees. When examining the potential benefits to employees, one must consider whether the problems that tiered structures present would be more or less severe than the concessions that would occur in the absence of such structures. For the high-tier employees, the comparison of tiers with alternative methods of reducing or controlling labor costs (i.e., layoffs, wage/benefit concessions, or one of the newer forms of compensation discussed in chapter 1), becomes critical. For employees in tiered situations, an employer's use of tiers to facilitate expansion may even result in greater job security. Overall, the literature suggests that employees on both the low and high tiers do not see any personal benefits to them resulting from tiers, particularly in the long run (Bernstein and Schiller 1985; Bowers and Roderick 1987; Salpukas 1987).

Potential Benefits for Unions

Several potential benefits for unions may result from tiers. It appears that tiered structures have been responsible for keeping more jobs in the unionized sector than would have otherwise existed. This, of course, relates to the process of concessions, described previously by Cappelli (1985b), where labor cost moderation is exchanged for improved job security. Further, when a company implements tiers as a part of a strategic business plan facilitating expansion, new unionized jobs may be created. For example, Seaberry (1985) reports the case of a midwestern supermarket chain where a two-tier plan helped the company to expand and add about 3,000 new jobs. The *Wall Street Journal* (October 14, 1985) reports that tiers were responsible for over 300 jobs created at the Rochester Delco Products General Motors plant. Ploscowe (1986) states that tiers lower labor costs without resorting to layoffs and may provide the employer with an incentive to hire new employees. Certainly, the creation of new jobs and the preservation of the existing ones would appear to benefit the union.

It has also been argued that two-tier plans are politically much easier for the union to sell to the membership and obtain ratification than other kinds of concessions. Ploscowe (1986) notes three advantages tiers have over other concession forms: (1) tiers do not cost current members anything, since they provide a vehicle to preserve the contract gains achieved over the years; (2) new members are more likely to support the union if they know that the implementation of tiers led to the creation of their jobs; and (3) tier systems result in more, not fewer, members for the unions.

Potential Benefits for Employers

There are several major interrelated benefits for employers that may result from the implementation of tiers. Tiered structures may save the employer money and facilitate expansion, both of which allow employers to compete more effectively. Ross (1985) cites the examples of American Airlines and Lockheed Aircraft. After negotiating tiers, these companies subsequently expanded and increased employment, thus lowering their average hourly labor cost.

An employer's labor cost savings will be large in industries with a high turnover of workers who are unskilled or require little or no training. The BNA data indicate that tiered plans are indeed concentrated in the industries characterized by rapid turnover; the industry with the greatest number of tiered agreements, for example, is retail food, where turnover is great. Dalton and Kesner (1986) argue that turnover under two-tiered agreements may result in "windfall" savings for a company as employees on the low tier replace much more expensive employees on the high tier. The cost savings will not be great, and may not even exist, in industries or companies experiencing declining employment.

Tiers offer an advantage to employers compared to across-the-board cuts, as the employer can reduce labor costs without losing valuable employees (Ploscowe 1986). Such employees, who would be on the high tier, would not have their compensation reduced, and thus would be less likely to search for alternative employment. Companies experiencing declining employment would appear to need across-the-board wage or benefit cuts to lower their average labor costs.

A related benefit to the employer is that tiers can reduce the costs of early retirement plans (Fogel 1985). In a tiered employment situation, employees who retire early are replaced by employees on the low tier, similar to what occurs with employee turnover. The result is that the company saves money over what it would have cost without the tiers. In some cases, companies have expanded early retirement plans for the purpose of obtaining greater cost reductions (Jacoby and Mitchell 1986).

It should be noted that even when tiered structures are eliminated, the potential cost savings may continue into the future. Wessel (1985) cites an example of a drugstore chain in which a two-tier plan had been in effect for 16 years. After that length of time, the wage difference between the two tiers had been nearly eliminated. The high-tier employees had received much lower increases than the low-tier employees, and management estimated that the average hourly wage cost was 8 to 10 percent lower than it would have been had tiers not been implemented. Similarly, Salpukas (1987) cites an example of a supermarket chain which provided wage increases to low-tier employees and lump-sum payments rather than wage increases for the high-tier employees. The tiers were to be merged after the high-tier rates had been frozen for six or seven years. Thus, when unions attempt to eliminate tiers, an employer can obtain additional labor cost savings through concessions of the high-wage tier employees. The BNA (1988) notes that an employer can obtain cost savings by playing off employees on one tier against those on the other tier in alternating contracts.

Potential Problems and Concerns Associated with Tiers

Several potential problems or concerns that may result from the implementation of tiered structures are identified in the literature. This discussion of potential problems focuses on those specific to employees, unions, and employers. Few of the potential problems have been the subject of academic scrutiny or examined empirically. Many are interrelated and appear to have their basis in the commonly held viewpoint that tiers, with their unequal pay for equal work, are unfair wage discrimination. As was the case with potential benefits, it is recognized that major problems resulting from tiers that affect one group of participants also may affect the other groups. For example, although it is often stated in the literature that lower employee morale resulting from tiers may impact adversely on both union and management in the form of increased grievances or lower productivity (Bowers and Roderick 1987; Essick 1987; Salpukas 1985; Wessel, 1985), lower employee morale is discussed in the section on potential problems for employees. A discussion of the potential problems/concerns includes public policy issues related to the union's duty to provide fair representation and to promote equal employment opportunity.

Based on a review of the literature, it appears that few of the potential problems associated with tiered systems become a major concern or political issue until one of the following two conditions is met: (1) the percentage of low-tier employees in any particular bargaining unit is relatively high, or (2) the low-tier employees gain enough seniority so that the other distinctions between them and the high-tier employees, such as skill, knowledge and familiarity with the job, disappear (Bernstein and Schiller 1985). Also, potential problems are likely to surface beyond the initial contract in an employment situation with temporary tiers or after several years for a permanent tiered contract (Balliet 1984; Flax 1984; Liggett 1984). With a strong economy and a tight labor market, however, problems with recruitment and turnover may arise even where tiers have not been in effect for a long time (Ross 1985; Salpukas 1987; Wessel 1985). In some cases, it appears that management has made changes to or eliminated tiers to alleviate the problems perceived as resulting from tiers.

Potential Problems for Employees

The potential problems for employees caused by tiers generally are thought to be related to lower morale (Bowers and Roderick 1987; Ploscowe 1986; Ross 1985; Salpukas 1987); the lower morale is certainly of great concern to the employer and union. Essick (1987) found that 38 percent of the managers from two-tier firms reported that tiers had had either a somewhat negative effect on morale or a significantly negative effect on morale. He also found that 17 percent of the managers surveyed reported that tiers had either a somewhat negative or significantly negative effect on the number (i.e., had increased the number) and significance of grievances filed. It should be noted that Sichenze (1989) found that "there are no reports of increased grievances, and no grievances have been filed that focus on two-tier provisions" (p. 493). Jacoby and Mitchell (1986) report that one-half of the managers from firms with tiers stated that tiers would result in a decline in employee morale.

Often cited as a problem is the job site friction between those on different tiers or between groups of workers opposing each other (Bernstein and Schiller 1985; Harris 1983c; Salpukas 1987). Balliet (1984) states that even if contract language protects more senior employees from easy replacement, two-tier agreements are almost certain to create severe strains within the worker/union community of interest. Salpukas found managers who believed that the low-tier employees often did just what was required on the job and no more, sometimes refusing to help the high-tier employees. Ross (1985) found high-tier employees who reported that occasionally low-tier employees refused to do a task because they were earning less. Bowers and Roderick (1987) state that workplace safety could become worse because of tiers. As a result of the morale problems and the constant arguing and complaining arising from a tiered plan, Ploscowe (1986) reports that one of his management clients had him negotiate away the tiers in exchange for work-rule concessions.

Possibly leading to both increased friction between groups and low morale for high-tier employees are the perceived threats to their job security, given the economic incentive to substitute lower-cost new employees for those on the high tier (Bernstein and Schiller 1985; Bowers and Roderick 1987; Ploscowe 1986). While seniority provisions generally protect the high-tier employees from being laid off, there are two widely cited examples in the retail food industry of high-tier employees being laid off and essentially replaced by low-tier employees (Bernstein and Schiller 1985; Bowers and Roderick 1987; Wessel 1985). Also, Wessel notes that equalizing tiers usually means that the high-tier employees' raises are sacrificed.

Potential Problems for Unions

The potential problems for unions relate to the belief that tiers create a different (and perhaps lower) class of members, with the low-tier employees having different interests than the high-tier employees. Thus, many observers contend that tiers are divisive and challenge the concept of union solidarity. Harris (1983c) discusses both the union and management perspectives on this divisiveness and the treatment of low-tier employees as creating "a bitter second class of workers" (p. 33). Craft, Abboushi, and Labovitz (1985) note that tiers, as a form of labor union concession, create new group differences in the union "that may stimulate factional fights and divisions within the ranks" (p. 174). In Wessel's (1985) discussion of this problem, he notes that tiers had caused such problems for the United Food and Commercial Workers International Union (UFCW) that it adopted a national policy opposing tiers for, among other reasons, "their inherent divisiveness" (p. 9). Balliet (1984) notes that union adoption of such clearly discriminatory wage packages is likely to heighten divisions within the rank and file and the union leadership. Ross (1985) notes that nothing could be more destructive to union solidarity than a pay structure giving unequal pay for equal work.

With the division of the union into classes and the weakening of union solidarity, it is unlikely that high-tier employees would be willing to strike along with low-tier employees to increase the low-tier rates if the high-tier rates did not receive an equal increase. Balliet (1984) further argues that if management attempted to lower the high-tier rates to those of the low tier, the low-tier employees would be unlikely to support a strike to prevent that. He believes the low-tier employees would have little interest in protecting the higher rates "of those who originally negotiated their inferior status" (p. 7). As noted previously, management can play off employees who are on different tier levels against each other in successive contract settlements, likely increasing the divisiveness among employees.

Thus, it is not surprising, as Ploscowe (1986) notes, that even the economic advantage to the current members and the potential for increasing union membership through employer expansion may be outweighed in some cases by the political damage to the union caused by tiers. Tiers may cause conflict within the union generally and problems at the bargaining table, leading to union-management conflict (Bowers and Roderick 1987). Wessel (1985) documents a case where a tiered agreement exacerbated a feud within a union. Ploscowe notes that tiers "may ultimately breed a radicalized and disaffected class of members more interested in overthrowing union leadership than in preserving the status quo" (p. 27).

If the low-tier employees become a majority of the bargaining unit, the union could be thrown into political turmoil. Ploscowe (1986) found some union officials who shared this concern and who conceded the possibility that the low-tier employees could vote the current leadership out of office or decertify the union. Bowers and Roderick (1987), recognizing these potential problems, even go so far as to suggest that implementing tiers may now be a union-busting technique used by management.

As tiered contracts have become more prevalent and unions have gained more experience with tiers, union leader fears about them have increased. Union leaders also are aware that high-tier employees are more concerned about their job security than previously. Ploscowe (1986) believes such concerns had led unions to become much less willing to accept tiers than previously.

Potential Problems for Employers

Some of the potential problems for employers appear to be related to the local labor market and the level of the low-tier pay scales, particularly the potential for increased turnover and for difficulties in recruitment. Turnover may be higher for low-tier employees than for similarly situated employees in firms without two-tier plans. Sichenze (1989) reports that turnover in the heavily tiered retail food industry was more than twice as high as the historical rate had been, going beyond the tightening of the labor market that occurred in the late 1980s. Wessel (1985) reports that the pay scale for low-tier employees at Hughes Aircraft Co. was so low that new workers did not stay. Ross (1985) reports that Giant Food found two-thirds of its new employees quit before the end of three months. American Airlines found some of its low-tier pilots quit and went to other airlines without a two-tier plan (Bernstein and Schiller 1985). In a study of a tiered employment situation that used a strategy of turning over low-tier employees rapidly, Granrose, Applebaum, and Singh (1986) found that unit labor costs were higher in those locations where turnover was higher. Essick (1987) obtained data on employee resignations from 76 companies with two-tier plans. A comparison of the data the year before the plan was implemented with the most recent 12-month period found essentially no difference, suggesting that tiers did not result in increased turnover.

Turnover is not always viewed as a problem, however. In companies whose workers are unskilled or require little or no training, turnover may be desirable as it keeps employees on the lower steps of the pay scales, thus helping to reduce labor costs (Dalton and Kesner 1986; Ross 1985). Obviously, savings from increased turnover have to be balanced against the increased costs of recruitment, training, and the lower productivity of new employees while they learn their jobs.

In a growing number of instances, often related to improvements in the economy and a tightening of the labor market, the two-tier systems have made recruitment difficult for employers. American Airlines had such difficulty recruiting pilots at its initial starting rate on the low tier that it had to raise the scale (Salpukas 1987; Wessel 1985). Giant Food had to raise the low-tier starting rate to attract new employees because the nature of the labor market in which it operated changed (BNA, March 2, 1988; Salpukas 1987). Those changes to the tiers at American Airlines and Giant Food were also introduced to reduce turnover. Lockheed could not recruit enough applicants at its California facility for some job classes at the starting rates and thus let applicants bargain individually for a higher rate of pay (Ross 1985).

Some employers found that the qualifications of applicants appeared to have declined after tiers were introduced (Salpukas 1987), though it can be argued that this is related to a tightening of the labor market (BNA, March 2, 1988). Salpukas even notes that some labor experts believe tiers for skilled workers will disappear due to labor market factors.[8] Ploscowe (1986) states that a careful investigation of prevailing wages in the relevant labor market must be conducted to determine that an adequate labor supply can be attracted at the desired rate.

An additional potential problem for the employer, as for the union, is the worsening of union-management relations. Thirty-two percent of the companies that Essick (1987) surveyed reported that tiers had had a somewhat negative or significantly negative effect on the overall labor relations climate. In contrast, 20 percent reported a somewhat positive or significantly positive effect on the climate.[9] Overall, a higher percentage of the respondents perceived a negative effect of two-tier wage systems on the labor relations climate, with the rest (49 percent) being neutral. Similarly, Jacoby and Mitchell (1986) report that 36 percent of the managers in firms with tiers perceived that two-tier plans had led to a decline in the climate of union-management relations, while 13 percent perceived it had led to an improvement. Based on the available survey data, it appears that most managers believe tiers result in a worsening of the labor relations climate.

Perhaps the most critical potential problem that tiers may create for employers is lower productivity. The prior discussion of the potential problems for employees, i.e., job site friction and morale problems, indicate that low-tier employees may put less effort into the job (Ross 1985; Salpukas 1987). If correct, this would result in lower productivity than would have otherwise been the case. However, unlike the issue of turnover and recruitment, there is little evidence that tiers result in less productive employees, with the exception of the special case of Hughes Aircraft Co. (Bowers and Roderick 1987; Wessel 1985). There, it appears that poor morale, low-tier employee dissatisfaction, and a lack of teamwork resulting from the implementation of wage tiers contributed to such low productivity and quality that contract payments were temporarily suspended by the Air Force. Subsequently, the low-tier starting rate was raised and the permanent plan converted to a temporary one. The available literature does not discuss whether those changes resolved the problems.

The only multiple-employer study using a productivity-related criterion is that of Essick (1987). He examined absenteeism, a variable that Katz, Kochan, and Gobeille (1983) found was negatively related to direct-labor efficiency and product quality, both of which have been viewed as indicators of productivity (Greenberg 1975; Siegel 1983). Essick analyzed absenteeism rates and other hard empirical data from companies with tiers, both before and after tiers were implemented. He concludes that, overall, his findings did not support the view that two-tier plans adversely affect the workforce.[10]

Essick (1987) and Jacoby and Mitchell (1986) also examined managerial attitudes about tiers and productivity. Essick found that 24 percent of the surveyed managers reported that tiers had had either a significantly positive or somewhat positive effect on employee productivity, 67 percent reported tiers had had a neutral effect, and only 9 percent reported tiers had a somewhat negative or significantly negative effect on employee productivity. Jacoby and Mitchell found that 13 percent of the managers they surveyed thought that tiers had improved employee productivity, 63 percent believed tiers had had no effect, and 24 percent believed that productivity had declined as a result of tiers. Thus, many surveyed managers believed that the implementation of tiers did not adversely affect productivity.[11] It should be emphasized, however that the survey data presented above only capture the subjective perceptions of managers. These studies and the Hughes case, while not providing a definitive answer concerning the effects of tiers on productivity, suggest that the relationship of tiers to employee productivity may vary depending on the situation. Nonetheless, the predominant belief expressed in the literature is that low-tier employees are less productive than those on the high tier (e.g., Ross 1985; Salpukas 1987).

Potential Public Policy Problems

Two legal public policy issues appear to be potential concerns/problems related to tiered-employment agreements: (1) Do tiered agreements violate the union's duty of fair representation? and (2) Do these agreements lead to legal problems related to equal employment opportunity (EEO)? While these issues in relation to tiered agreements have not been ruled on by the courts, they have been the subject of research and debate by scholars.

Duty of Fair Representation

Under the duty of fair representation (DFR) doctrine, a union must abstain from arbitrary, unfair, discriminatory, or bad-faith behavior in its responsibilities as the members' representative and fairly represent their interests. The DFR doctrine means a union is liable to all of its members and provides a safeguard against majority abuse of the interests of the numerical minority of the bargaining unit (*Harvard Law Review* 1985). Two-tier agreements potentially represent a threat to the capability of the union to safeguard the class of new low-tier employees in the bargaining unit. The doctrine currently provides only a small number of restrictions on agreements, such as two-tier agreements, that discriminate at the time of entry into the bargaining unit.

In several major cases, the Supreme Court outlined the nature of the DFR, generally avoiding a rigid definition of DFR, but instead opting for a flexible standard based on good faith. In *Ford Motor Co. v. Huffman* 345 U.S. 330 (1953), a union was allowed a "wide range of reasonableness . . . in serving the unit it represents." The Court stated that the tests were actions that could be described as manifesting "complete good faith" and "honesty of purpose." Thus a union did not violate its DFR merely if its conduct had some unfavorable effects on certain groups in the bargaining unit. If a union has acted in good faith with an honesty of purpose in attempting to reconcile the competing interests of different groups, it may favor one group over another. In *Gray v. Asbestos Workers Local 51* 416 F.2d 313 (6th Cir., 1969), the Circuit Court ruled that a job applicant enjoyed no right to fair representation, thus limiting application of the DFR to members of the bargaining unit only. Using the standard in *Gray,* any contracts into which tiers were introduced (not those that continued tiers) would not violate the union's DFR, as the new hires were not in the bargaining unit when the contract was bargained.

Two cases under the Railway Labor Act, *Steele v. Louisville and Nashville Railroad* 323 U.S. 192 (1944), and *Tunstall v. Brotherhood of Locomotive Firemen and Enginemen* 323 U.S. 210 (1944), approved discrimination on bases relevant to the union's statutory purposes. In stating that a union could not bargain differences based on irrelevant factors, the Courts went on to state what might be permissible and that variations could be based on differences that were relevant to the authorized purpose of the contract. Yet the set of "relevant" distinctions in terms of employee expectations yields virtually no restriction on the union's discrimination at the time the new employee enters the bargaining unit.

Summers (1984) states that such "relevant" differences could include those based on seniority, skill, and the type of work performed. Ploscowe (1986) notes that seniority, or date of hire, has always been a basis for the allocation of certain benefits under a collective bargaining agreement; thus it is unlikely that a Court would view differences based on that distinction to be arbitrary. In *Foxworth v. Airline Pilots Association* 83 Lab. Cas. (CCH) 10,498 (S.D. N.Y., 1978), the court stated that "it is not a breach of the duty of fair representation to provide special grandfather benefits on the basis of an employee's date of assignment."

In an analysis of the DFR in relation to tiered agreements, Liggett (1984) examined those court cases and others attempting to determine whether a contract that continues tiers previously negotiated violates the union's DFR to those low-tier employees continuing their employment. Liggett asks two questions relating to the DFR and tiered agreements. First, does the protection provided for one group's interests adversely affect another group's interests in a manner that violates the sense of permissible distinctions as found by the Court? Second, does the protection provided for a group's interests adversely affect another group's interests in a manner that violates the criterion set out by the court in *Huffman*? Liggett concludes that a union has failed in its duty of fair representation in the negotiation of a permanent two-tier agreement; permanent tiered agreements are much more vulnerable to DFR charges than are plans that merge. In addition, the availability of options other than tiers, i.e., across-the-board decreases for all members of the bargaining unit, raises questions concerning the defenses of "honesty of purpose" and "complete good faith" available under *Huffman*. Although the establishment of permanent tiers may be inconsistent with the fair representation doctrine, both the BNA (January 10,

1985) and Jacoby and Mitchell (1986) interpret Liggett's analysis to mean that tiers would likely withstand a DFR suit.

Equal Employment Opportunity

Equal employment opportunity (EEO), as stated in Title VII of the 1964 Civil Rights Act as amended, prohibits employment discrimination on the basis of race, color, religion, sex or national origin. The courts have held in several cases that an employment practice must not have a disparate impact on a "protected class," generally considered to be those of minority races, females, or foreign born, unless the employment practice is based on a business necessity (Lopatka 1977). The courts have held that there are three tests to determine the legitimacy of a business practice. It must serve a business purpose; that purpose must be sufficiently compelling to override the effects of any disparate impact; and there must be no alternative practices to equally or better accomplish the business practice with less disparate impact (Lopatka 1977).

Tiers have become an EEO concern because the lower tier could contain a disproportionate number of members of protected classes, such as women and minorities. Ploscowe (1986) suggests that this EEO concern is legitimate because the percentage of females and minority race employees is increasing in industries with tiers. Bowers and Roderick (1987) note that the continuing movement of women into the workforce suggests a potential EEO problem for tiers, as women would not be on the high tier.

A wide range of views regarding EEO is found in the results of two managerial surveys regarding tiers. Essick's (1987) survey of companies found that, of those with tiers, 5 percent stated that two-tier wage systems had a somewhat or significantly negative effect on the number and significance of EEO grievances filed, while 93 percent said it had a neutral effect. The Jacoby and Mitchell (1986) data gathered from managers at firms with two-tier plans showed that 51 percent agreed with the statement: "Legal problems for employers are created by two-tier plans if new hires are disproportionately female and minority workers." The remaining 49 percent of the respondents disagreed with that statement.

For two-tier systems, the question of concern is: "If women and minorities are disproportionately employed in the low tier, would they have grounds to win an EEO complaint?"[12] Rosenblum (1984) of the Equal Employment Opportunity Commission argues that a tiered structure would likely be safe from discrimination claims under Title VII of the 1964 Civil Rights Act so long as the lower tier was implemented without race or gender bias. Rosenblum's argument is supported by a law professor quoted in Flax (1984), who noted: "If such plans can be shown to have a serious business consideration rather than being a covert attempt by one group to do in another, I'd be surprised if responsible courts failed to uphold them" (p.77). Rosenblum further argues that even if women or minorities were disproportionately concentrated in the low tier, tiers negotiated in exchange for job security measures and agreed to in good faith, not as a way to get around the EEO laws, would probably be viable in an EEO suit.

There is still the possibility that low-tier employees will file a suit, even if the suit were not viable (Bowers and Roderick 1987; Jacoby and Mitchell 1986). Certainly, employers and labor unions should be concerned with the employee perceptions concerning EEO issues. The feelings of not being fairly represented and of being discriminated against also have the potential to lead to low morale and productivity problems (Bowers and Roderick 1987; Flax 1984).

The Incidence of Tiers

The review of the literature and the examples discussed above suggest several conditions that appear to have influenced the incidence of tiered settlements. The following conditions seem most relevant: the nature of the competition affecting the employer and its industry; the nature of the local and national economies; the nature of employment trends in the company and its industry; and the industry's collective bargaining structure. These conditions affected the needs and goals of unions and management, and therefore their willingness to negotiate and maintain tiers.

Certainly, it appears that the implementation and maintenance of tiers in several industries have been closely related to the competitive environment in that industry. For example, tiers are more common where an employer is confronted with competition from companies (generally nonunion) with lower labor costs. Also, the relationship between tiers and concession bargaining suggests that when the local and national economies are stronger, with relatively low unemployment rates and therefore a lower number of union contract concessions, fewer new tiers are negotiated.

Additionally, the literature suggests that the nature of employment trends within an industry or company may be related to the incidence of tiers. For example, tiers are more likely to be found in industries or companies that are expanding or companies that have a high amount of turnover. Similarly, industries, and companies within them, with a very stable workforce or declining levels of employment have a lower incidence of tiers.

The nature of the industry's collective bargaining structure also appears to be related to the implementation of tiers. The broader the bargaining structure, i.e., industrywide or companywide versus individual plant bargaining structures or those based on a local union's jurisdiction, the less likely are tiers to be found. In broader structures, where unions have organized the product market to a greater extent, unions possess greater bargaining power and thus are more able to resist management pressure to negotiate tiers. The nature of the bargaining structure appears to be less of a factor today, however, as industrywide and pattern-setting bargaining have become less common during the 1980s (Kochan, Katz, and McKersie 1986).

The previous discussion of the potential problems perceived to be associated with tiers provided several examples of management either eliminating or substantially modifying the tiered compensation systems. In each situation, management moved to reduce what it viewed as a disadvantage or cost associated with tiers. The descriptions of those cases indicates that the tiers were eliminated or modified to accomplish the following goals: improve employee morale; facilitate employee recruitment; decrease employee turnover; and improve product quality. Tiered compensation plans are more likely to be eliminated or modified to reduce the difference between the tiers where management believes that the costs have exceeded the benefits to the company.

Further, if management is already experiencing difficulties in recruiting employees, they may decide not to negotiate disparate compensation rates in the first place.

Recent Trends

To ascertain whether the BNA two-tier settlements reported in table 2.2 were new or modified plans and thus how prevalent tiers are, it is necessary to determine when such plans came into widespread use. While it is not certain when two-tier contracts first appeared on the American industrial relations scene, Flax (1984) states that two-tier contracts go back to the thirties. Balliet (1984) argues that it was only with the advent of widespread employer demands for contract concessions in the 1980s that two-tier provisions became common enough to attract much attention. Using data on concession settlements, Jacoby and Mitchell (1986) estimate that in 1982, less than 1 percent of all settlements were two-tier agreements. It is apparent, however, that some currently existing tiered plans were negotiated before then. For example, roughly 20 percent of Essick's (1987) 1986 sample had six or more years of experience with such plans.

It seems then, that the major increase in the number of new tiered-settlements took place around 1982. Given the large increase in the percentages of settlements with wage tiers as reported by the BNA and the three-year length of the majority of contracts (BNA, October 8, 1987), it appears that almost all of the 1983 and 1984 settlements would represent new plans. Also, it appears that enough of the two-tier settlements in 1985 would be new to represent an increase over the number of new settlements for 1984. By 1986, many of the earlier tiered agreements would have come up for renewal, with or without modification. It is probable that employers which had sought dual wage rates the most would have already negotiated them. Thus, the decrease in the number of new two-tier plans starting in 1986 is likely greater than that which is assumed when one interprets the BNA data in table 2.2 as representing new plans only, as many of the preexisting plans could have been modified.

The BNA's data also reveal that an increased proportion of the new plans are temporary rather than permanent (BNA, March 1, 1988;

February 23, 1989; Thomas 1988). Unions appear to be largely respon-sible for this recent trend. For example, the policy statement issued by the executive board of the UFCW in February, 1985, strongly discouraged permanent wage tiers while not ruling out temporary wage tiers (Bernstein and Schiller 1985). Based on his experience as a manage-ment negotiator, Ploscowe (1986) concluded that unions "will not readily negotiate a permanent two-tier structure, [but] will continue to negotiate temporary dual pay plans" (p. 27).

The available data also show a trend toward the elimination of ex-isting tiered compensation structures. The BNA data base contains 4 settlements in which tiers were eliminated in 1985 and 3 in 1986, but 15 in 1987 and 5 in 1988. While there has been an increase in the number of settlements eliminating wage tiers and a decrease in the number of newly negotiated tiers, the BNA data indicate that for both 1987 and 1988 there were still five times as many settlements (127 total) in which tiered plans were negotiated or modified (without elimination) as there were plans (20 total) that were eliminated.

In addition, it can be calculated from the BNA data that 27 of the temporary plans negotiated in 1987 were new plans, 6 lengthened the wage progressions, and 1 shortened them (BNA, March 1, 1988). In 1988, 14 new temporary plans were negotiated, 1 lengthened the wage progressions, and 6 shortened them (BNA, February 23, 1989).[13] Adding the number of new plans to the number of those with lengthened progressions indicates that for each of those two years, there were more than two times as many settlements in which tiers were newly instituted or extended as there were settlements which eliminated tiers. Even with the decline in the number of new plans being negotiated, more tiers currently are being either newly negotiated or modified to contain lengthened wage progressions than are being eliminated. Thus, it can be assumed that both the number of contracts with tiers and the number of workers employed on the low-wage tier are still increasing.

Others have misinterpreted the BNA data as indicating the imminent demise of two-tier structures. Newspaper reports, such as those by Crawley (1988) and Lewis (1989) seem to have misinterpreted the BNA yearly figures as representing the total percentage of contracts existing with tiers in them rather than the percentage of contracts with tiers negotiated in a given year. Even the BNA (1988) has suggested that "since [1985], the prevalence of plans has declined" (p. 55). It appears that some of these reports have been overly influenced by the prevailing attitudes expressed in the literature concerning the "unpopularity" of tiers (e.g., BNA 1988) in their assessments of the incidence of tiers.

The Future of Tiers

The literature suggests several factors likely to affect the future penetration of tiered compensation structures. Bernstein and Schiller (1985) argue that employees who were willing to accept tiers previously, when unemployment was higher and the economy was not as healthy, will be less willing to accept their low-tier status. In addition, in many bargaining units, low-tier employees will reach sufficient numbers to exert increased pressure on both employers and union leaders for the elimination of tiers (Borum, Conley, and Wasilewski 1987).

These changes and greater union knowledge about the impact of tiers appear to have made unions (both those that had negotiated many tiers and those that had not) increasingly reluctant to negotiate such plans (Ploscowe 1986). For example, the UFCW, which had negotiated many two-tier plans, recognized the unpopularity of tiers with its members when it adopted a bargaining goal in 1985 that opposed permanent tiers and supported working toward the equalization of the rates (BNA, March 2, 1988).[14] Further, union leaders are expected to find none of the other new compensation strategies discussed in chapter 1 as inherently unfair as two-tier plans (BNA 1988).

The results from the BNA annual surveys of employer bargaining objectives for 1988 and 1989 (BNA, March 2, 1988; October 6, 1988) reveal subtle changes in management views of tiers, which will likely affect the prevalence of tiers in the future. These surveys indicated that, of the employers with labor agreements expiring in 1988, 95 percent of those with wage tiers planned to continue them, versus 81 percent of those with agreements expiring in 1989. Of employers without tiers, 18 percent planned to negotiate them in 1988 versus 12 percent in 1989. These findings seem to support the view that the rate of decline for new tiered compensation plans will continue to increase and that more plans will be eliminated. It may be that many of the employers who most strongly desired to implement tiers and were able to convince their unions to do so have already negotiated them.

Changes in the economy and labor force since the early 1980s will also likely play a part in determining the prevalence of tiers. An important short-term change was the economic recovery from the 1981-82 recession, which resulted in unemployment rates in 1988 almost half the size of those earlier in the decade (BNA 1988; BNA, January 25, 1989). The improved economy and lower unemployment at the end of the 1980s, by themselves, probably made management less willing to negotiate tiers, as tiers make it more difficult to attract new employees. Also, the BNA (1988) recognized that a long-term demographic change, i.e., the "baby bust," would eventually lead to a shortage of new entrants to the labor force. When the effects of this demographic change are combined with those taking place in the economy, they concluded that

> the demographics of a middle-aged workforce have elevated employee recruitment and retention to a similar status [as labor cost containment]. The problem has become even more complicated—how does an employer hold down labor costs to remain competitive without losing its employees to its competitors [p. 23].

In contrast to the difficulties in recruitment and retention associated with tiers (resulting from the lowering of the entry wage level), all of the other new forms of compensation can facilitate recruitment and retention through means of additional employee incentives. O'Dell and McAdams (1986) argue that two-tier plans are the one new compensation strategy that does not enhance the use of a participative human resource strategy. Thus, it is not surprising that the BNA data indicate that as new wage tiers were becoming less common, lump-sum payments have become more common.[15] Lump-sum payments are often accompanied by participative employee human resource strategies and profit sharing plans (Brophy and Walsh 1987; Uchitelle 1987). Overall, the factors discussed here will likely continue to be related both to the decrease in the number of new tiers being negotiated and to the trend toward the elimination of tiers.

Although the above discussion may be interpreted by some as suggesting that tiers will rapidly fade away in the near future, this seems unlikely, as a sizable but decreasing proportion of management have an interest in implementing or maintaining tiers. Beyond the interest expressed in the BNA annual surveys of management collective bargaining objectives, that interest is documented in the 1986 survey data reported by Essick (1987) concerning management intentions for tiers. His survey focused only on tiers and provides some additional insight beyond the BNA annual surveys. He found that more than 60 percent of the 311 companies without tiers reported that they would consider adopting a two-tier plan in the future. Of the 123 respondents with tiers (28 percent of the survey group), about two-thirds intended to increase the use of tiers by extending the number of employee groups covered, by widening the pay difference between the tiers, by converting temporary tiers to permanent tiers, and/or by implementing benefit tiers. Insofar as management attempts to achieve these goals, tiers will still remain a major collective bargaining issue.

Essick (1987) concludes his analysis with the following prediction.

> Because American companies continue to face increasing competition, both at home and abroad, two-tier wage systems are expected to grow in popularity as an innovative approach to controlling labor costs [p.232].

Ploscowe (1986) offers the following strong arguments concerning the future of tiers.

> Both management and labor will continue to negotiate two-tier contracts because of increased competition from nonunion operators and the growing wage disparity between union and nonunion employees. The question is not whether, but how, management and labor will respond to this pressure. Labor costs will be reduced, whether by wage and benefit concessions, layoffs, work rule changes, two-tier contracts, or a combination thereof. Labor, although finding two-tier contracts distasteful, will continue to find the other alternatives completely unacceptable [p.28].

Salpukas (1987), while recognizing that tiered compensation systems are under attack, similarly notes that "with the increasing competition from deregulation and lower-cost nonunion or foreign companies, they are not going to disappear anytime soon" (p. 1). He quotes airline executives who stated that they would maintain tiers as long as nonunion competitors maintained low fares and possessed lower labor costs than established unionized carriers. Sichenze (1989) states that "two-tier labor contracts appear to represent a restructuring of the total wage package in the retail food industry—one that will continue into the immediate future" (p. 494). None of the above predictions, however, appears to have considered the other new compensation strategies as a viable alternative to tiers. Also, with the exception of Salpukas (1987) and Sichenze (1989), little attention has been given to the tightening of the labor market or to the change in the workforce demographics.

One prediction by Jacoby and Mitchell (1986) was slightly less optimistic. Based on a late 1984 and early 1985 survey of managers, Jacoby and Mitchell report the management belief that the number of two-tier wage structures would increase substantially in the short run. They conclude that two-tier plans will likely outlast the era of concession bargaining. Jacoby and Mitchell state that such plans are likely to be temporary plans, however, as the managers believed the collective bargaining process would eventually merge the permanent tiered wage scales into one unified scale. Our own conclusions concerning the future of tiers will be presented in chapter 8.

NOTES

1. Essick (1987) reports that approximately half of his 123 respondent companies with tiers had permanent wage tiers. Also, his survey revealed that 25 percent of two-tier systems cover employee benefits, while relatively few companies reported having tiers for employee benefits only. However, unlike other sources that sampled more broadly, 71 percent of his respondents with tiers were in manufacturing versus approximately 57 percent sampled by the BNA in 1988. In addition, 49.6 percent of the tiered companies Essick surveyed had less than 1,000 employees, and thus would not be included in any of the Bureau of Labor Statistics analyses of major collective bargaining settlements. Thus, it appears that the Essick data on the types and forms of tiers is not representative.

2. It should be recognized that some of the individual companies or individual industries that will be discussed in the following sections are exceptions to the generalizations reached concerning the two sectors. Also, since individual data by company were not readily available, aggregated data by sector or industry must be used in examining patterns of wage changes and tier implementation.

3. Given that there were only 10 two-tier manufacturing contracts in the BNA sample for 1988 (versus 38 in 1987), no conclusions are drawn concerning the business strategy employed.

4. The BNA service sector 1988 data are based on 35 contracts. It is highly likely that in 1988, based on the similarity of the 1988 settlements in that sector to the 1985 settlements, tiers again were used primarily as part of a strategy for expansion.

5. The BNA (March 27, 1987; March 15, 1989) data show lump-sum payments in 36 percent of their sample of all nonconstruction agreements in 1988, 32 percent in 1987, and 33 percent in 1986, compared to 19 percent in 1985 and 6 percent in 1984.

6. Our placement of industries into the industry groups is as follows: (1) manufacturing industries subject to competition from imports and/or nonunion companies; electrical machinery, fabricated metals, food processing, furniture, lumber, machinery except electrical, paper, printing, and stone, clay and glass; (2) industries affected by pressure from the government to cut costs; transportation equipment and postal (this is the only group that includes both manufacturing and service sector industries); (3) service sector industries affected by deregulation; airlines, communications, motor transportation, rail, and utilities; and (4) other service sector industries subject to competitive pressures; health services, insurance and finance, other services except health, and wholesale and retail. It is recognized that some of those industries, or some companies within a particular industry, could be placed into a different group as more than one force may have led to the establishment of tiers in any one instance.

7. By 1987, the airline industry had moved into a second phase of deregulation that involved multiple mergers and subsequent changes in the competitive climate. The analysis of Cappelli's (1985a) data focuses on the role of tiers in the premerger era.

8. Survey data from Essick (1987) indicates that tiered agreements have the greatest frequency for production workers, but very few cover skilled trades and maintenance workers. Cappelli and Sherer (1987) note that tiered plans offer little advantage in skilled areas, given that the strong external labor market makes it comparatively easy for such employees to find alternative employment.

9. One can only speculate as to why some managers perceived that tiers had resulted in an improved labor relations climate. Some possible reasons would be that the implementation of tiers: (1) had enabled the union and management to avoid other types of concessions; (2) had prevented facilities from closing; (3) had enabled the company to expand; or (4) had been bargained in ex-

change for something else the union wanted. With any of these reasons, the labor relations climate could have improved.

10. Sichenze (1989) also found no reports of increased absenteeism, tardiness, or sick leave usage.

11. Sichenze (1989) notes that while there were no clear-cut productivity figures, the labor cost figures of the companies where she interviewed did not indicate that employees' work-related behaviors were impacted.

12. The 1989 Supreme Court decision in *Ward's Cove Packing Co., Inc. v. Atonio* 109 S. Ct. 2155 (1989) qualified the interpretation of disproportionate section and employment practices. The burden on the plaintiff to prove the allegation of discrimination has been substantially increased.

13. In 1985, the BNA reported that 5 percent of the settlements lengthened the progressions and another 5 percent shortened them (BNA, February 24, 1986). In 1986, 14 percent of the settlements lengthened the progressions (BNA, February 26, 1987).

14. In the short run, however, the BNA reported that the UFCW has had to settle for a narrowing of the compensation gap between the tiers.

15. Refer to the data in table 2.2 and in note 5 for the proportion of settlements containing tiers and lump-sum payments, respectively, in each year after 1984.

3

Labor-Management Relations in the Retail Food Industry

The study of tiers in the retail food industry is useful because of the variety of tier forms, the large number of labor agreements containing tiers, and the extended length of time tiers have existed there. The purpose of this chapter is to present a brief introduction to this industry, its labor-management relations, and the resulting changes in the bargaining process and outcomes, such as tiers. This chapter lays the groundwork for the next chapter, which examines in depth a specific retail food company that negotiated tiers. Together, these two chapters provide the context for the survey results presented in the later chapters.

This chapter is divided into three major sections. The first section looks at the history of the retail food industry through the 1960s, focusing on the evolution and development of the industry, its subsequent unionization, and the structure of bargaining there. The second section examines the effect of market saturation and increased competition on the industry. The last section focuses on the resulting changes in the bargaining process and outcomes that have occurred in the past two decades. This and the following chapter incorporate information obtained from an extensive number of interviews with officials from the unions, companies, and others involved in the industry.

Before looking at the history of the retail food industry, it is useful to define some of the terms commonly used to describe stores and their organization (Food Marketing Institute (FMI) 1986). The term "independent" is used to refer to an operator of 10 or fewer retail stores. The term retail "chain" is used to define an operator of 11 or more retail stores. A "supermarket" is viewed as any store, owned by a chain or independent, having self-service grocery (and usually self-service in other departments), whose annual sales volume is $2,000,000 or more. This definition has been upgraded in the retail food industry from time to time.

The unions representing retail food employees are often referred to in shortened form. For example, the term "Retail Clerks" comes from the Retail Clerks International Association (later Union). In the past, this union usually represented all food clerks in grocery stores, except those in the meat department. The term "Meat Cutters" is derived from the Amalgamated Meat Cutters and Butcher Workmen of North America and refers to meat department employees in grocery stores. The United Food and Commercial Workers International Union (UFCW) was formed in 1979 by a merger of the Retail Clerks and Meat Cutters Unions. Some UFCW local unions were formed where former Retail Clerks and Meat Cutters locals merged. In other geographic areas, there are separate Retail Clerks and Meat Cutters locals. The International Brotherhood of Teamsters, Chauffeurs, Warehousemen and Helpers usually represents the truck drivers and the warehouse employees within the retail food industry.

History of the Retail Food Industry Through the 1960s

The Development of the Industry

Prior to the 1850s, retail food sales were the exclusive domain of small family businesses, but at about that time, the structure of food retailing in the United States began to evolve through a series of major changes. As a result of these changes, food retailing shifted from a large collection of small family businesses to a more consolidated industry. The first of these changes was the "chain store movement," which began in 1859 with the Great Atlantic and Pacific Tea Company (National Commission on Food Marketing (NCFM) 1966).

The chains involved in this movement reorganized food wholesaling, integrated food wholesaling and retailing, and substantially improved the efficiency of physical distribution (NCFM 1966). By combining wholesaling and retailing, chains were able to substantially lower costs through relative economies of scale. Thus, their profit margins were greater and their prices lower than the typical small family businesses with whom they were competing (Northrup and Storholm 1967). Chain stores eventually had their greatest expansion between 1910 and 1930.

The number of chain stores reached a peak in the early 1930s, with 80,000 total stores, controlling nearly one-third of the nation's total retail food business (NCFM 1966). The depression, along with severe competition, eventually halted the expansion of the chain stores. These same two economic factors, however, contributed to the development of the supermarket in the independent sector and its subsequent expansion. Supermarkets, which introduced modern mass retailing, were large low-overhead stores that combined several departments, such as meat, produce, and dairy, with the traditional grocery line of products. Most of them were self-service (NCFM 1966).

Following World War II, increased consumer mobility and income, the establishment of shopping centers, a strong desire for convenient one-stop shopping by many families, and the elimination of less efficient independents all contributed to the further growth of supermarkets. Thus supermarkets were able to increase their share of the retail food market from 28 percent in 1948 to 69 percent in 1963 (NCFM 1966).

The chains, and subsequently many independent operators converted many of their neighborhood stores to supermarkets in order to reduce retailing costs. Also, to compete more effectively, many of the independent operators joined together with other independents into groups known as "affiliated independents." The affiliated independent group is characterized by a wholesaler-retailer interdependence in which the two parties typically enter into an agreement. The retailer receives the advantage of economies of scale through the concentrated purchasing power exercised by the wholesaler, who in turn receives the assurance of selling the retailer goods for resale (NCFM 1966).

Unionization of the Industry

When the structure of food retailing was altered, the degree of unionization of the retail food industry also changed. Prior to 1900, the Meat Cutters' retail membership had been confined to grocery and specialty meat stores (Estey 1968). Founded in 1890, the Retail Clerks had only 5,000 members in 1933 (Northrup and Storholm 1967). The Retail Clerks grew rapidly to 246,000 members in the following 20 years and to 444,730 by 1966 (Northrup and Storholm 1967). Estey (1968) argues that as the small independent stores were combined into chains and subsequently converted into supermarkets, the working environment became more conducive to unionization than it was elsewhere in the retail industry.

Throughout the history of the retail food industry, the small family-owned store has been difficult to unionize because of the personal relationships and frequent contact between employee and employer. The chains and supermarkets are very large-scale businesses. A single supermarket may employ over 100 people, and some of the chains employ several thousand workers in one metropolitan area. With the passage of the Wagner Act (National Labor Relations Act) in 1935, the larger chains and supermarkets became ready targets for unionization. Their size meant that the per capita cost of union organizing was lower, and they provided the Retail Clerks with a basis for bargaining power. Generally, the Retail Clerks could not obtain such bargaining power in other parts of the retail sector or in family-owned grocery stores where small size combined with the relative lack of employee skills meant that the entire workforce could be easily replaced in the event of a strike.

Estey (1968) notes that an additional factor that may have contributed to the unionization of chain groceries and supermarkets was their employment of highly skilled meat cutters. The meat cutters' skill, in association with a highly perishable food product, made them a focal point from which unionization spread to other employees. Once the meat cutters were organized, the task of organizing the less skilled and less strategically located food clerks was greatly simplified.

Northrup and Storholm (1967) report three primary factors that led to the organization of employees by the Retail Clerks and Meat Cutters. First, these two unions received support from the Teamsters, whose driver and warehouse members controlled the supplies upon which the retailers depended. When the Teamsters' members failed to cross the picket lines at the retail stores, thus halting the flow of goods, the stores were forced to close. Although the Teamsters represent a small percentage of employees in the retail food industry, they have had a very influential role in the development of its labor relations.

Second, Northrup and Storholm state that when a union received recognition from a chain, it generally bargained both the union shop clauses (which provided for automatic extension of membership to new employees of existing stores in the bargaining unit), and accretion clauses (which extended the union shop to stores built or acquired in the future). As recognition was traditionally granted on a local marketwide and/or areawide basis, the rapid increase in union membership appears attributable to employer expansion, since much of the growth of major grocery chains through the 1960s occurred by opening new stores or by acquisition of existing nonunion stores (Estey 1968).

A third technique utilized by the unions in organizing employees was the establishment of direct contact with employers seeking to open the door to unionization of the chains. In this way, the unions often "organized the employer" as opposed to soliciting the votes of the employees (Estey 1968). Additionally, the unions cooperated with the retail food industry on a number of lobbying activities, including opposing anti-chain legislation (Northrup and Storholm 1967). In some areas, this cooperation certainly led to a decrease in the opposition to unionization.

The Structure of Retail Food Bargaining

With the radical changes in structure and the subsequent unionization of the industry, labor costs became the most significant operating cost in the retail food industry (Merwin 1984; Northrup and Storholm 1967). Such costs, including both direct and fringe benefits, represented 11.5 percent of gross sales in 1985 (FMI 1986); costs were generally higher for the major national chains than for the regional chains and independents (Merwin 1984; Northrup and Storholm 1967). Differences in labor costs may result in differences in food prices or company profitability. The industry gross profit margin on sales in recent years has averaged between 20 and 24 percent, while the net profit has averaged only about 1 percent.

To circumvent the possibility of competitors obtaining an advantage due to lower labor costs and to protect themselves in the event of a strike, major chains in many geographic markets organized themselves into multi-employer bargaining associations. These associations negotiated one contract with each of their unions, with identical terms covering all the member employers. This helped to stabilize labor costs among the different companies operating in a market (Northrup and Storholm 1967). Even chains who did not belong to a multi-employer group could usually be counted on to follow the pattern set by the other employers.

In addition, multi-employer bargaining prevented other association members from taking advantage of a strike. Northrup and Storholm (1967), assessing labor relations in the industry in the 1960s, note that a strike was a situation feared by individual chains. They cite three reasons why losses to supermarkets in a strike are "severe, immediate, nonrecoverable and can result in permanent defection of customers" (p. 21). First, sales that are not made during a strike are lost forever. Second, the perishable inventory is likely to be damaged. Third, because food shopping is habitual behavior, customers who are diverted from their regular store are likely to continue shopping at the new source after a settlement. With a strong multi-employer group, such a permanent loss of business was less likely to occur because the customer options would be more limited. With the apparent benefits of multi-employer bargaining, it is not surprising that between 60 and 80 percent of the Retail Clerks membership were included in multi-employer bargaining arrangements.[1]

Although many of the companies were included in the multi-employer bargaining units, there were many other factors that contributed to relatively unstable labor relations in this industry. Northrup and Storholm (1967) report that, within the multi-employer groups and with other retailers who might have followed the pattern those groups set, there were often conflicts between the regional chains and the national chains, given that the former had relatively limited resources and thus had less ability to pay wage increases and/or withstand a strike than national chains.

Second, the affiliated independent groups, many of whom were nonunion, were active in many of the markets. If they were unionized, whether or not they paid the same wage rates as the chains, they generally provided benefits at a level below that of the supermarket chains and almost always had work rules that provided them with savings that members of the multi-employer group did not have. Thus, such affiliated independent groups had no interest in being a part of a multi-employer group.

An additional problem resulted from the fact that, in most retail food markets, some portion of the employees were organized by the Meat Cutters, some by the Retail Clerks, and still others by the Teamsters. In some of the retail food markets, still other unions had recognition. As a result of this condition, there was constant pressure on the employers to increase labor costs, since each union would try to obtain a "superior" contract with the multi-employer group.

Market Saturation and Increased Competition

Changes in Growth Patterns

In the late 1950s and early 1960s, the growth patterns within the retail food industry in many geographic areas changed as markets became overcrowded or saturated (Merwin 1984; NCFM 1966). Merwin's description of what took place when a chain opened a supermarket on the fringe of a fast-growing city prior to the saturation point showed how this change in growth affected labor costs. A recently opened supermarket would typically have relatively low labor costs. Employees would be hired at the bottom of the seniority ladder, and thus they would be at the bottom of the compensation progression.

During this same time period and prior to a realization that the industry growth patterns were changing, companies often negotiated labor agreements that would substantially increase their labor costs. In those labor agreements, companies would often trade lower wage increases for more restrictive contract language and greater benefits (Retail/Services Labor Reports (RSLR),[2] April 6, 1982). For example, the A&P agreement of double time and then triple time as a Sunday premium was based on the belief that it would never operate on Sundays. In addition, employers often added fourth, fifth, and sixth weeks to their vacation schedules, because there were very few employees who had the seniority necessary to take the longer vacations.

When a geographic area became saturated, as many areas of the country outside the Sunbelt and the West did, the new supermarkets no longer replaced small independent stores; instead they took business away from other already established supermarkets, possibly even from those owned by the same chain. As the chains altered their business strategies in an effort to compete for customers, some of the stores opened on Sundays and most stores lengthened their hours of operation. When the markets ceased to expand, the labor costs increased as employees moved up the seniority ladder and few new employees were hired. Many such stores were no longer profitable, as the operating costs began to increase faster than inflation-adjusted sales (Merwin 1984).

Store Closings

The intensification of competition coupled with increased labor costs threatened company profits, particularly in the markets that had become saturated. Thus, A&P, which at the time was the largest supermarket chain with about 3,600 stores, announced in 1975 that it would be closing 1,200 stores (RSLR, May 1, 1975). For the most part, these were the older, smaller stores, although A&P intended to cease operations completely in some areas. It should be noted that there is a shared perception among industry observers that the A&P store closings were not related to the high labor costs.

A&P and some of the other companies found, however, that closing stores did not necessarily lead to an improvement in company profitability. Because many employees had rights to transfer between stores within an area, the retention of the expensive senior employees and the layoff of less expensive newer employees led to an increase in the average labor costs in the area. A&P also noted that some of its strongest competition in certain areas came from stores that had been sold to independents and regional chains (RSLR, January 1, 1982). These independents and regional chains were often not unionized, which gave them a further advantage of lower costs and more flexible work rules (Northrup and Storholm 1967; Ray 1980). Competition also came from small convenience stores (Northrup and Storholm 1967), and later on from nontraditional outlets, such as drug stores and service stations, which sold some grocery items.

By 1980, a total of 7,000 stores had been closed and about 100,000 unionized jobs had been lost (Ray 1980). It needs to be recognized that when all stores in a given area were closed, the major chains had alternative opportunities to adjust their business strategies to address the problems represented by market saturation and increased competition. The operational losses from the stores, if any, were necessarily eliminated through the closings. Further, when a major chain closed a store, the chain could sublease it to an independent operator at a rate higher than the cost of the original lease. Because of the chains' financial resources and credit ratings, they generally obtained relatively long-term and inexpensive leases for a store (RSLR, April 6, 1982).

As wholesalers of goods to individual stores, the largest national chains would keep open an individual store that was not profitable (Merwin 1984), as it helped protect total company profits. The national chains could also wholesale food products to stores that were purchased by the independents or, alternatively, they could sell all of the stores in an area to wholesalers who then would sublease the stores to independents. A notable example of the former was when a major chain sold several of its stores in a midwestern state in 1981 to an independent operator and then continued to supply those stores with goods of its own brand (RSLR, February 9, 1982). An example of the latter occurred in 1984, when Kroger closed all its 44 Pittsburgh area stores after UFCW members rejected a proposal to reduce wages by two dollars per hour (RSLR, February 20, 1984). Kroger subsequently sold the stores to a wholesaler who subsequently sold them to independents to be supplied by the wholesaler.

Another approach was for a national chain to form a joint venture with a wholesaler to offer a full line of food products and to supply services, as occurred in 1984 in a midwestern state (RSLR, May 28, 1984). There, the chain closed about 30 percent of its stores in that state, sold them to independent operators (none of which became unionized), and then supplied the chain's products to the independent stores through a new wholesaling joint venture.

In some situations, even the closing of marginally profitable stores allowed companies to increase profitability through such means as wholesaling and, at the same time, put substantial pressure on the UFCW local unions through temporary or permanent loss of membership. In addition, the unions incurred the costs associated with organizing the stores when they reopened. In the Pittsburgh area, the UFCW was successful in organizing 18 of the 26 former Kroger stores that reopened by August 1984 (RSLR, August 20, 1984). Another six of those stores were organized by the United Steelworkers of America; the six stores, according to the UFCW, paid lower rates than those organized by the UFCW.[3]

The store closings also applied substantial competitive pressure to the remaining chains, even if the sold stores were subsequently unionized. As a result of these store closings, the percent of the retail food market held by major national chains declined dramatically in the 11 years from 1973 to 1983 in cities with decreasing population growth (Merwin 1984). Merwin reports that the most dramatic drops were found in Baltimore, where the national chains' market share went from 82 to 39 percent, and in Pittsburgh, where the share dropped from 48 to 29 percent.[4] A significant outcome resulting from these changes was the breakdown of the multi-employer bargaining structure in many cities. The previously existing pattern wherein most companies in a city applied the same negotiated settlement became less common.

Changes in Bargaining Process and Outcomes

Increased Management Willingness to Take a Strike

While there had always been strikes in the industry (Northrup and Storholm 1967), their frequency increased after the wage-price controls instituted by President Nixon ended. During the 1970s and 1980s, there was a greater willingness on the part of management to take a strike as the companies attempted to hold the line on their labor costs. Management's ability to take a strike had been enhanced by product innovations and changes in technology, i.e., prepackaged meats, checkout line scanners. Such developments facilitated the operation of stores by supervisory staff and by replacements of the regular workforce during a strike. In addition, many management officials believed that the public had become less supportive of unions in general, and that customers would be willing to cross picket lines to shop.

The aggressive bargaining stance taken by the management of Safeway Stores Company, currently one of the largest national chains, resulted in several strikes in the late 1970s and early 1980s. In a 1980 speech, the then presiding chairman, Peter McGowan, cited important lessons learned from a 1978 Teamsters' strike and a 1980 Retail Clerks' strike, both in northern California (RSLR, November 27, 1980). Essentially, Safeway management perceived that they had "won" those strikes because contract restrictions were removed and additional clauses were avoided, thus reducing labor costs over what they would have been otherwise. Interestingly, at the time of McGowan's speech, Safeway was involved in three additional strikes. The company maintained that they had not been damaged in the marketplace by those strikes, but instead had maintained their market share.

Changes in Wage Settlements

Table 3.1 presents estimated retail food industry negotiated settlement figures for first-year wage increases and the Consumer Price Index (CPI) changes for selected years in the late 1970s and the early 1980s. Based on these figures, it appears that management officials were able to reduce the rate of increase in labor costs to below that of the change in the inflation rate. Also, the settlement figures for the late 1970s are shown to be relatively high in comparison to the later settlements. During this time period, many retail food companies exchanged the greater wage increases for lower premium rates for Sundays, reductions in vacations and other paid time off, the elimination of other restrictive contract language (RSLR, April 6, 1982), and the implementation of some tiers.

During the early 1980s, the profits of most of the chains were further reduced by such factors as a recession, an increase in nonunion supermarkets, and a decrease in the inflation rate, which caused inventory profits to disappear (*Business Week,* March 19, 1984). These factors, along with management's reaction to the changes in the economic environment, caused the unions to settle for somewhat less in 1981. At the end of 1981, the director of collective bargaining for the UFCW acknowledged that the union was making concessions that it probably would not have made previously (*Business Week,* December 28, 1981).[5] He contended that the union was more concerned with job security and predicted that the union would therefore probably settle for lower wage increases in 1982 (*Business Week,* December 28, 1981). This prediction was subsequently confirmed. The settlement figures were even less in 1983 and were greatly reduced in 1984.[6]

Table 3.1
Overall Inflation Rate and Estimated Negotiated First-Year Wage Increases in the Retail Food Industry

Year	Inflation rate[a]	Percent increase in base wage
1978	9.0	11.0[b]
1981	8.9	10.1[c]
1982	3.9	5.5[c]
1983	3.8	3.6[c]
1984	4.0	.4[d]

a. Changes from December to December in Consumer Price Index, *Economic Report of the President,* U.S. Government Printing Office, Washington, D.C., various years.
b. *Business Week,* December 28, 1981.
c. *Business Week,* August 27, 1984.
d. *RSLR,* February 25, 1985.

Implementation of Tiers

During the 1960s, an additional method, which later became known as "tiers," was instituted to reduce the increase in labor costs. Because the retail food industry was among the earliest to implement tiers (before the term "tier" came into widespread use), "two-tier wage structures" would not appear in the earlier labor agreements or in industry reports in the Bureau of National Affairs Retail/Services Labor Reports. Most early references to tiers only mentioned "new-hires" or restrictions on "new hires."[7]

The following paragraphs examine some examples of the forms that tiers, as a bargaining outcome, have assumed in this industry. These tier forms were used both as part of a strategy of expansion and as part of a strategy of economic survival. Sichenze (1989) argues that tiers in this industry effectively capped the upward climb of wages and benefits and permitted food retailers to compete more effectively in a changing environment. Individuals familiar with the industry provided examples of where the union was presented with a choice: either to negotiate tiers (or other labor cost-reducing mechanisms) and thus allow a particular chain to expand at less cost, or not to negotiate, and a nonunion subsidiary will be established to carry out the expansion. Those individuals also believed that in many instances where an employer wanted to expand into an adjacent market, that choice was implied even when it was not stated. Unions that desired to represent those new stores logically agreed to tiers.

Wage and Location Tiers

A thorough examination of reports from the RSLR, along with information obtained from interviews, suggests that the first retail food wage tiers appeared in 1974. The tiers implemented at this time were accompanied frequently by substantial wage increases for high-tier employees. An illustrative example was the 1974 Meat Cutters settlement, which covered storewide units of A&P and Kroger in Kentucky and southern Indiana. As a result of this settlement, high-tier food clerk wages went from $4.41 per hour to $5.76 per hour over a three-year period. In addition, they received three unlimited cost-of-living adjustments (COLA), which moved them to a $6.17 hourly rate, for a total three-year increase of 40 percent. The employees hired after the expiration of the prior contract received 25 cents less per hour than previously hired employees, a differential that was maintained as they progressed through the rate progressions (RSLR, November 12, 1974; RSLR, December 1, 1977). The 1977 contract renewal, which contained wage tiers for A&P and Kroger, maintained the 25 cent per hour differential between the high- and low-tier employees.[8]

The 1977 contract renewal for Kroger contained location tiers, which established a five cent per hour differential in wages based on the geographic area of the store and whether or not an area had unionized competition. The differential based on a location tier was implemented in approximately 17 Kentucky towns that had no unionized competition. The RSLR reports that a Kroger spokesman believed that the location tier was a recognition by the union that a unionized company should receive differential treatment when going head-to-head with nonunion competition.

The 1980 contract renewal for southern Indiana and Kentucky between Kroger and the UFCW widened the existing area differential to 10 cents per hour and continued all the other tiers previously in effect (RSLR, June 12, 1980). By 1986, after A&P had almost completely pulled out of that market, Kroger reported that wage tiers were the only thing allowing Kroger to continue operating in that area. Overall, Sichenze (1989) found wage tiers for one or more job classifications in 91 percent of the retail food contracts that she examined, and 88 percent of those were permanent.

Employment-Status Tiers

Employment-status tiers, which were often implemented in combination with wage tiers, typically had an adverse effect on the compensation of part-time employees. For example, relatively low rates were established at Kroger for new-hire part-timers in Ohio in 1979, and previously hired part-timer rates were capped (RSLR, August 2, 1979). In another part of the state, new-hire rates for part-time delicatessen clerks differed by as much as $1.05 per hour from rates of those previously hired (RSLR, August 23, 1979). In Pittsburgh, in early 1978, Kroger and the Retail Clerks negotiated a contract that reduced the increases current part-time employees would receive when progressing to full-time status. Sichenze (1989) found that benefit tiers existed in 86.5 percent of the contracts she analyzed, and were applied to all job classifications, unlike wage tiers, which are often applied to specific job classifications.

Benefit Tiers

Some of the contracts mentioned above also contained tiers that affected employee benefits. Both the 1980 southern Indiana and Kentucky contract for Kroger employees and the 1984 contract covering Kroger employees in a midwestern state reduced Sunday and holiday work premiums from double time to time-and-one-half for all new hires (RSLR, June 12, 1980). A national chain in another midwestern state cut its pension contributions in 1984 for all new hires (RSLR, August 28, 1984). Also, a 1983 midcontract modification in the same midwestern state instituted copayments for insurance for all new hires in a regional chain, whereas previously hired employees had no copayments (RSLR, January 7, 1985). Sichenze (1989) found that benefit tiers existed in 86.5 percent of the contracts she analyzed, and were applied to all job classifications, unlike wage tiers, which are often applied to only specific job classifications.

Job-Duty Tiers

Two-tier wage structures were also frequently negotiated within the nonfood job classes based on employment date. Ross (1985) found that supermarkets in the San Francisco Bay area had negotiated what was called the "nonfood clerk tier" in 1974 (referred to here as a job-duty tier). Employees in the nonfood job class received about two-thirds the pay of the food clerks while doing identical work (the employees in these two job classes did handle different products). A similar nonfood job class was implemented for retail food employees in Baltimore in 1982. Other areas of the country, such as the Los Angeles area, have also used nonfood job classes (Wessel 1985).

Changes in the UFCW's Position Toward Tiers

As the number of contracts with tiers negotiated with the UFCW increased,[9] the number of employees on the low tier also increased. Ploscowe (1986) notes that the increased numbers of low-tier employees began to cause many political problems for the union; after such employees became a majority, there was increased political pressure to stop the extension of tiers or to eliminate them. At its executive board meeting in February 1985, the executive board of the UFCW adopted a collective bargaining goal to eliminate multi-tier wage and benefit structures, because the union viewed tiers as inherently discriminatory to newer UFCW members (RSLR, March 3, 1985). UFCW President William H. Wynn operationalized this goal by saying "we're going to equalize wage rates." Wynn was willing, however, to accept temporary tiers with lower starting rates that would be raised to the top rate within a given period of time (Bernstein and Schiller 1985). The executive board did not establish a time period within which equalization must be reached, but instead permitted each local union to bargain with management. The stated UFCW goal appeared to strengthen the union's resolve not to expand previously implemented tiered compensation structures or to initiate new ones.

The first and biggest major test of this resolve surfaced during an eight-week strike/lockout affecting more than 1,100 grocery outlets and 22,000 employees in southern California during November and December of 1985 (RSLR, November 11, 1985). Here, the contract proposals (which involved two-tier wage structures) of the Food Employer's Council (FEC), the multi-employer bargaining group for the major southern California grocery chains, was rejected by the Meat Cutters locals and the Teamsters.

This incident came to symbolize the nationwide importance that tiers represented for this industry and the conflict regarding their implementation and use. The FEC contended that tiers were "consistent with settlements across the country," and would not affect the wages of employees already on the payroll. A union spokesman responded that "it is important for us to protect workers of the future. The first step in destroying a union is to negotiate a lower rate for new members, and we are not going to give in on this two-tiered rate" (RSLR, December 9, 1985). The unions threatened to take the strike nationwide by pressuring chains with stores outside of southern California, such as Safeway and Lucky Stores. The final settlement between the unions and the FEC represented a compromise on tiers; the unions avoided granting any permanent two-tier wage structures, and management obtained some of the desired cost savings possible with temporary and job-duty tiers (RSLR, January 1, 1986).

Conclusions

The unionized retail food industry has been attempting to adjust to a continually changing competitive environment. Wage tiers were first implemented in the industry in the 1970s in anticipation of possible future economic difficulties and for the purpose of gaining a competitive advantage. They were generally accompanied by relatively large increases in compensation for previously hired employees, which suggests that those tiers were part of a strategy of expansion. By the early 1980s, however, the strategy was altered due to changes in the external environment that reduced profits for the industry. During this period, the negotiation of tiers was usually accompanied by other concessions, which suggests that they may have been a part of a survival strategy, at least in certain markets. After 1985, when the UFCW position on tiers changed, the unions and management found themselves in considerable conflict over their implementation.

NOTES

1. Testimony by the president of the Retail Clerks, *Multiemployer Association Bargaining, Hearings before the General Subcommittee on Labor of the Committee on Education and Labor.* U.S. House of Representatives, 88th Cong., 2nd sess., 1965, p. 10. Cited in Northrup and Storholm (1967), pp 124-125.

2. The Retail/Services Labor Reports (RSLR), a weekly publication of the Bureau of National Affairs, Inc., discusses labor relations developments affecting the retail sector. It is the only such publication for that sector.

3. In contrast to the situation in Pittsburgh, stores in the Midwest that were sold to unionized chains and those that were sold to nonunion independents eventually ended up operating as nonunion stores.

4. In 1984, the market share held by national chains in Pittsburgh went to zero after Kroger closed all its stores in the area.

5. Management officials thought that the 1979 formation of the UFCW from the Retail Clerks and the Meat Cutters had ended wage competition and was bringing more realism to bargaining (*Business Week,* December 28, 1981).

6. The 1984 settlements, however, were closely related to the strength of the economy in different areas of the country and to company profitability, with small increases in the Sunbelt and concessions in other areas of the country.

7. Sichenze (1989) notes that most of the early tiered provisions affected benefits and work-rules rather than wages.

8. The 1977 A&P contract renewal lowered the starting rate from $3.73 to $3.25 for food clerks hired after a given date. In the 1977 Kroger contract renewal, the COLA payments applied only to those employees who had been on the payroll for six months when the increase was to be made.

9. The Bureau of National Affairs (BNA) surveys of contracts have consistently found that the UFCW has negotiated more than twice as many settlements mentioning two-tier wages as any other union. BNA reported 124 such settlements for the UFCW for the years 1983 through 1987 (BNA, March 1, 1988). Due to the decentralization in the retail food industry and the individual agreements for each local geographic area, the UFCW has a very large number of contracts. Unions operating in other industries, such as the airline industry, as shown in table 2.2, likely have a much greater proportion of their membership working under tiered agreements than the UFCW.

4
Tiers and the
Mayway Food Market Company

This chapter looks at the implementation, expansion, and maintenance of tiers at Mayway—the fictitious name for the retail food company at which our detailed case study and employee survey were conducted.[1] As part of this examination, the chapter discusses the history of the union-management relations at Mayway. The chapter also describes the environment of the state where the focal company operated, along with the bargaining developments that affected the process and outcomes of retail food bargaining there and led to the widespread adoption of tiers by other companies.

Historical Development of Mayway's
Union-Management Relations

In 1934, the Mayway Company opened its first grocery store in a town in a midwestern state. Between the time of the company's founding and 1951, Mayway expanded slowly, opening four more stores in the rural areas of the state. In the early 1950s, after the rumor of a Teamsters' organizing effort reached management, the company chose not to resist an effort by its employees to organize an independent union not affiliated with the American Federation of Labor-Congress of Industrial Organizations (AFL-CIO). All of the company's nonexempt employees, including truck drivers, warehousemen, and those in the food and meat departments, were then represented by that one independent union. The company benefited by only having to bargain with one union, instead of having different groups of its employees organized by the Retail Clerks, Meat Cutters, and Teamsters. With such a diverse bargaining unit, however, Mayway's union appeared more susceptible to competition and conflict among its different constituencies.

Company Expansion

In the early 1960s, Mayway opened its first store to carry a large line of general merchandise in addition to groceries. Soon after that store's opening, a Retail Clerks local union filed with the National Labor Relations Board (NLRB) seeking a separate bargaining unit for that store on the grounds that it was a new operation distinct from the supermarkets. In deciding the case against the Retail Clerks local, the NLRB certified the already existing bargaining unit and the company's recognition of the independent union. The NLRB also validated the accretion agreement between the parties, thereby extending the union's recognition to any stores the company opened.

This decision would come to have a major impact on company expansion and the subsequent negotiation and implementation of tiers. Had the Retail Clerks local won this case, the new stores with general merchandise (GM) departments would not have been added automatically to the bargaining unit. If the decision were reversed, the independent union's desire for increased membership might have been thwarted by the organizing efforts of other unions. Also, if the union were forced to compete for membership with other unions, it would have been less likely to agree to the lower rates for the general merchandise job classes (the job-duty food/nonfood tier) because it would have wanted to deprive other unions of a potential campaign issue.

Given that very few general merchandise retailers were unionized, it was necessary for Mayway to establish lower rates for general merchandise (GM) clerks than comparable food clerks so as to be competitive with other general merchandisers (even though the duties and skills required for both job classes were often identical). This new pay difference formed a job-duty tier. As a result of the NLRB decision, it was nearly impossible for other unions to organize all of the company's employees (as all the stores would have to be organized at the same time), and it was easier for Mayway to maintain the wage differences between the job-duty food/nonfood tier.

At the time of the NLRB decision, the company had 17 stores and about 1,000 employees in the rural areas of the state. By 1974, however, it had expanded into the state's largest metropolitan area and had 25 stores and about 6,000 employees in the bargaining unit. All of the additional stores carried general merchandise lines, and many of the older stores had been expanded to carry or had been replaced by new stores carrying such lines. This addition of general merchandise lines accounted, in part, for the large increase in employment.

When Mayway opened its first store in the metropolitan area, another Retail Clerks local filed a petition with the NLRB to represent the employees at that store. In this case, the outcome was different; the NLRB ruled against the company and independent union, noting that the new store served a different trade area with separate economic and marketing considerations. The NLRB decision was upheld by the Courts in 1977 and invalidated the accretion agreement. That decision would lead to conflict between Mayway and the union representing its employees, as the company insisted that the union obtain recognition at each new store through NLRB-conducted elections.

Affiliation of the Union with the Retail Clerks

In the early 1970s, a faction known as the ''dissident group'' developed within the union. This group favored closer ties with organized labor, including affiliation with the Retail Clerks, and more distance from the company. In 1975, a union membership vote to affiliate with the Retail Clerks was defeated, although the closeness of the vote (49.5 percent to 50.5 percent) and the significant organized opposition to the affiliation were indicators of considerable conflict among the union members over the methods of achieving union and member goals. The employees who sought affiliation with the Retail Clerks, particularly those in the dissident group, wanted to more readily exchange information with other unions and sought the technical assistance provided by the international union. They believed that through affiliation with the Retail Clerks they would have more bargaining power to obtain desired work rules. In addition, affiliation with an AFL-CIO union would prevent other AFL-CIO affiliates from organizing within its jurisdiction and taking its members.

The company was concerned that its dealings with the employees at Mayway would be significantly altered if the union representing its employees affiliated with the Retail Clerks. With such an affiliation, the employees could have been divided along the geographical jurisdictional lines of the Retail Clerks, thereby forcing the company to deal with several Retail Clerks local unions. The independent union helped the company maintain flexibility by restricting its dealings to one union. Also, the company believed that if it was required to deal with the Retail Clerks, it might be forced into multi-employer bargaining. If that were the case, the resulting labor contracts would likely be less responsive to the particular needs of Mayway. The independent union, which represented all of Mayway's unionized employees and no employees outside of Mayway, was not considered as an outsider as would be a union affiliated with the AFL-CIO.

In 1977, the union elected all of its officers from the dissident group, replacing an administration that had led the union for about 20 years. During bargaining for the 1977 wage reopener, which was marked by a membership vote to strike and lengthy negotiations, the conflict between the new union administration and management intensified. The new union administration aggressively sought affiliation with the Retail Clerks, and in 1978 they conducted a campaign for affiliation. Mayway still opposed such an affiliation, and the election campaign became very fractious; support for affiliation was seen as prounion and anticompany. In the subsequent election, votes favoring affiliation with the Retail Clerks outnumbered those opposed by a three-to-two margin, and the Retail Clerks International Union granted its new local union a jurisdiction covering all employees of Mayway within the state.[2]

One month after the vote, the company refused to bargain with the union and requested the NLRB to determine whether it was legally bound to bargain with the new Retail Clerks local union. The company claimed there were allegations by certain employees about irregularities in the conduct of the 1978 affiliation election. In a subsequent strike vote, characterized by the Retail Clerks local as a vote for its existence,

90 percent of those voting favored striking when the contract expired. A federal mediator, however, averted a strike by helping to obtain an agreement to extend the existing contract. Subsequently, the NLRB ruled that the union election for affiliation with the Retail Clerks would stand. After the union had won the vote and the NLRB decision, the union officers began to portray the company in more positive terms, so as to reduce the union-management conflict. As a result, many who had supported the affiliation with the expectation of radically changing the company employee relations policy were disappointed; the most senior employees subsequently encouraged members to become more negative toward the union.

The 1978 Negotiations and Agreement

The 1978 contract negotiations were influenced primarily by two conditions. First, there had been an increase in the market share held by nonunion retail food employers in the rural market area of Mayway.[3] Second, the level of conflict between the union and management had increased. While historically the independent union had negotiated slightly higher wages than the unionized competition, by early 1978 the top rates of its employees were slightly lower than the rates negotiated by some of Mayway's competitors. Thus, a priority of the new Retail Clerks local was to obtain parity with those rates through relatively large wage increases. Another priority of the union was to gain provisions and rights in operational areas that were similar to what other Retail Clerks locals had in their contracts but which had not been a concern of the independent union. The company's intentions in bargaining were to avoid multi-employer bargaining, to keep its pension and insurance plans out of any multi-employer plans, and to lower the costs of carrying out its strategic business expansion plans.

The November 1978 three-year contract implemented a two-tier wage structure that established a new lower wage scale for all retail store employees in the bargaining unit hired after the date of the contract (except skilled meat cutters and department heads).[4] The 1978 tiered agreement also included the negotiation of separate area-based scales of low-tier rates (i.e., (1) for the urban area—including the major metropolitan and cyclical subareas, and (2) for the rural area) as a result of differences in the external competitive environments in the state. In the major metropolitan subarea, the unionized chains controlled over 80 percent of the retail food market compared to 30 percent in Mayway's rural market area. Thus, a higher scale was established for the urban area than for the rural area, so as to more closely approximate the pay rates of the competition in those different areas. Large savings also would be obtained in the future as a result of combining the full- and part-time rate schedules for new GM employees. This change, which represented a form of an employment-status tier, essentially made it impossible for the ''new'' part- or full-time GM clerks to receive rates equivalent to those obtained by the current full-time GM employees. The new contract, however, gave part-timers the right to bid on full-time openings. Previously, Mayway could bypass the long-term, part-time employees and hire full-timers from outside the company.

Unlike most two-tier contracts, the low-tier wage rates at Mayway also applied to most previously hired employees who changed departments after the effective date of the contract. Promotions within the same department (food or GM), however, allowed employees to move among the high-tier rates only where there were no separate scales for full- and part-time employees. Thus, under the contract, high-tier, part-time GM clerks could not move onto the high-tier, full-time GM clerk rate schedule but, for example, could move into the higher-paying, low-tier cashier job class in the food department.

Given the wage increases and other improvements the union obtained in this contract for the current employees, however, the union and its members did not consider this contract as concessionary. For example, the union received increases of between 9 and 10 percent for the first year for most job classifications. These increases put them equal to the highest rates in the state and above the rates of the regional chains in the rural area. Also, while not joining any multi-employer plans, Mayway agreed to match the benefits contained in the multi-employer Retail Clerks plans.[5]

In addition to settling the new contract, the parties resolved the issue of how future stores would be added to the bargaining unit, with the union given recognition for all new Mayway stores opened within the market area of any Mayway store in the state. By this time, the union had organized the stores in the metropolitan subarea, and would thereafter receive recognition for new stores opened there. The union also obtained an implicit agreement that the company would continue to expand its operations by building new stores. With new stores added to the bargaining unit, employees in the previously opened stores would have increased opportunities to raise their income, both by taking higher-paying positions in a new store and by moving up to vacated positions within their same store. In addition, the union argued that the job security of the previously hired employees would increase as new stores opened. Such employees had employment rights over less senior workers in the new stores in their geographic area in the event of layoffs.

Overall, it is unlikely that the union would have agreed to the two-tier structure if future stores would not be added to the bargaining unit. Also, in retrospect, it is unlikely that the union would have been able to receive such large pay and benefit increases and that the company would have been able to expand as it subsequently did, had the two-tier wage structure not been negotiated.

State-Level Environment

The previous sections have shown the historical context in which Mayway and its union negotiated various tier forms. Implementation of tiers permitted the company to control labor costs, resulting in savings that facilitated its strategic business plan of expansion both into new lines of products and into new stores. It enabled the union to increase its membership and to obtain large pay increases for the current employees in the high levels of the tier forms. The following section describes the state-level environment in which Mayway and its union operated and the changes occurring in that environment.

Geographic Areas

Based on population density and economic characteristics, the state in which Mayway operated can be divided into two areas: urban and rural. The urban area has been and continues to be dominated by one manufacturing industry long marked by economic cycles that significantly affect employment in the area. The urban area may be broken down into two major subareas: the major metropolitan subarea and the "cyclical industrial" subarea. The major metropolitan subarea consists of a prominent metropolitan center and suburban areas containing more than one-half of the state's population. The other urban subarea (cyclical industrial) is contiguous to the metropolitan subarea but was not combined with it for census bureau purposes. Many of the employers in each subarea have been very closely allied to the urban area's major manufacturing industry.

The rest of the state will be referred to as part of the rural area. The principal industries in the rural area are agriculture and tourism, although it should be recognized that this area is not completely devoid of manufacturing development. The rural area does not contain any cities with a population of over 250,000.

The Major Unionized Chains

Table 4.1 shows the characteristics of the major unionized chains in the state in the mid-1970s and in 1986. The mid-1970s was chosen because it was the time when Mayway opened stores outside of its traditional rural market area. At this time, the different competitive economic environment encountered by Mayway began to strongly influence its union-management relations and to affect the negotiation of tiers. The date of 1986 has been included in this table because the surveys were mailed to employees at selected Mayway stores at that time.

As can be seen in the table, there were eight major unionized chains in the state in the mid-1970s; two of the unionized chains were national and six of the unionized chains were regional. The greatest concentration of unionized stores was in the metropolitan subarea, which contained five major national and regional operators. Mayway operated

Table 4.1
Characteristics of the Major Unionized Chains in the State in the Mid-1970s and 1986

Chain	Geographic area of operations	Mid-1970s		1986	
		Number of stores	Unionized store employees	Number of stores	Unionized store employees
National					
I	Metropolitan	58		41	
	Cyclical industrial	14		4	
	Rural	33		12	
	Total	105	6,500	57	4,100
J	Metropolitan	68		40	
	Cyclical industrial	14		10	
	Rural	2		2	
	Total	84	3,450	52	2,250
Regional					
A	Metropolitan	58	3,000	19	1,100
B	Metropolitan	79		84	
	Rural	1		1	
	Total	80	5,300	85	6,000
C	Metropolitan	46	3,900	20	1,500
D	Cyclical industrial	25	800	24	600
E	Rural	25	550	21	450
Mayway	Metropolitan	2		8	
	Cyclical industrial	2		5	
	Rural	21		24	
	Total	25	6,000	37	16,000
Totals for all chains		448	29,500	315	32,000

only two stores in the metropolitan subarea at that time and thus was not considered by the other chains to be a major operator there.[6] Although not discernible from table 4.1, the three major regional metropolitan chains bargained on a multi-employer basis (Company A, which had some out-of-state operations, Company B, and Company C). Along with the two national chains, the three regional chains established a pattern of collective bargaining agreements that was followed throughout much of the state.

In the cyclical industrial subarea, there were stores operated by each national chain, Mayway, and Company D. As can be seen, Company E and Mayway were the two largest regional chains in the rural area. There were also three smaller regional unionized chains that operated in the rural area, as well as numerous smaller nonunion chains and nonunion stores.

By 1986, changes in the environment led each national chain and most of the regional chains to close stores and reduce the employment of unionized store employees. Most of the stores that had been closed eventually were reopened by lower cost nonunion independent operators. This contributed to an increase in nonunion competition and thus to continuing pressure on the unionized chains to control labor costs. While many chains closed stores and/or operated under bankruptcy protection between the mid-1970s and 1986, Mayway increased the number of stores in each geographic area of operation and greatly increased the number of employees per store. Further, data from industry market surveys indicate that Mayway's share of the retail food market was at least three times greater, on the average, per store than for any competitor with stores in the same area.

Although the total number of unionized chain stores in the state declined substantially during this period, the total number of unionized retail store employees increased. This increase in the total number of unionized employees was largely attributable to Mayway's expansion and the increased employment within both its new and older stores. It can be calculated from table 4.1 that the average number of employees per store at Mayway was about six times as many as at the next largest regional chain.[7]

Figure 4.1 summarizes many of the major events that occurred after the mid-1970s in the years when contracts were renegotiated or modified in midterm at Mayway. Table 4.2 illustrates the impact of the events on the wage rates paid at the end of selected years.[8] The table shows top rates of hourly pay for the cashier and GM clerk job classes. These two job classes represented about one-half of Mayway's retail store employees. Cashiers were also selected because they were employed by all of the competition. It should be recognized that there was generally no class equivalent to the GM clerks employed at Mayway's competition. Also, all of the rates included in the table were taken from contract settlement data with the exception of the nonunion top rates, which are based on estimates. The effects of the store closings, chains operating in bankruptcy, increased competition, and the breakdown of pattern-setting bargaining on the rates is apparent in both the existence of a range of top rates and the freezing of many of the top rates between 1984 and 1987 at both Mayway and its competition.

Another result of the many store closings and changes in employment levels was a reduction in the number of Retail Clerks local unions operating in the state between the mid-1970s and 1986 from five to two. The independent union representing employees at Mayway had affiliated with the Retail Clerks in 1978. In 1980 and 1982, the two Retail Clerks local unions operating in different parts of the rural market area of Mayway merged into the union representing Mayway's employees. The resulting Retail Clerks local then represented all of the unionized employees of Mayway plus other employees of other companies in the rural market area of Mayway. In 1983, there were mergers of the two Retail Clerks local unions based respectively in the cyclical industrial subarea and in the largest rural section of the state into the Retail Clerks local based in the metropolitan subarea. The resulting local did not represent any of Mayway's employees, even where they were employed in the urban area. The two remaining Retail Clerks unions, however, represented workers in different stores of the same employer other than Mayway, such as the two national chains and Company B. There were also separate Teamsters locals and a statewide Meat Cutters local representing employees in the retail food industry.

Figure 4.1
Time Chart of Major Events Surrounding the Bargaining Rounds

	State economy	Nonunion operations	National chains	Regional chains	Mayway
1977/78	Strong	Increase in rural market share	Moderate wage increases	Company A bankrupt, closes stores, moderate wage increases for others	Union affiliation with Retail Clerks, wage tiers and higher urban rates instituted, subsequent expansion
1980/81	High unemployment	Small increases in market share	Large wage increases, many stores outside of metropolitan subareas sold	Large wage increases, except for Company A	Differentials between tiers increased, ratio of expansion slows
1982/83 midterm modifications	Highest unemployment, population decreasing with outward migration	Larger increase in market share	Wage freezes and contracts extended for one year	Company C bankrupt, cuts rates, rest freeze wages and extend contracts for one year	Benefit tiers instituted, rate of expansion increases
1984	Decreasing unemployment	Large increase in urban market share	Company I cuts wage rates and closes 35 stores, Company J freezes rates	Wages frozen for three years	Differentials in wage tiers reduced, benefits reduced and benefit tiers eliminated, top rates frozen with lump sums given, expansion continues
1986/87	Strong, unemployment much lower, population increasing again	Stable market share	Companies I and J initiate wage and employment-status tiers, J expands	Company C essentially goes out of business, A and B expand and initiate wage and employment-status tiers	Employment within stores increases, some wage tiers eliminated, differentials reduced, rate of expansion slows

Table 4.2
Top Pay Rates Paid at the End of Selected Years

	1977	1978	1981	1984	1986[a]	1987
Cashier						
Urban						
Mayway HT[b]	6.90	7.56	9.16	10.95	10.95	10.95
Mayway LT[c]	---	7.46	8.46	10.25	10.25	10.25
Competition	6.86	7.56	8.81/9.91	9.00/10.37	9.56/10.37	8.37/10.37
Rural						
Mayway HT	6.90	7.56	9.01	10.15	10.15	10.15
Mayway LT	---	6.96	7.71	8.70	8.70	8.70
Competition	5.80/6.86	6.37/7.56	7.61	7.83	8.13	6.00/8.13
GM Clerk-Mayway						
Part-Time HT	4.09	4.44	5.60	6.35	6.35	6.35
Full-Time HT	4.42	4.79	6.04	7.04	7.04	7.04
All Urban LT[d]	---	3.75	4.50	5.20	5.20	5.20
All Rural LT[d]	---	3.68	4.35	5.20	5.20	5.20
Nonunion Competition	2.30/4.50	2.65/4.85	3.35/6.00	3.35/6.00	3.35/6.00	3.35/6.00

a. 1986 rates are those in effect at the time the survey was mailed to Mayway employees.
b. HT=high-wage tier.
c. LT=low-wage tier. No such rates were in effect in 1977.
d. The GM Clerk low-wage tier rates eliminated all part- and full-time distinctions.

State Bargaining Developments

During the late 1970s, problems began to arise in the statewide pattern of bargaining settlements, and these affected subsequent contracts at Mayway. In November 1978, one of the larger regional chains (Company A) in the metropolitan subarea filed for bankruptcy as a result of overexpansion. The federal District Court in March 1979 permitted the company to unilaterally change the terms in its labor agreements and institute a two-year wage freeze. As a result, there were increased competitive pressures on the other chains with higher wages operating in that area.

The 1980 Urban-Based Agreements

In 1980, new contracts were negotiated between the remaining four metropolitan subarea chains and the UFCW locals.[9] In addition to the bankruptcy at Company A, there were several other indications that problems were imminent for the 1980 contracts. First, one of the national companies requested lower rates outside of the metropolitan subarea and expressed its dissatisfaction with the rates paid in the urban-based contracts.[10] Second, when the two-year wage freeze at Company A terminated, the company negotiated new contracts with the unions that provided a $1 per hour wage cost advantage over the other metropolitan chains. Third, the market share of the five major chains deteriorated as a result of the increased competition from both other union and nonunion stores, and by early 1981 they were suffering significant financial losses. In addition, concurrent with the serious economic decline of its most important industry, the state was experiencing a high rate of unemployment.

The 1981 Mayway Agreement

In the 1981 negotiations, Mayway and the union examined the possibilities of paying the same rates established by the other unionized urban chains. They concluded, however, that the 1980 urban contracts would be so costly, the contracts would have to be modified before expiration. Thus, in the urban area, Mayway and the union agreed to have lower high-tier rates than the other chains were paying. In the rural area, the high-tier rates were increased above what the other rural-based chains were then paying, but they were increased less than the urban-area, high-tier rates.

In contrast to the 1978 negotiations, the 1981 negotiations at Mayway were marked by only slight disagreement; the settlement was ratified by a two-to-one margin. In exchange for a more explicit company strategy of expansion, the union agreed to maintain the two-tier wage structure and increase the rate differences between the tiers. During the term of the prior contract, the lowered labor costs resulting from the two-tier plan had facilitated the expansion plan involving five new stores. The new stores added about 1,500 employees to the bargaining unit, thereby satisfying the union goals of increased membership and greater job security.

Midterm Agreement Reopenings in 1982 and 1983

Nonunion stores continued to increase their market share at the expense of the unionized chains throughout 1981. Documenting that increase, the trade publication, *Grocer's Spotlight,* reported that independent stores, which were over 90 percent nonunion, increased their statewide market share from 54 percent to slightly over 60 percent during 1981. In addition, some of the unionized chains had implemented two-tier wage structures. Others were paying lower rates than were negotiated in the statewide patterned contracts, further increasing the competitive pressures among the major unionized chains. Also, the state's population declined during the high unemployment in 1982 and 1983 as people moved elsewhere to find work. Those problems in the state's economy, along with the increased competitive pressures, led to concessions at the chains whose contracts were negotiated in 1980 and 1981 before those contracts expired.

With many concessions occurring across the state,[11] Mayway tried to convince its employees that it also needed concessions in order to compete more effectively. Although the union officers did not agree that the competitive situation of Mayway warranted concessions, they agreed to reopen the contract in late 1982. The agreement to reopen the contract was based on union officers' perception that contract changes at the time would result in a contract more advantageous to the union in 1984. The final contract modifications resulted in new work rules establishing a benefit tier effective with contract ratification in April 1983.[12] Also, a new form of job-duty tier was formed with the implementation of a new job class, central service clerks, in all stores opened after the date of ratification. Because these newer stores had changed the organization of the departments from that of the older stores, this job class had more flexible duties and a generally lower pay scale than the job classes that had previously performed that work. Thus, due to changes in the economic environment, a different strategy and greater union contract concessions were needed for Mayway to remain competitive. Although the company strategy shifted, expansion remained critical in Mayway's business strategy; contract modifications encouraged the company to open four new stores, which added about 900 employees to the bargaining unit.

The 1984 Bargaining Renewals

A severe recession led to a static level of grocery sales for the chains and independents from the beginning of 1982 through 1984. Also, between 1980 and 1984, there had been a decline in the market share from 75 percent to 50 percent for the five major chains operating in the metropolitan subarea. This change in market share, along with substantial losses for each operation, led each chain involved there to seek immediate solutions. Such problems suggested that bargaining in 1984, when the agreements negotiated in 1980 and 1981 expired, would be critical.

The Urban-Based Agreements

Increasing the pressures on all the major chains operating in the state, but particularly those in the metropolitan subarea, was the announcement in May 1984 by the largest national chain that it would sell all of its stores in the state to independent operators if it failed to obtain the necessary contract terms when the 1980-1984 contracts expired.[13] Prior to negotiations with the UFCW locals, the national chain stated that it would like to maintain some stores in the state rather than sell them to independent operators, but whether it pulled out of the state depended on how well the unions were able to adapt to the company's needs in bargaining. In July, after the members voted a proposed agreement down, the national chain closed the 70 stores. The leadership of the International UFCW and the two locals reacted to the closure by resuming negotiations for the purpose of reopening some stores. In August, the national chain and the two unions reached a three-year agreement and the company reopened 45 stores.[14]

As predicted by the urban unions, the other companies tried to obtain the same contract terms as the national chain. In the middle of October, following the recommendations of the union negotiators, members employed at the other urban chains overwhelmingly voted not to ratify similar contracts. The union negotiators noted that, unlike the contracts of the national chain, the rejected contracts had no guarantees to keep stores open during the life of the contract.

Subsequently, the largest chain in terms of urban market share became the pattern-setting target for the following agreements. Although the new contract placed this regional company at a competitive disadvantage compared to the national chain, the Retail Clerks local soon reached similar settlements with the other unionized solvent chains operating in the urban area (not including Mayway).[15] Further, those chains were forced to compete with the stores that the national chain had sold and which were reopened mostly as nonunion entities. Thus the 1984 urban-based negotiations led to four different levels of wage rates among the unionized chains operating in the urban area. The highest urban rates were the high-tier rates negotiated by the rural-based local union and applied to Mayway's urban stores. The four different levels of the unionized chains' wage rates resulting from the urban negotiations, as well as greater nonunion competition, placed additional pressure on Mayway to control labor costs in order to remain competitive.

The Mayway 1984 Agreement

The bargaining of the competing chains had a major impact on the negotiations at Mayway. No settlement could be reached at Mayway until the participants could determine the terms of the national chain's contracts, the number of stores that would remain open, and how they would affect the competitive environment. Bargaining to renew the agreement covering Mayway's employees had begun in April 1984, but was suspended in May until it could be determined how many stores would be closed. Mayway and the union agreed to extend their contract expiring in July until they had reached a settlement. In these negotiations, Mayway sought to eliminate double time on Sunday and holidays, reduce paid time off, contain health care costs, and pay few, if any, wage increases. The company also wanted the new contract to facilitate its immediate expansion plans of opening four new stores within the urban area. The union's goals were to protect its members' current wage levels and to reduce, or at least avoid widening, the differences between the wage tiers. Also, the union wanted to increase job security, which essentially meant assisting the company in carrying out its expansion plans.

The negotiated settlement appeared to meet the goals of both union and management. It should be recognized, however, that there was considerable employee discontent concerning the terms of the agreement, as reflected in the December ratification vote in which only 53 percent voted to approve the contract. Major employee discontent developed over the freezing of top rates for all job classes for the entire three-year term of the contract and over the fact that Sunday double time was eliminated. With freezing of the top rate of the wage progressions (for both the high- and low-wage tiers), employees paid at the top rate of their job class would be given four lump-sum payments during the life of the contract. The lump-sum payments would vary in amount according to job class and the number of hours worked, but were 15 to 20 cents per hour worked for the largest job classes.

The settlement also established that starting rates would be lowered by up to 78 cents per hour for both those food job classes where two-tier rates did not exist and for the low-wage tier food job classes. In addition, most food department rate progressions were lengthened by at least one year; every low-tier GM wage progression was lengthened except one.[16] New baggers hired after the effective date of the contract were placed on a lower and longer wage progression, and the previous

bagger wage tiers were combined into one schedule. Also, many starting GM rates in the urban area were lowered and were made equal to
the starting rates in the rural area.

The contract reduced pay for holiday work from double time to time-
and-one-half. Sunday double time was phased out over the term of the
contract, so that by February 1987, all Sunday hours would be paid
at straight time. Since Sunday hours would no longer be paid at a
premium, the union negotiated the option for them to become part of
the regular weekly work schedule. Previously, by working Sundays,
part-time employees could work the same number of hours as full-timers,
although they could not receive the same benefits. The settlement on
Sunday hours led the company to promote many part-time employees
to full-time positions with required Sunday work. Consequently, the
number of full-time employees increased by almost 20 percent.

Work rules governing health care costs were also changed significantly. The insurance copayments required of employees hired after April
1, 1983 (those on the low benefit tier), were extended to apply to all
employees. Thus, while the benefit tier was eliminated, the company
cost for benefits was lowered. In exchange, health care coverage was
significantly improved and also extended to 2,200 part-time employees
who had previously had no such coverage. As a result, the differences
in benefits within the employment-status tier were reduced.[17]

A new job-duty tier was instituted when the job class of specialty
food clerk was established with duties related to operating salad bars
and handling bulk food, duties which had previously not been performed.[18] The top rate of this new class was between four and five dollars
per hour below that which the five major chains operating in the
metropolitan subarea would have to pay for a person with the same job
duties, as their contracts severely restricted the type of work that could
be paid below the cashier's rate. Observers argued that this was an example of where the union would gain in accommodating Mayway; so
many employees were hired to perform these duties, they constituted
an additional 10 percent of the retail food store workforce by 1986.

Overall, the 1984 settlement resulted in major changes to the tiered
compensation plan in effect at Mayway. Taken together, all of the con-

tract changes facilitated the company's efforts to moderate labor costs and to continue in its expansion plans. When viewed in the context of the wage freeze, this contract incorporated a greater use of union concessions by management than in 1983. From the union's perspective, however, relative to the 1981 contract, the percentage difference between the top rates of the two-wage tiers was reduced. As calculated from the data in table 4.2, the percentage reduction becomes somewhat larger when factoring in the hourly lump-sum payments (which were the same for each wage tier). These changes, along with the changes in the bagger classification, allowed the union to contend that it was working toward the elimination of wage tiers.

In combination with the previously existing two-tier wage structure, it can be calculated that the changes in the wage tiers alone resulted in an average savings for a new store of between $2 and $4 million in payroll costs during the first four years of operation. The wage rates in table 4.2 show that each contract negotiated after Mayway instituted the two-tier wage plan resulted in greater absolute dollar labor cost savings (over time the savings also increased due to turnover). The savings resulting from the implementation of the job-duty tier with the different food and nonfood rates (cashier versus GM clerk) are also readily apparent. Overall, the two tier forms shown in the table, along with the implementation of temporary tiers and the employment-status tiers generated such large labor cost savings for Mayway that it was able to expand considerably. In 1987, the use of wage tiers alone would save Mayway more than 27 million dollars a year on its retail store employee payroll, or over 13 percent of that payroll, compared to the identical employment situation with all employees paid as though they were on a unitary wage scale that used only the high-tier rates. The discussion in chapter 2 suggested that tiers may be accompanied by lower productivity, particularly on the part of the low-tier employees. Analyses presented in chapter 7 and appendix C, however, provide no clear evidence that the maintenance of tiers has negatively affected productivity at Mayway.

Further Changes

By late 1985 and early 1986, the economy in the state had improved markedly, the unemployment level had dropped, and the state's population had begun to increase. Mayway opened four new stores during this time, all in the urban area, and had two more under construction there. Further, the company converted most of its 1985 fall and holiday temporary positions to permanent positions in the beginning of 1986. This increased the average unionized workforce in each store about 20 percent over the previous year's level. While Mayway expanded its employment, one of the regional chains in the metropolitan subarea closed 20 stores at the end of 1985 and early 1986. Many of these stores were subsequently sold to other unionized companies, while others were not reopened.

Urban Area Changes

Major changes in the retail food industry continued in the urban area in late 1986 and 1987. One of the larger regional chains in the metropolitan subarea (Company C) went into bankruptcy. By the end of 1987, only one of its stores remained in operation. In contrast, several other companies expanded during 1987, the first significant expansion in several years for a major chain other than Mayway.

During the same period, the UFCW contracts originally negotiated in 1984 had to be renegotiated. The largest regional chain in the metropolitan subarea appeared to lead the way in the settlements. After a one-week strike in August 1987, the company and the UFCW locals agreed on a new contract that established both a wage- and an employment-status tier.[19] The goal of that company and the other urban chains was to reduce the number of full-time employees and increase the number of part-time employees. In order to equalize the ratio of part- to full-time workers, no new full-time employees would be hired. Further, the contract established that full-time employees could be involuntarily moved to part-time positions. If any full-time positions became available in the future, employees who had previously held full-time positions would have the first rights to those positions. Thus, the new contract established a *de facto* employment-status tier. The other companies operating in the metropolitan subarea subsequently obtained similar contracts.

The Mayway Agreement

The major issue in the urban area for the other chains, the ratio of part- to full-timers, was not an issue in the 1987 negotiations at Mayway, since the company had obtained considerable flexibility in this respect when the union representing its employees was independent of the AFL-CIO. The union's major goal in bargaining was to increase wages, which had been frozen since the 1984 contract. In addition, there was considerable interest in closing the gap between the two wage tiers. The company was primarily interested in obtaining greater flexibility in relation to job assignments. Company expansion within the union's jurisdiction no longer appeared to be an immediate concern.

The new 1987-1991 contract provided pay increases of between 2.5 to 5 percent for all job classes effective November 1988, with smaller increases scheduled for 1989 and 1990.[20] For some job classes, lump-sum payments of varying amounts based on hours worked would be paid in 1989 and 1990. Wage tiers were completely eliminated for baggers, the lowest paid job classification generally filled by entry level employees or workers who wanted a temporary position. A significant outcome of this contract was that the gap between the tiers was also narrowed for most job classifications.

The number of job classifications was reduced by about one-third with the establishment of new combined job classes, including one which bridged the food and GM departments. Most important, in the urban area, the gap between the high- and low-wage tier was eliminated for cashiers and food clerks, moving about 2,500 employees up to the high-tier rates over four years.[21] However, a third, lower wage tier level for those two job classifications was instituted in the new contract effective September 1988, using the same rates as paid in the rural area.[22] Thus, while the 1987-1991 contract made significant changes in wage tiers, the principle of wage tiers remained intact as they were retained for all retail store job classifications except the most and least skilled classes.

Summary

The implementation and development of tiers at Mayway can be seen, first, as primarily a function of the adoption of a strategic business plan of expansion in the 1960s and 1970s, and second, as a part of concession bargaining in the 1983 and 1984 agreements. Whether accompanied by major union concessions or not, the negotiation and implementation of tiers at Mayway prior to 1987 was a vital component in the company's expansion strategy. By 1987, the economy and the competitive environment had improved enough so that the union was able to obtain gains for its members and reduce or eliminate some of the differences between the wage-tier levels. In addition, in 1987, the company appeared to have no immediate plans for expansion within the state and the local union's jurisdiction.

Thus the evolution of tiers at Mayway can be placed within both the framework developed in chapter 1 concerning *why* tiers are implemented and the framework adapted from Holley and Jennings (1988) explaining *how* tiers and other collectively bargained settlements are determined. It has been shown repeatedly in this chapter that the economy and the competition were important factors in the negotiation of tiers at Mayway. It has also been shown that the contract settlements that implemented new tiers or changed previously existing tiers in order to moderate labor costs were frequently obtained in exchange for work rules (agreements) improving employee job security, i.e., creating new jobs by building new stores. Through such agreements, management obtained labor cost changes that facilitated the execution of its strategic business plans for expansion, and the union leaders sufficiently satisfied their members with higher wages and greater job security so that their political positions were protected. The union also increased its membership through labor agreements that assisted the company's expansion.

NOTES

1. The material included in this chapter is based on interviews with knowledgeable individuals concerning the labor relations aspects of the company and industry, newspaper reports, and reports in the *Retail/Services Labor Report* (RSLR). Because the author agreed to anonymity for the local union and company participating in the study, these parties will be identified by fictitious names, i.e., Mayway. Also, to protect the anonymity of the parties, no citations are made to specific newspaper articles or to specific RSLR issues.

2. While there was no organized employee opposition to the affiliation, the movement toward affiliation exacerbated the divisions within the membership, as the warehouse employees, truck drivers, and many of the most senior employees opposed affiliation.

3. The market share of the unionized stores in this area went from more than 60 percent in 1970 to about 30 percent in 1978. This was a factor in the negotiations, given that nonunion competitors typically paid close to the minimum wage, with a top rate much less than the top rate for a similar job in a unionized company and generally only $1 to $2 per hour above minimum wage. Further, the costs of benefits were considerably less for nonunion companies, as they used proportionately more part-time employees (who received few if any benefits).

4. Keeping skilled meat cutters and department heads off of wage tiers is fairly common among retail food employers (Sichenze 1989). By doing so, Mayway facilitated keeping a core of skilled employees who could assist in the training and supervision of new employees. J. Walsh (1988) argues that supermarkets need a core of employees who are trained to do all of the jobs, who know the shortcuts, and who can train and supervise new workers. Excluding this core group from "tiering" also means that new hires can move more readily into the core group.

5. This resulted in a doubling of the GM pensions and increased the food employee pensions by two-and-one-half times. Insurance benefits were also increased, with the company agreeing to match both the current and future benefits negotiated in the Retail Clerks plan.

6. Its stores there were relatively new, were not organized by the same unions as the other five chains, and did not follow the pattern of collective bargaining settlements in that subarea. In addition, each of the other five chains had corporate or regional offices and warehouses in the subarea, while Mayway did not.

7. The greater employment per store at Mayway in 1986 is largely attributable to two factors. First, about 45 percent of the company's employees were in general merchandise departments, compared to less than 5 percent at the other retail food chains. Second, about 75 percent of the company's employees were part-timers, compared to 10 to 30 percent in the other chains.

8. The figures for 1977 represent the last settlement at Mayway prior to the implementation of the two-tier wage structure. While no contract was bargained at the company in 1986, the rates are shown in table 4.2 for the date the surveys were mailed to Mayway employees.

9. The three-year contracts between both the Retail Clerks and Meat Cutters locals of the UFCW and the four chains in the urban area each contained increases of $2.60 in regular and limited (capped) cost-of-living adjustment (COLA) payments as well as two unlimited COLA increases in the second and third years of the contracts. All the contracts also increased labor costs by granting more paid days off. These contracts contained much greater wage increases than the 1974 and 1977 urban-based contracts (about 44 percent including the unlimited COLA increases versus 34 percent) or the 1978 Mayway agreement (24 percent).

10. Company I's dissatisfaction with the contract led it to sell its warehouse and 21 stores in the rural area to Company D in October 1980.

11. In the urban area, the concessions consisted of wage freezes and one year contract extensions for the solvent chains. Bankrupt firms received wage reductions. In the rural area, concessions were likely to consist of wage reductions. Company D received contract concessions including wage reductions of about $1.00 per hour. Even with those contract changes, Company D was unable to operate profitably in the rural area, and by the end of 1983, it no longer operated any rural stores.

12. New employees on the low-benefit tier paid a portion of their health care insurance premiums, and any Sunday hours would be paid at time-and-one-half rather than double time.

13. It was perceived by the competition that any stores sold would likely become nonunion independents—with much lower labor costs. Thus, in reaction to the threats of the largest national chain, the other national chain (Company J), announced that if all the sold stores became independent, it would consider closing all of its operations in the state. Therefore, the negotiations at the other three chains whose UFCW contracts expired in early August were suspended until the situation with the largest national chain was resolved.

14. The contract contained a 13.5 percent wage cut and also reduced the amount of paid time off. On the other hand, the unions got the company to agree to reopen 45 stores and guarantee that 40 of them would remain open for the life of the contract.

15. After much conflict, including a nine-day strike at the largest operator in the metropolitan subarea, similar agreements were reached between the remaining chains and the Meat Cutters. Those agreements set meat clerk rates slightly above the food clerk rates, but had other equivalent provisions as in the Retail Clerks contracts.

16. As an example of how these changes affected the wages of new employees, in September 1983, an urban cashier began at $5.50 per hour and took three years to reach the top hourly rate of $10.95 per hour. From late December 1984 to September 1987, the urban cashier progression started at $5.25 per hour and took four years to reach the same top rate. No one employed at the time of the contract ratification in any job classification received a wage cut as a result of the lengthened progressions or lower starting rates. These changes in the progressions and starting rates represented the implementation of temporary wage tiers within the permanent low-wage tier.

17. The company also obtained savings in exchange for increased employee flexibility in scheduling days off, when the personal days and sick days were combined into one category. Employees with eight years seniority had such days reduced from twelve to eight. Employees with less than eight years seniority but hired before April 1, 1983, had such days reduced from eight to six, and employees hired after March 31, 1983, from eight to four.

18. Another change in the job class structure was that the central service clerk job class created in the 1983 contract modifications was eliminated, with those positions reassigned to GM clerk positions at the courtesy desk. That contract change would apply to all stores opened after April 1, 1983, plus any stores undergoing a major renovation in the future, as all those stores changed the location and functions of the courtesy desk. For those stores, this change meant that about 7 percent of the jobs would be moved from the higher paying food-tier job classifications to the lower paying nonfood-tier GM job classifications.

19. The top rate for clerks and cashiers remained frozen at $10.37 per hour for the life of the contract, but lump-sum bonuses were to be paid. All new clerks and cashiers would earn a top rate of $2 per hour less. The company offered a one-time payment of between $5,500 and $18,000 (depending on job class and employment status) to employees who voluntarily gave up their jobs.

20. A tentative agreement expiring in September 1991 was reached in September 1987. That agreement was rejected by the membership by a vote of 5,147 to 3,316. The major reason given for

its rejection was that about 60 percent of the employees (those at the top rate of their wage progressions) would receive no raise until two full years had passed. The contract was subsequently renegotiated and ratified in December by a vote of 7,030 to 3,101. The major differences between the rejected and ratified contracts were that most of the raises were moved forward a year and that some of the job classifications received larger increases.

21. The high-wage tier employees in both classifications received increases of about 2.5 percent in November 1988, with lump-sum payments based on hours worked of 2 percent of base pay in November 1989, and 3 percent in November 1990. The low-wage tier employees were scheduled to receive raises in their base rate in 1988, 1989 and 1990, at which point the high- and low-wage tier rates would be equalized at $11.15.

22. The starting rate of the new third tier for cashiers was $4.60, 12 percent below the previous starting rate. After 48 months, through both moving up the wage progressions and across the board increases, the third-tier rate was scheduled to reach $9.29, approximately 17 percent below the unified high- and low-tier rate.

5
Sample Characteristics, Research Design, and Data Analysis

A goal of this study is to better understand the attitudes, behaviors, and characteristics of employees in a tiered employment situation. The literature indicates that managers make assumptions about employee attitudes, behavior, and performance in tiered employment situations that often conflict with those of union leaders (Flax 1984; Harris 1983c; Ross 1985; Salpukas 1985). Even where managers and union leaders are reported to agree on the effects of tiers on employees, that agreement is generally based on anecdotal, impressionistic evidence rather than scientific evidence (Salpukas 1987; Wessel 1985). Thus, the results of our survey of employee attitudes in a tiered employment setting should help both parties in making more informed decisions in the future.

This chapter begins with descriptions of the economic and employment characteristics of the relevant areas and the stores whose employees we surveyed. That is followed by a discussion of the survey development, administration, and characteristics of the respondents. The chapter also examines the four tier forms at Mayway and concludes with a description of the techniques used to analyze the survey data. The next two chapters present the results of the analyses pertaining to the research questions and hypotheses.

Area Descriptions

The areas of the state in which Mayway operates differ substantially in terms of their economic characteristics, population density, and the nature of labor relations in the retail food industry. In order to control for the effects of the different environments, the survey design incorporated six economically different geographic areas (groupings of counties) from which the 17 stores were chosen. In each of these county groupings, individuals were surveyed both from stores opened before (old stores) and after (new stores) the two-tier structure was implemented at Mayway. Each of the six county groupings is discussed, focusing on only the most relevant information. Tables 5.1 and 5.2 present selected economic characteristics of the urban and rural areas' county groupings respectively.[1]

Urban Area County Groupings

Cyclical Industrial

The two cyclical industrial counties were among the top three counties in the state in terms of their rate of population decrease between 1980 and 1985. Their economy was highly dependent on a cyclical heavy manufacturing industry, which had substantially reduced its employment levels in the 1980s and which had many employees on layoff status at the time of the survey. Employees from two old stores and three new stores were surveyed in this county grouping, i.e., subarea.

Outer Suburban

The two outer suburban counties had remained largely stable in population between 1980 and 1985. Also, note that the unemployment rates for these two counties were the lowest of those considered in this study. Moreover, both counties are characterized by a high percentage of managerial and professional specialty employees and high per capita income. The two stores surveyed in this county grouping (one old and one new) were on the outer fringe of the metropolitan subarea and also served other areas that were more rural. Each is located about 40 miles from the downtown of the largest city in the state.

Suburban

The two counties included in the suburban county grouping, which were also part of the metropolitan subarea, had the largest population of those considered, although each had suffered slight declines in population between 1980 and 1985. Similar to the urban counties, the suburban unemployment rate had decreased noticeably between 1980 and

Table 5.1
Selected Characteristics of the Urban Counties Where the Surveyed Employees Worked

Characteristic	County groupings					
	Cyclical industrial		Outer suburban		Suburban	
	County 1	County 2[a]	County 1	County 2[a]	County 1	County 2[a]
Occupation						
Managerial & professional specialty	18%	19%	32%	24%	19%	20%
Technical, sales & administrative support	26%	28%	30%	28%	31%	33%
Service	13%	15%	14%	11%	15%	13%
Farming, forestry & fishing	1%	2%	1%	2%	0%	1%
Precision production, craft & repair	15%	14%	9%	17%	12%	16%
Operators, fabricators & laborers	28%	23%	14%	18%	22%	18%
Per capital income in dollars						
1970	4,060	3,834	4,367	4,199	4,443	4,494
1980	10,171	9,269	11,261	10,067	9,993	10,846
1984	13,181	11,495	14,670	13,291	12,303	14,498

Table 5.1 (continued)

| | Cyclical industrial | | Outer suburban | | Suburban | |
Characteristic	County 1	County 2[a]	County 1	County 2[a]	County 1	County 2[a]
Population						
1970	445,589	219,743	234,103	58,967	2,670,368	625,309
1980	450,499	238,059	264,748	100,289	2,337,891	694,600
1985	433,900	216,900	262,300	101,800	2,174,300	689,700
Unemployment rate						
1970	5.3%	4.8%	5.0%	4.7%	6.0%	4.8%
1980	17.7%	14.0%	7.6%	11.7%	13.8%	14.0%
1985	12.3%	10.3%	6.1%	7.1%	9.6%	9.5%

(County groupings)

a. Indicates a county where no "old stores" were surveyed.

1985. The three surveyed stores (two old and one new) were located 10 to 20 miles from the downtown of the largest city.

Rural Area County Groupings

Rural Center

The average county population and per capita income for the rural center counties were the lowest of any of the county groupings included in the study. These counties had the highest proportion of employment devoted to agriculture of any county grouping. The two surveyed stores (one old and one new) were located in towns of under 25,000 in population. It should be noted that a large service-oriented employer operates in both towns.

Balanced

The economy of the balanced county grouping was marked by its diversity, including a relatively large percentage of the workforce in managerial and professional positions, technical sales and administrative support positions, and blue-collar occupations. There were two old stores surveyed in one of the counties and one new store in the other. The county containing the new store had lost population between 1980 and 1985, while the other had experienced slight population growth.

Stable Industrial

Both surveyed stores in the stable industrial counties were located in the same community of about 25,000, which straddled two adjacent counties. The counties had a diversified industrial base and each was among the 10 fastest-growing counties in the state between 1980 and 1985. Similar to the other rural counties, the per capita income was low in comparison to the urban counties.

Table 5.2
Selected Characteristics of the Rural Counties Where the Surveyed Employees Worked

| | County groupings | | | | | |
| | Rural center | | Balanced | | Stable industrial[b] | |
Characteristic	County 1	County 2[a]	County 1	County 2[a]	
Occupation					
Managerial & professional specialty	15%	23%	25%	21%	18%
Technical, sales & administrative support	23%	25%	31%	27%	25%
Service	14%	13%	14%	13%	13%
Farming, forestry & fishing	6%	8%	2%	3%	4%
Precision production, craft & repair	13%	15%	11%	13%	15%
Operators, fabricators & laborers	29%	15%	17%	23%	25%
Per capital income in dollars					
1970	3,237	3,856	4,081	3,996	3,631
1980	7,807	8,749	9,854	8,474	8,549
1984	9,921	11,369	12,817	11,149	11,651

Population					
1970	45,848	81,951	201,550	163,940	194,756
1980	51,815	89,948	212,378	171,276	238,729
1985	52,800	89,400	215,500	163,800	252,467
Unemployment rate					
1970	7.0%	5.1%	4.7%	5.2%	5.4%
1980	11.2%	9.7%	9.4%	13.0%	8.7%
1985	15.2%	10.8%	7.1%	11.1%	8.7%

a. Indicates a county where no "old stores" were surveyed.

b. The data for the two counties in this area have been combined because the city in which the stores were located was in both counties.

Characteristics of the Surveyed Stores

Figures for selected economic and employment characteristics[2] for each surveyed store organized by county grouping are presented in tables 5.3 and 5.4. These tables also show the overall mean figures of each characteristic for all urban and rural stores, respectively. In table 5.5, the means of the same characteristics are shown for both the old and new stores. Some of these characteristics, along with additional characteristics, will be used in the analyses of the relationship of tiers to productivity (see appendix C).

Urban and Rural Store Differences

Analysis of the data in tables 5.3 and 5.4 indicates that the urban stores had significantly ($p < .001$) more employees and more sales floor space than the rural stores. Also, the greater number of employees in the urban stores, along with the more recent expansion of the company there, meant such stores had a significantly greater proportion ($p < .001$) of low-wage tier employees than found in the rural stores. In addition, the average hourly rate and wage and the unitary hourly rate and wage were significantly ($p < .05$) higher in the urban stores than the rural stores. As discussed in the previous chapter, the latter differences reflect the generally higher pay scales in the urban area.

Old and New Store Differences

Tests of the data in table 5.5 indicate that old stores had a significantly ($p < .001$) lower percentage of employees on the low-wage tier than did new stores. Because of that difference, there were several other significant differences between the old and new stores. Employees in old stores had significantly higher pay ($p < .05$), were older ($p < .05$), and had more seniority ($p < .001$). The old stores also had significantly ($p < .05$) more employees and sales floor space than the new stores.

Table 5.3
Selected Economic and Employment Characteristics of Urban Area Stores in 1986

Characteristic	Cyclical industrial					Outer suburban	
	Store 1[a]	Store 2[a]	Store 3	Store 4	Store 5	Store 6[a]	Store 7
Number of employees	475	451	266	321	338	515	397
Average seniority (years)	5.10	5.14	3.24	3.27	3.24	4.39	2.27
	(4.66)	(4.67)	(2.86)	(3.04)	(3.55)	(5.69)	(2.97)
Wage tier (% low tier)	71.2	72.7	96.2	94.4	89.1	78.1	94.2
Employment-status tier (% part-time)	79.8	81.0	81.9	82.8	85.9	77.9	83.9
Job-duty tier (% GM)	42.2	42.7	45.1	43.2	38.7	43.8	43.6
Average age (years)	29.07	29.63	28.40	27.39	27.52	27.14	26.22
	(9.76)	(9.84)	(9.83)	(7.39)	(8.22)	(8.40)	(9.27)
Percent female	62.9	61.3	59.2	59.3	61.3	61.2	59.6
Percent minority	12.9	13.3	16.2	4.1	9.1	5.0	4.3
Average hourly rate	6.72	6.83	6.12	6.37	6.37	6.37	5.68
	(3.05)	(3.08)	(2.75)	(2.87)	(2.84)	(3.01)	(2.57)
Average hourly wage	7.06	7.10	6.33	6.64	6.61	6.65	5.95
Unitary hourly rate	7.38	7.46	7.10	7.22	7.16	7.03	6.62
	(2.89)	(2.93)	(2.79)	(2.81)	(2.81)	(2.91)	(2.67)
Unitary hourly wage	7.71	7.73	7.33	7.49	7.42	7.32	6.92
Sales floor space in square feet	193,000	183,000	140,000	140,000	140,000	225,000	138,000

Table 5.3 (continued)

Characteristic	Suburban			Overall urban mean
	Store 8[a]	Store 9[a]	Store 10	All stores
Number of employees	614	594	439	441
Average seniority (years)	3.75	3.85	2.71	3.69
	(4.28)	(3.33)	(2.72)	(.97)
Wage tier (% low tier)	77.7	82.3	95.0	85.0
Employment-status tier (% part-time)	77.6	82.5	77.7	81.1
Job-duty tier (% GM)	46.7	40.3	44.6	43.2
Average age (years)	26.96	28.52	27.42	27.83
	(9.80)	(10.05)	(10.63)	(1.02)
Percent female	65.4	69.2	62.4	62.1
Percent minority	4.9	5.3	5.8	7.6
Average hourly rate	6.07	6.59	6.06	6.32
	(2.97)	(2.97)	(2.83)	(.35)
Average hourly wage	6.37	6.82	6.29	6.58
Unitary hourly rate	6.78	7.32	6.91	7.09
	(2.89)	(2.85)	(2.90)	(.27)
Unitary hourly wage	7.08	7.54	7.18	7.37
Sales floor space in square feet	248,000	242,000	110,000	176,000

a. Represents an "old store" opened before the two-tier wage structure was negotiated.
Standard deviations are in parentheses.

Table 5.4
Selected Economic and Employment Characteristics of Rural Area Stores in 1986

Characteristic	Rural center		Balanced			Stable industrial		Overall rural mean
	Store 11ᵃ	Store 12	Store 13ᵃ	Store 13ᵃ	Store 15	Store 16ᵃ	Store 17	All stores
Number of employees	231	275	339	453	289	156	337	297
Average seniority (years)	4.67	3.05	5.27	5.39	2.75	7.37	3.59	4.54
	(5.65)	(3.57)	(5.85)	(6.47)	(3.10)	(7.23)	(5.75)	(1.55)
Wage tier (% low tier)	71.0	90.9	70.8	72.8	93.4	62.8	85.2	78.1
Employment-status tier (% part-time)	82.5	74.6	83.5	78.3	73.8	85.7	63.6	78.4
Job-duty tier (% GM)	48.7	41.5	41.4	43.1	48.8	48.1	42.7	45.0
Average age (years)	30.19	25.53	28.72	29.21	26.07	34.09	29.44	29.00
	(11.40)	(7.45)	(10.15)	(10.69)	(8.00)	(13.51)	(12.04)	(2.77)
Percent female	73.6	57.7	62.7	58.0	61.9	76.5	68.9	65.7
Percent minority	0.0	8.3	12.2	12.1	9.5	5.9	7.0	7.8
Average hourly rate	5.78	5.73	6.12	5.94	5.53	6.49	5.19	5.81
	(2.59)	(2.32)	(2.69)	(2.64)	(2.27)	(2.72)	(2.14)	(.40)
Average hourly wage	6.08	5.97	6.37	6.14	5.74	6.61	5.34	6.04
Unitary hourly rate	6.43	6.86	6.82	6.75	6.66	7.31	6.12	6.70
	(2.54)	(2.51)	(2.64)	(2.55)	(2.51)	(2.37)	(2.32)	(.37)
Unitary hourly wage	6.72	7.18	7.08	6.97	6.93	7.44	7.08	6.94
Sales floor space in square feet	126,000	125,000	145,000	168,000	130,000	67,000	120,000	126,000

a. Represents an "old store" opened before the two-tier wage structure was negotiated.
Standard deviations are in parentheses.

Table 5.5
Means of Selected Characteristics of Old and New Stores

Characteristic	Overall "old store" mean	Overall "new store" mean
Number of employees	426	332
Average seniority (years)	4.97	2.99
	(1.01)	(.38)
Wage tier (% low tier)	73.2	92.3
Employment-status tier (% part-time)	81.0	79.1
Job-duty tier (% GM)	44.6	43.3
Average age (years)	29.29	27.21
	(2.03)	(1.19)
Percent female	65.7	61.2
Percent minority	8.8	6.5
Average hourly rate	6.31	5.88
	(.38)	(.41)
Average hourly wage	6.58	6.11
Unitary hourly rate	7.02	6.83
	(.36)	(.36)
Unitary hourly wage	7.29	7.09
Sales floor space in square feet	177,000	130,000

Standard deviations are in parentheses.

Survey Development

Many items included in the survey were developed to address the eight research questions posed in this study.[3] In addition, more general items were developed or adapted from other sources, to test the six hypotheses related to issues such as employee morale, performance, satisfaction with tiers, union support, and perceived fairness of tiers. All of the survey items and the sources of the scales that were not developed specifically for this study are shown in appendices A and B.

One-on-one interviewing with Mayway employees not surveyed was carried out to ensure that the questionnaire instructions were stated clearly and that each item was understood in the manner intended by the researchers. As a result, some of the instructions and wording of items[4] were changed and clarified. The items and sections were ordered to facilitate the respondents' understanding of the concepts examined.

Survey Administration and Response

In March 1986, one of the two survey forms was mailed to the employees at the 17 Mayway stores. The first form was mailed to employees in five of the six county groupings to collect data relating to both the research questions and the hypotheses. The second form, sent to employees in the suburban county grouping, contained items relating only to the hypotheses.[5] An additional mailing in April asked those who had not returned the survey to do so.

Of the 6,490 potential respondents, 265 employees were considered ineligible for this study because they were found to be in job classifications that did not have wage tiers (n=110),[6] or because, through a change in job classification, they were no longer paid on a high-wage tier pay scale (n=155).[7] Of the 1,703 surveys returned, 1,599 surveys (25 percent of potential respondents) were used in the analyses (1,117 of the first survey form and 482 of the second). Surveys were eliminated because the respondents were in job classifications that contained no wage tiers (n=34), had moved from a position on the high-wage tier to one on the low-wage tier (n=44), or because the surveys were returned with excessive missing data (n=26).

Comparisons were made between the population of potential respondents and the respondent group on several characteristics to assess the representativeness of the data (see table 5.6). Several significant differences between the total population and the survey respondents were found. The respondent group contained significantly higher proportions of food department employees, high-wage tier employees, and females than the population. Also, the respondents were approximately one year older, had about 11 months more seniority with the company, and had a higher rate of pay (with an average difference of approximately 50 cents per hour). The respondents and the population did not differ on store status (whether a store was opened before or after the two-tier structure was implemented) or area (rural or urban). While it appears that there was some response bias, the data were judged to be adequate for the purposes of this study.[8] There were adequate numbers of respondents from each level of each tier form, so that meaningful examinations and tests of differences within each form could be conducted. The relatively small magnitude of the differences between the respondent group and the population, along with the large sample size, will permit findings to be generalized both to Mayway as a whole and to other companies with tiers.

Table 5.6
Demographic Profile Comparison of Survey Respondents and Population

Characteristic[a]	Respondent (N = 1599)	Population (N = 6225)
Wage tier (% high tier)	23.1**	17.3**
Store-status (% new store)	40.6	41.5
Job-duty (% food)	57.9*	54.8*
Age (years)	29.06**	27.82**
	(9.39)	(9.60)
Seniority (years)	4.69**	3.77**
	(4.79)	(4.42)
Payrate ($/hour)	6.50**	6.01**
	(2.80)	(2.73)
Sex (% female)	70.9**	63.7**
Area (% rural)	30.2	32.1

*Indicates a characteristic where the respondents differ from the population at the .05 significance level.
**Indicates a characteristic where the respondents differ from the population at the .001 significance level.
Standard deviations in parentheses.

a. Accurate population data are not available for the employment-status tier form in 1986.

Tier Forms at Mayway

The collective bargaining agreements at Mayway resulted in four outcomes that met the criteria[9] for being a tier form—the wage tier, the store-status tier, the employment-status tier, and the job-duty tier. Each tier form resulted from a change in the labor agreement and reduced the compensation for some employees who were hired or changed positions after a certain date. Note that each of the tier forms consists of two levels, with every employee on either a high or low level of each of the four forms.[10] The percentage of employees in the low-wage, employment-status (part-time), and job-duty (GM department) tier forms is shown for both old and new stores (store-status) in tables 5.3 through 5.5, along with other store characteristics.

The wage tier at Mayway resulted from the implementation of new, low-wage tier pay scales for employees who entered job classifications after the two-tier plan was negotiated in 1978. This tier form, unlike the other three, is classified as a permanent tier form, given that the low-wage tier pay scales would not merge with the high-wage tier pay scales over time unless the contract were changed.

Wage tiers had been in effect at Mayway for over seven years at the time the survey was administered. By then, all employees on the high-wage tier, and many of those on the low-wage tier, had reached the top rate of the pay progression for their job classification. Many of the employees on the low-wage tier, however, were still on the lower steps of the pay progression. Thus, for this sample those on the low-wage tier can be divided into two groups: those at the top rate of their pay progression and those still advancing on their pay progression.

Martin and Lee (1989), in an empirical study of the standards used by employees to evaluate pay in a tiered employment situation, treated low-tier employees not at the top rate as a distinct group. They argued that this group, as the most recently hired, would not be as aware of all the psychological, economic, and political ramifications of a tiered wage structure as employees in the other groups. They found that low-wage tier employees not at the top rate knew significantly less ($p < .001$) about the labor agreement and pay structure than the other employees.

The second form, store-status, is based on whether employment is in stores opened before the implementation of the two-tier wage structure (old stores) or in the stores opened afterward (new stores). The store-status form results in lower compensation on the average for the new-store employees, who were mostly hired after the wage tier was negotiated (with the exception of a small percentage of high-wage tier transferees). Given the lower average pay in the new stores compared to the old stores, workers employed in new stores are considered as a low-tier group. One should note that employees could voluntarily move from an old store to a new store and vice versa without a change in pay scale or wage tier.

The store-status tier form is of considerable interest because of the large number of employees hired in the stores built after the negotiation of the two-tier plan. The establishment of new stores was based on implicit and explicit agreements, whereby the company would carry out its plans for expansion in exchange for the negotiation (and maintenance) of the two-tier plan. The new-store employees directly benefited from the two-tier plan through the creation of their jobs.

The new stores were comprised predominantly of low-wage tier employees, most of whom had never worked in a store with a majority of high-wage tier employees. Certainly, their experience with tiers and their socialization to the tiered employment situation would differ from that of old-store employees on both wage tier levels. Further, interviews with union officials indicated that the more senior employees in the old stores (who were on the high-wage tier) negatively affected the low-wage tier employees' attitudes toward the union. In the new stores, high-wage tier employees who had transferred from old stores generally improved their work situation by obtaining the more desirable work schedules or higher-paying positions. Such experiences could lead to differences in attitudes toward tiers between the new- and old-store employees.[11]

The employment-status tier, the third tier form at Mayway, is based on the established differences in weekly earnings, benefits, and hours between the part- and full-time employees. All employees at Mayway began in part-time positions and could move into full-time positions only as openings occurred. There was a career line progression from part- to full-time positions; however, some employees (even those on the high-wage tier with the most seniority) desired the flexibility of a part-time position and did not aspire to a full-time position.[12] At the same time as the implementation of the two-tier plan, the wage progressions were lengthened for many part-time positions, and where previously separate wage progressions had existed for part- and full-time positions, these wage progressions were combined for the low-wage tier employees. The newly established wage progressions were equal to or lower than those of the previous part-time, high-wage tier schedules. Thus, after the implementation of the plan in 1978 both the high- and low-wage tier employees in many job classifications continued to receive the lower, part-time pay rates after progression to full-time status within their same job classification. Because of their lower compensation rates, their decreased ability to increase their pay rates upon promotion to full-time status, and their lower weekly income relative to full-time employees, the part-time employees at this company are considered to be in another low-tier group.[13]

The fourth tier form, the job-duty tier form, manifests itself in the difference in compensation between food and nonfood job classifications. The general merchandise (GM) department employees, who are paid considerably less yet perform many of the same duties as the food department employees, constitute another low-tier group at Mayway. There was a very strong and well-defined career line from GM department positions to the higher paying food department positions.

The last three tier forms should be viewed as temporary, since employees could move from the low level to the high level as openings became available. Note that any movement from a full-time to a part-time position, or from a food department position to a general merchandise position, would almost always be accompanied by a decrease in income, even if the employee's wage tier level did not change.

For the respondents, the relationships among the four tier forms can be seen in tables 5.7 and 5.8. Table 5.7 provides a cross-tabulation of the wage tier form (broken down into low-wage tier employees not at the top rate of their pay progression, low-wage tier employees at the top rate, and high-wage tier employees) with the low and high levels of the other tier forms. Within the low-wage tier, there were nearly

Table 5.7
Cross-Tabulation of the Wage-Tier Form
with the Low and High Levels of the Other Tier Forms

Wage tier	Total	Store-status		Employment-status		Job-duty	
		New	Old	Part time	Full time	GM	Food
Low-wage tier not at top rate	912	435	477	838	74	482	430
Low-wage tier at top rate	318	157	166	238	80	100	218
Total low-wage tier	1230	592	638	1076	154	582	648
Total high-wage tier	369	58	311	201	168	90	279
Total	1599	650	949	1277	322	672	927

Table 5.8
Correlation Matrix of the Tier Forms, Pay Rate, and Seniority

Tier forms and variables	Wage tier	Store-status	Employment-status	Job-duty	Pay rate
1. Wage tier (1=low, 2=high)					
2. Store-status (1=new, 2=old)	.28***				
3. Employment-status (1=part-time, 2=full-time)	.34***	.02			
4. Job-duty (1=GM, 2=food)	.20***	.00	-.05**		
5. Pay rate	.59***	.11***	.27***	.60***	
6. Seniority	.84***	.20***	.39***	.24***	.74***

NOTE: **$\le$.01; ***p$\le$.001. N=1599.

three times as many respondents not at the top of their wage progression as there were those at the top rate. The cross-tabulation indicates that roughly equal proportions of low-wage tier respondents from both groups were employed in old and new stores (approximately 50 percent); for the high-wage tier respondents, 84 percent were in old stores. Fewer than 10 percent (n=58) of the new-store employees were on the high-wage tier. The cross-tabulation also indicates that 92 percent of the low-wage tier respondents not at the top rate were in part-time positions compared to 75 percent for the respondents on the low-wage tier at the top rate. In comparison, there were only slightly more part-time (55 percent) than full-time respondents on the high-wage tier. Finally, only among low-wage tier respondents not at the top rate were GM department employees in a majority (53 percent). In contrast, only 24 percent of the high-wage tier respondents were in the GM department positions.

The correlation matrix of the four tier forms (the wage tier form is divided into only high and low levels) and related variables in table 5.8 shows that seniority (upon which all of the tier forms are at least partially based) is significantly (p < .001) positively correlated with each tier form. As should be expected, the four tier forms are also significantly positively correlated with pay rate. Only weak correlations are found among the three tier forms of store-status, employment-status, and job-duty. The wage-tier form has the highest correlation of any tier form with each of the other three and with seniority.

Data Analysis

To address the research questions, several analyses were conducted for the purpose of exploring the survey data. First, descriptive statistics were determined for each relevant item. These descriptive statistics consisted of an overall percentage and a percentage derived for the high and low levels of each of the four tier forms, comprising a total of nine separate percentages. These percentages are discussed in the results section of chapter 6. Second, the results of a factor analysis were used to determine several scales, each consisting of items tapping a similar underlying dimension.[14] Examination of the internal consistency of the various clusters of items along with the concepts defined by them determined the final composition of the scales derived. The investigation of those scales was carried out using four-way analyses of variance (ANOVAs) to determine if there were any significant differences between the two levels within each of the four tier forms.

A two-step process of analysis was employed with the hypotheses given their directional nature and the fact that multiple items or scales were used in testing them.[15] First, a multivariate analysis of variance (MANOVA) was carried out for each hypothesis[16] to determine whether or not the items or scales as a group differed significantly within each tier form. If any tier effect was significant in a MANOVA, four-way univariate ANOVAs were run to determine the nature and direction of the significant differences between the two levels within each of the four tier forms for each item or scale.

Following the rationale of other research in this area (Martin and Peterson 1987), the four tier forms in this study were entered into the ANOVAs and MANOVAs in the following order: job-duty, employment-status, store-status, and wage.[17] This ordering provided for a conservative test of attitudinal differences as a function of wage tier, because differences in the other tier forms that might not be present in other companies with two-tier wage plans were taken into account first. All tier effects shown in the results of the ANOVAs were adjusted for job-duty, employment-status, and store-status. Thus, differences in those three tier forms were not confounded with the effects of wage tier status. Similarly, the effects shown for store-status were not confounded by differences in employment-status and job-duty, and so forth. Tests for significant differences for the scales related to the research questions and for each hypothesis were carried out by entering the tier forms in the order described above.[18]

Two complete sets of analyses were used for both the research questions and the hypotheses. The first was based on the total sample. The second set included only that portion of the sample paid at the top rate of their pay progression.[19] The latter set of analyses was conducted to remove some of the effects of seniority from the scale analyses and the hypothesis tests. Because each of the four tier forms was so closely related to seniority, it was possible that any significant difference found within a tier form would be tapping into a relationship between seniority and the examined employee attitudes, behaviors, and characteristics. The analyses that included only the respondents at the top rate of their pay progression included only those employed for at least two years, the length of the shortest pay progression, and in the three largest job classifications (cashiers, GM clerks, and food clerks), for 48 months.[20]

The second set of analyses eliminated most of the effects of changing seniority on pay within the low-tier groups. These analyses significantly ($p < .001$) reduced the correlation of pay rate with seniority from the .74 shown in table 5.8 to .30, as a result of the restriction of range on both variables. Given the differing characteristics of the two sets of analyses, it was useful to examine and compare the results of both sets of analyses to determine the relationship of tiers to the examined attitudes, behaviors, and characteristics. The analyses for the store-status, employment-status, and job-duty tier forms were conducted both including and excluding respondents not at the top rate of their wage progressions. Such analyses avoided the complexity of analyses involving more than three tier divisions, e.g., new-store employees not at the top rate, new-store employees at the top rate, old-store employees not at the top rate, and old-store employees at the top rate.[21]

Summary

This chapter began with an examination of the sample characteristics and followed with a discussion of the survey development, administration, and response. Also, the chapter discussed the four tier forms at Mayway, which met the criteria established for being a tier form. By examining the four tier forms, this study extends the research on tiers to forms beyond wage tiers. The chapter concludes with a discussion of the methods used to analyze the survey data presented in the next two chapters.

NOTES

1.The selection of the 12 counties was constrained by the differing nature of the counties and by the need to have old and new Mayway stores within each county grouping. The data shown in tables 5.1 and 5.2 indicate a high degree of similarity between the two counties within each grouping. Note that for some of the groupings, the two counties included are not contiguous.

2. The following are definitions of the relevant retail store payroll characteristics included in the tables.

Average Hourly Rate. The average hourly rate is the average pay rate of all workers employed within a store regardless of their full- or part-time employment status.

Average Hourly Wage. The average hourly wage is the cost of labor per hour to operate a store. It is computed by dividing the total weekly payroll for unionized employees by the total number of hours those employees worked that week. It is generally higher than the average hourly rate because higher-paid job classifications, such as cashiers, have to be on duty whenever a store is open, while the lower-paid job classifications, such as baggers, are more heavily employed at peak customer traffic times.

Unitary Hourly Rate. The unitary hourly rate is the same as the average hourly rate except that the pay rates of all employees are calculated as though they were on a unitary wage scale, which use only the high-tier wage rates. The unitary hourly rate is a hypothetical figure.

Unitary Hourly Wage. The unitary hourly wage is the same as the average hourly wage except that it is calculated as though the pay rates of all employees were computed from the high-tier wage rates.

3. The only previously existing survey items directly concerned with wage tiers were developed by Jacoby and Mitchell (1986), and these items have been adapted for this study to address one of the research questions.

4. For example, most of the Mayway employees were unfamiliar with the term "two-tier wage structure"; they referred to the employees on the high-wage tier as "onboards" (they were on board when the tiers were implemented) and those on the low-wage tier as "hereafters" (they were hired here after the tiers were implemented). Thus wage tiers were referred to in the survey as the "hereafter-onboard rate differences."

5. The second survey was partially funded by the ANR Pipeline Company Foundation and was designed to examine issues other than those included in the research questions.

6. Meat cutter and department head job classifications were not placed on permanent wage tiers; the surveys of respondents in these classifications were excluded from the study.

7. As discussed previously, employees originally on the high-wage tier who later moved to a different job classification in a new department, moved onto the low-tier rates for that new job classification (most of these employees moved from low-paying general merchandise positions to higher-paying food department positions). This is not typical of the way such changes are handled at other companies with wage tiers. An examination of the data indicates that employees who had changed wage tiers differed in several attitudes from both the high-wage tier employees and other employees on the low-wage tier. Because of these differences, and the small number of employees involved, the surveys of these employees were excluded from the study.

8. The population figures shown in table 5.6 do not include individuals who changed wage tiers or who were in job classifications that were not on permanent wage tiers. Thus the population size shown in table 5.6 is less than the total number of employees summed across the stores in

tables 5.3 and 5.4, and the population statistics may vary slightly from those computed from the latter tables.

9. The criteria established for this study are included in the definition of tiers presented in the introductory chapter.

10. Exceptions to this, as mentioned in footnote 6, were those in the meat cutter and department head job classifications. These job classifications represented 1.7 percent of the surveyed population.

11. Martin and Peterson (1987) found several significant differences in employment-related attitudes between the employees in old and new stores.

12. Survey results for this study indicate that the longer the respondents had been employed in particular part-time positions, the more they desired to work the same number of hours as they presently worked.

13. The reader is referred to the discussion provided for figure 1.3.

14. Factor analysis refers to a variety of statistical techniques whose objective is to represent a set of variables in terms of a smaller number of variables. Thus, it helps to reduce sets of variables to a smaller set of factors based upon the underlying patterns of relationships indicated in the data.

15. Significance tests for the individual survey items examined in the research questions are not reported given the large number of items. Because of the large number of comparisons involved, an increased number of significant differences may result from chance factors alone. The use of significance tests was deemed more appropriate when the items were combined into scales.

16. A MANOVA combines together all of the items or scales being tested in a hypothesis into one statistical procedure and analysis. This technique is commonly used when the dependent items or scales are closely related and are being used to test the same hypothesis. In addition to examining the main effects of the MANOVA, the direction of the differences of the means within each tier form must be examined in order to determine whether the hypotheses being tested are supported.

17. For the ANOVAs, we were only interested in the significant differences between levels within a tier form. We were not interested in the interaction effects that might indicate, for example, that high-wage tier employees in old stores had attitudes that differed significantly from high-wage tier employees in new stores. The results indicated that less than 5 percent of the interaction effects were found to be significant in the ANOVAs of the scales in chapter 6 and of the scales and items used in chapter 7. Only in the case where there was a very small proportion of the sample involved, as among high-wage tier employees employed in new stores (which was less than 20 percent of both the high-wage tier and new-store employee groups), did the direction of the mean differences within a tier form vary from those shown in the ANOVA results tables.

18. Exploration of the data was also carried out by entering the tier forms into the ANOVAs in the following order: store-status, employment-status, job-duty, and wage tier. The ANOVA results using the above order entry were essentially the same as those reported in chapters 6 and 7.

19. Of the 1,117 respondents who answered the first survey form, 280 were on the high-wage tier, 218 were at the top rate of the low-wage tier, and 619 were not at the top rate of the low-wage tier. Of the 482 who answered the second survey form, the figures were 89, 100, and 293, respectively.

20. Several methods are theoretically available to control for or adjust for seniority differences. Seniority could be entered into a regression equation along with the four tier forms as independent variables, and the items examined as dependent variables. Also, the same ANOVAs as were described in the text could be run again covarying (controlling for) seniority. These two methods,

which may be suitable in other situations, were not considered to be appropriate for this study given the very high correlation of seniority with the wage-tier form. This very high correlation suggested that such methods violated the homogeneity of regression assumption and led to unstable results.

Table 5.8 shows that the three tier forms of store-status, employment-status, and job-duty had correlations with seniority of a significantly lower magnitude ($p < .001$) than the wage-tier form did. Thus, ANOVAs not including the wage-tier form which covaried seniority were run. The pattern of significant differences found within a tier form with these ANOVAs was very similar to that found with just respondents at the top rate of their pay progression and shown in the results tables for those three tier forms. This suggests that mean differences that were significant for the total sample but no longer significant for the top-rated sample for the store-status, employment-status, and job-duty tier forms were related to employee differences in seniority rather than to their different location on a tier form.

21. In each set of analyses, the focus of the research questions and the hypotheses concerned the differences between low-wage tier employees and the high-wage tier employees. This research did not generally explore the differences that may exist between low-tier employees at the top rate and those not at the top of the wage progression, although such an investigation may be of theoretical interest.

6
Research Questions
Concerning Tiers

This chapter centers on the development and analysis of eight research questions for which survey questions were designed to gather data. Most of the research questions focus specifically on general employee views about the two-tier wage structure at Mayway. The questions are derived from the literature and also from discussions with union and management officials in the retail food industry and with observers of the industry. Unlike the hypotheses, which will be the focus of chapter 7, these atheoretical research questions do not contain directional predictions of differences between tier levels, even though such differences are of interest and will be discussed.

The first six research questions concern employee attitudes about the two-tier wage plan at Mayway and about tiers in general. They are organized into two sets of three questions each. The first set focuses on employee views of why the two-tier wage plan was originally negotiated at Mayway, how much various groups have benefited from its implementation, and the perceived effects of the plan on employment-related outcomes. The second set focuses on employee views of predictions about outcomes of future bargaining over the wage structure, attitudes toward selected changes in the compensation system and potential related outcomes, and general employee attitudes toward tiers. A number of survey items were developed to examine each of these research questions.

Given the distinct differences between the urban and rural areas and between the stores operating in those areas, it is important to determine the impact that such differences may have had on the measured employee attitudes. Such differences have been found to have a relationship to employee work-related variables in previous studies (Adams, Laker, and Hulin 1977; Hulin and Blood 1968). Thus the seventh research question focuses on differences among the geographic areas for the first six questions.

The eighth research question concerns the relationship of tiers to the potential public policy problem of equal employment opportunity.

Research Question Development

In chapter 2 we examined some of the goals the participants might possess when initially negotiating a two-tier wage structure. For example, the parties may be concerned with such matters as helping the employer to compete, allowing for employer expansion, increasing employee job security, obtaining union contract concessions while getting the contract ratified, protecting the high-wage tier employee pay, and helping to control labor costs. We also know that high-wage tier employees might be concerned that the implementation of tiers could give management an incentive to get rid of them. In this study then, one line of inquiry concerns the employee perceptions of the reasons why the structure was originally negotiated at Mayway.

We also discussed the potential benefits of tiered wage plans for each of the participant groups. In addition to the employer, union, and employees, the implementation of tiers in service industries could result in benefits for the customer in terms of better service. An additional area of interest thus pertains to the employee perceptions of how much various groups have benefited from the wage structure.

The reasons why the tiered plan was initially implemented should be linked to the employment-related effects of the structure. Survey items related to the third research question focused on employee perceptions of the effects that the wage structure has had on such employment-related outcomes as store expansion, job security, compensation, promotion opportunities, and ability to work more hours.

The preceding discussion leads to the first set of research questions. The specific questions examined are:

(1) What goals of the negotiating parties do employees believe the plan was negotiated to meet?

(2) To what extent do employees perceive that the various groups have benefited from the implementation of the plan?

(3) What employment-related effects do employees believe have resulted from the plan?

One area of focus for the second set of questions is the employees' predictions of various outcomes in future bargaining over the two-tier wage structure. The literature review provides the basis for the survey items selected to address this fourth question. Potential changes in the wage structure may range from no change, through a narrowing of the difference between the high- and low-tier rates, to an equalization of the rates. The implementation of a third wage tier also is a possibility in future bargaining. Other logical changes include those incorporating the concerns of both the high- and low-tier employees regarding the potentially differential treatment of employees on each tier level.

The fifth research question concerns employee attitudes toward changes in the tiered wage structure or other changes to the compensation system and the potential related outcomes. Rather than focusing on the likelihood of a potential change to the existing wage structure, this research question concerns the employee perceptions of selected means for dealing with tiers in the future and the relationship of these changes to potential outcomes affecting tiers. For example, what would be the employee attitudes toward such a change as the lowering of high-wage tier rates to the low-wage tier rates if it would assist in preventing the closing of stores? All of the items examined in this research question recognize that changes to tiers are often accompanied by other employment-related changes.

Also of interest are the employee attitudes toward selected statements relating to the existing wage structure and tiers in general. This sixth question concerns a variety of matters, including attitudes toward the company's and union's expectations for change and perceptions of the potential that tiers have for causing political problems for the union and tension among the union members. An additional survey item included in this broad research question examines employee perceptions of the relationship of tiers to the duty of fair representation.

The preceding discussion leads to the second set of research questions:

(4) What changes related to the plan do employees believe are likely to occur?

(5) What are the employee attitudes toward selected changes in the plan and the potential related outcomes?

(6) What are the employee attitudes about the company and union expectations, problems relating to the plan, and the relationship of tiers to the duty of fair representation?

One question, which overlaps with each set of research questions, concerns the differences among the employees in the geographic areas. The seventh research question examines whether differences exist for the first six research questions among the geographic areas of Mayway's operations. Given that such locality differences have been found to have a relationship to employee work-related variables, it is anticipated that the distinct differences between the urban and rural areas and stores in those areas could impact on the employee attitudes. This leads to the seventh research question.

(7) What are the differences in the employee attitudes examined in the first six research questions among the geographic areas of operation?

The final research question is based on the discussion in chapter 2 concerning tiers and the potential public policy problem of equal employment opportunity. Tiered compensation structures are an EEO concern because the lower tier could contain a disproportionate number of members from protected classes, such as women and minorities. It has been suggested that the percentage of females and minority race employees is increasing in industries that have implemented tiers, which leads to the eighth research question.

(8) Are the low-tier groups disproportionately comprised of women and minorities?

Results and Discussion

Discussion of the survey results as they address the research questions is organized into four major sections: the first two sections relate to the two sets of three research questions; the third section concerns area differences; and the fourth relates to the EEO issue. Descriptive statistics for each relevant item are shown in tables 6.1 to 6.3, 6.5 to 6.8, and 6.11. The first six of those tables also include a key word representing the name of the scale, if any, in which the item was placed. Tables 6.4 and 6.9 contain the results of the scale analyses of both the total sample and that portion of the total sample at the top rate of the wage progression.[1] The values shown in the tables are derived from the total sample analyses. While the values derived from the top-rate sample analyses may differ from those of the total sample, in no case did the direction of any significant difference vary from that shown. For ease of interpretation, the scale scores presented have each been divided by the number of items in the scale.[2] Table 6.10 includes means only for those scales found to differ significantly in either set of analyses between the urban and rural areas. Table 6.11 includes two items relating to EEO.

Views of Why the Plan was Negotiated, the Benefits, and the Effects

The data in table 6.1 relate to the first research question. The table presents employee estimates of the importance of each of 10 reasons or goals for the initial negotiation of the two-tier wage plan. The survey used a five-point response format that ranged from "not at all important" to "extremely important." Only the two highest responses, "important" and "extremely important," are shown. Responses are shown for the entire sample, as well as for the high- and low-levels within each tier form.

As can be seen, 60 percent of the employees perceived that saving the company money was important or extremely important to the participants in the negotiation of the two-tier wage structure. Of the remaining items, company expansion or contraction, helping the company to compete, protecting the jobs of union members or the wages of the high-wage tier employees, and helping to get the contract ratified were seen by 40 to 50 percent of the respondents as important or extremely important. Giving management an incentive to get rid of the high-tier employees was perceived as a prominent reason by only 29

Table 6.1
Perceived Possible Reasons for the Original Negotiation of the Two-Tier Wage Structure Related to Research Question 1
(Percent of respondents answering "Important" or "Extremely Important")

		Tier form and level								
		Wage		Store-status		Employment-status		Job-duty		Overall percent
Reason[a]	Scale label	High	Low	Old	New	Full time	Part time	Food	GM	
		n=264	n=807	n=571	n=500	n=217	n=854	n=621	n=450	N=1071
1. Save the company money	MGTGOALS	65	58	61	59	63	59	61	59	60
2. Allow the company to open new stores	MGTGOALS	50	46	45	51	52	46	47	49	47
3. Keep stores from closing	PROTECT	40	53	46	54	43	52	45	57	50
4. Help the union get a new contract ratified	RATIFY	49	48	49	47	48	48	47	50	48
5. Help the company get a new contract ratified	RATIFY	46	44	45	44	39	46	43	47	45
6. Help the company compete with unionized competitors	MGTGOALS	41	44	42	46	44	44	41	48	43
7. Help the company compete with nonunion competitors	MGTGOALS	45	39	40	42	46	39	38	45	40

8. Protect the jobs of the union members	PROTECT	43	52	47	54	49	47	48	52	50
9. Protect the wages of high-wage tier employees	PROTECT	49	48	46	52	47	50	50	47	48
10. Give management an incentive to get rid of high-wage tier employees	HTEFFECT[b]	48	23	33	24	34	27	32	24	29

a. All items were scaled from 1 (Not at all Important) to 5 (Extremely Important).
b. To facilitate interpretation, the scoring of this item was reversed when computing its scale.

percent of the respondents. The obvious disparity in perceptions between those on the high- and low-wage tier is evident for this item, with the former being more pessimistic.

Data pertaining to the second research question, concerning perceptions of how much each of six groups has benefited from the plan, are shown in table 6.2. The employees responded to a five-point response format that ranged from "not at all" to "very much." The percentage of respondents who reported that a group benefited "pretty much" or "very much" is included in the table. Overall, the respondents perceived that the company benefited the most from the plan, followed by the union. These perceptions are likely related to the effect of the wage structure on company savings and the facilitation of its expansion plans, both of which have allowed Mayway to compete more effectively. Also, the wage structure has been responsible for keeping more jobs for the union than would have otherwise existed.

While the overall percentage indicates that the high-wage tier employees were seen as benefiting "pretty much" or "very much" from the plan by over one-third of the respondents, the percentages suggest that respondents from each of the four low-tier groups thought that the high-wage tier employees had benefited considerably more than the high-tier groups perceived that they had. It appears that the low-tier groups perceive that the negotiation of the two-tier plan had resulted in no immediate costs to the high-tier employees. Very few of the respondents perceived that the remaining three participant groups—low-wage tier employees, employees in general at the respondent's store, and customers—had benefited "pretty much" or "very much."

Data concerning the third research question, employee perceptions of the effects of the two-tier wage structure on selected employment-related outcomes, are presented in table 6.3. Respondents used a five-point scale ranging from "definitely decreased" to "definitely increased" to report the perceived effects of the wage structure. The table shows the percentage of respondents who answered "probably increased" or "definitely increased" for each of the items. The overall percentages for the first three items relating to job security suggest that most respondents perceived little positive effect resulting from the two-tier

Table 6.2
Perceptions of How Much Various Groups Have Benefited from the Two-Tier Wage Structure Related to Research Question 2
(Percent of respondents answering "Pretty Much" or "Very Much")

		Tier form and level								
		Wage		Store-status		Employment-status		Job-duty		Overall percent
Group[a]	Scale label	High	Low	Old	New	Full time	Part time	Food	GM	
		n=264	n=807	n=571	n=500	n=217	n=854	n=621	n=450	N=1071
1. The company	No scale	91	75	79	79	87	77	80	78	79
2. The union	No scale	55	41	48	42	47	44	45	44	45
3. High-wage tier employees in general	HTEFFECT	10	46	31	42	23	40	31	44	37
4. Low-wage tier employees in general	OTHERSBENF	11	10	10	10	13	9	10	10	10
5. Employees in general at the respondent's store	OTHERSBENF	6	11	9	11	8	10	10	10	10
6. Customers	OTHERSBENF	10	18	15	18	16	17	16	18	16

a. All items were scaled from 1 (Not at all) to 5 (Very much).

Table 6.3
Perceived Effects of the Two-Tier Wage Structure on Employment-Related Outcomes Related to Research Question 3
(Percent of respondents answering "Probably Increased" or "Definitely Increased")

Effect[a]	Scale label	Tier form and level								Overall percent
		Wage		Store-status		Employment-status		Job-duty		
		High	Low	Old	New	Full time	Part time	Food	GM	
		n=264	n=807	n=571	n=500	n=217	n=854	n=621	n=450	N=1071
1. The job security of high-wage tier employees	HTEFFECT	15	37	28	37	22	35	29	35	31
2. The job security of low-wage tier employees	No scale	44	33	36	35	36	35	39	31	36
3. The respondent's job security	OPPORTUNITY	12	27	20	28	18	25	23	24	23
4. The number of hours the respondent is able to work in a week	OPPORTUNITY	9	18	15	18	10	18	15	18	16
5. The respondent's current hourly pay rate	EARNINGS	9	12	11	13	11	12	11	13	12
6. The respondent's current weekly earnings	EARNINGS	9	12	10	12	11	12	10	12	11

7. The respondent's current fringe benefits	EARNINGS	12	13	12	16	13	12	12	14	13
8. The dollar amount of the respondent's future raises	EARNINGS	13	13	12	11	15	13	12	15	13
9. The respondent's promotion opportunities	OPPORTUNITY	5	13	10	11	13	12	9	15	11
10. The closing of stores by the company	NUMSTORES[b]	4	6	6	4	4	6	5	5	5
11. The opening of stores by the company	NUMSTORES	79	67	71	75	72	71	79	68	71

a. All items were scaled from 1 (Definitely Decreased) to 5 (Definitely Increased).
b. To facilitate interpretation, the scoring of this item was reversed when computing its scale.

plan on their own or others' job security. Other items, relating to pay, fringe benefits, promotion opportunities, and the number of hours the respondent is able to work in a week, were seen by very few as having been increased. Responses to the last two items strongly suggest that employees believed that the two-tier wage structure led to the opening of new stores and did not lead to store closings.

Overall, there are some patterns to be seen in the responses, both for the individual items in the three tables (6.1 through 6.3) and for the scales developed from the first set of research questions and presented in table 6.4. The items reflecting the stated goals of management in implementing the two-tier plan were to save the company money, to allow the company to expand by opening new stores, to help the company compete with both unionized and nonunion competitors, all of which are included in the Goals of Management scale. All of the items in that scale focus on improvement of the human resource function's contribution in the attainment of Mayway's competitive strategic objectives.

The ANOVA results of that scale for both the total sample and for those at the top rate of their wage progression suggest that the high-wage tier employees were more aware of the stated rationale for implementing the plan and its role in the firm's business strategy. This difference in the understanding of the stated goals management wished to achieve in the initial negotiation of the plan appears related to differences in experience with the plan. In contrast to the low-wage tier employees, the high-wage tier employees were employed when the plan was negotiated and had the opportunity to vote on its inclusion into the first contract. Also, the lack of any significant differences for the Negotiation for Ratification scale was not surprising, given that the goal of getting a new contract ratified is not unique to negotiating a two-tier wage structure.

Another pattern in the responses both for the individual items and for the scores of the next four scales shown in the table (Other Groups Benefiting, Effects on Compensation, Effects on Opportunities, and Effects on High-wage Tier Employees) suggests that the employees perceived very few benefits or positive effects resulting from the plan. As can be seen in table 6.4, the overall mean for each of these four scales is relatively low. The lowest overall mean is for the scale Other Groups Benefiting, relating to benefits for the low-wage tier employees, employees in general, and customers. The ANOVA results of this scale for the total sample, but not for the top-rate sample, indicated that the high-wage tier employees had significantly less favorable perceptions concerning the benefits of the wage structure for the other groups. The scale with the second lowest overall mean was Effects on Compensation. For this scale, there were no significant differences within any tier form, as all of the tier groups shared in the perception that the existing structure had not resulted in increased compensation for the respondents.

The overall mean score on the Effects on Opportunities scale, relating to opportunities in terms of increasing the respondent's job security, the number of hours possible to work in a week, and promotion opportunities, suggests that low-tier respondents generally were more favorable concerning the impact of the two-tier wage structure on opportunities. For this scale, three of the high-tier groups in both sets of analyses had significantly less positive perceptions about the effects of the plan on opportunities than did the low-tier groups. For the employment-status tier form, the full-time respondents at the top rate were more favorable concerning the effects on opportunities.

The Effects on High-Wage Tier Employees scale, consisted of items that focused specifically on the plan's effects on high wage tier employees. The analyses for this scale revealed significant differences in the perceptions between most of the high- and low-tier employee groups. The high-tier employee groups perceived that their employment situation had been damaged by the two-tier plan giving management an incentive to get rid of them and thus decreasing their job security. This supports the statements of Bernstein and Schiller (1985), Bowers and Roderick (1987), and Ploscowe (1986), that the responses of the high-tier employees may be related to perceived threats to job security, given the economic incentive to substitute them with lower-cost new employees.

Additional perceptions of employees concerning the effects of the wage structure on job security can be seen in the responses to items 1 and 2 in table 6.3. The responses to these items indicate that employees in each wage tier group perceived that their group's job security had

Table 6.4
Analysis of Scales Related to the First Set of Research Questions

Scale label and title	Scale reliability	Wage		Store-status		Employment-status		Job-duty		Overall percent
		High	Low	Old	New	Full time	Part time	Food	GM	
		n=264	n=807	n=571	n=500	n=217	n=854	n=621	n=450	N=1071
MGTGOALS: Goals of Management	.71	3.40*	3.28*	3.28	3.34	3.39	3.28	3.28	3.35	3.31
RATIFY: Negotiation for Ratification	.82	3.28	3.29	3.30	3.28	3.26	3.29	3.24	3.35	3.29
OTHERSBENF: Other Groups Benefiting	.75	1.83**	2.08**	1.96	2.08	2.01	2.02	1.97	2.08	2.02
EARNINGS: Effects on Compensation	.70	2.17	2.31	2.24	2.32	2.23	2.29	2.24	2.23	2.27
OPPORTUNITY: Effects on Opportunities	.89	2.54***	2.83***	2.69**	2.83**	2.82	2.74	2.72*	2.81*	2.76
HTEFFECT: Effects on High-Wage Tier Employees	.52	2.38***	3.31***	2.92***	3.27***	2.84***	3.14***	2.95***	3.27***	3.08

PROTECT: Negotiations for Protection	.70	3.13***	3.34***	3.20	3.40	3.20	3.31	3.23*	3.36*	3.29
NUMSTORES: Effects on Number of Stores	.51	3.73	3.64	3.64	3.68	3.72	3.64	3.69	3.61	3.66

NOTES: The scores of the eight scales range from 1 to 5, with higher scores representing more important or positive values (3 is the scale midpoint). Asterisks indicate the significance level of the difference between the two tier levels in the total sample analyses. Underline indicates a significant difference (p < .05) when that portion of the sample paid at the top rate of its pay progression is examined.

*p < .05
**p < .01
***p < .001

been increased to a lesser extent than the other group perceived that it had. Further, while about 50 percent of the respondents perceived that a possible reason for the original negotiation of the wage structure was to protect the high-wage tier employees (see items 8 and 9 in table 6.1), only 20 percent[3] of that group perceived that they had benefited to any great degree. In contrast, 46 percent of the low-wage tier employee group surmised that the high-wage tier employees had benefited to a great degree from the plan.

Focusing specifically on the store-status form, the significant differences found in both sets of analyses for the two scales, Effects on Opportunities and Effects on High-wage Tier Employees, indicate that the new-store employees had more positive perceptions relating to the effects of the plan. Given the relatively high number of high wage tier employees in the old stores, it is not surprising that the old-store respondents believed that the two-tier wage structure had a more negative effect on the high-wage tier employees. The old-store respondents were also significantly less favorable about the impact of the wage structure on their opportunities. While the mean scale scores for the new-store employee group were relatively low, it appears that opening new stores or work locations (which represents increases in opportunities and job security for new-store employees) may reduce some of the overall negative employee perceptions following the implementation of a two-tier wage structure.

The responses to the items in the Negotiation for Protection scale indicate that nearly one-half of the respondents perceived that one set of reasons the plan was originally negotiated was to provide employee protection by keeping stores from closing, protecting union jobs, and protecting high-wage tier employee wages. The responses to the items in table 6.3, however, that focused on protecting union jobs (items 1, 2, and 3, concerning job security) and protecting high-wage tier employee wages (items 5, 6, and 8, concerning earnings) indicate that employees, particularly those in the high-tier groups, did not perceive that the plan had accomplished those goals.

The scores for the scale, Effects on Number of Stores, are the highest of the four scales concerning the specific effects of the two-tier plan.

These were the only scores that were positive within both levels of the four tier forms. The results indicate that each group of employees believed the negotiation of wage tiers had resulted in more stores being open. In other words, it appears that the employees were aware of the relationship between the implementation of tiers (i.e., Mayway's human resources strategy) and the firm's strategic business objective of expansion.

Views Concerning Possibilities for Changes in the Plan and Related Issues

The data in table 6.5 pertain to the fourth research question and present employee estimates of the likelihood of each of seven possible changes to the existing wage structure over the next two contract negotiations. Employee responses to each item were based on a five-point response format that ranged from "not at all likely" to "extremely likely." The percentage of respondents who answered "likely" or "extremely likely" is shown for each of the potential bargaining outcomes. As seen in the table, the respondents perceived that the most likely change to the two-tier plan in future bargaining was the creation of a new third tier. Nearly one-half of the respondents believed that this change was likely or extremely likely. "No change in dollar differential between the high- and low-wage tier rates" was viewed as second most likely to occur.

Only one-quarter or fewer of the respondents perceived the remaining changes listed in the table as likely or extremely likely to occur. Equalization was perceived as more likely when accompanied by a freeze of the high-wage rates, as opposed to either lowering them or increasing both rates according to different schedules. Finally, the responses to items 6 and 7 show that approximately equal percentages of respondents perceived that either the high- or the low-wage tier employees would receive greater increases.

The data presented in tables 6.6 and 6.7 pertain to the fifth research question and show the employee attitudes toward selected changes in the existing compensation structure and the potential related outcomes. Ten statements were presented to the employees with responses to each item based on a seven-point response format ranging from "strongly disagree" to "strongly agree." The percentage of respondents answer-

Table 6.5
Predicted Outcomes of Future Bargaining Over the Two-Tier Wage Structure Related to Research Question 4
(Percent of respondents answering "Likely" or "Extremely Likely")

		Tier form and level								
		Wage		Store-status		Employment-status		Job-duty		Overall percent
Outcome[a]	Scale label	High	Low	Old	New	Full time	Part time	Food	GM	
		n=264	n=807	n=571	n=500	n=217	n=854	n=621	n=450	N=1071
1. Implementation of a new, third wage tier with the next contract	No scale	46	46	47	45	46	46	48	42	46
2. No change in dollar differential between high- and low-wage tier rates	No scale	24	29	28	27	26	28	27	29	28
3. Freeze high-wage tier rates, allowing low-wage tier rates to increase and become equal	NARROWRATES	40	20	25	23	31	23	28	20	25
4. Lower high-wage tier pay rates to equal low-wage tier rates	NARROWRATES	28	14	19	16	23	17	21	14	18

5. Raise high-wage tier rates less than low-wage tier rates, resulting in equal-ization over time	NARROWRATES	14	13	14	13	14	13	14	13	14
6. High-wage tier employees will receive greater percentage increases than low-wage tier employees	NARROWRATES[b]	12	23	17	23	19	21	18	22	20
7. Low-wage tier employees will receive greater dollar increases than high-wage tier employees, but the rates will not be equalized	NARROWRATES	21	17	17	18	21	17	19	16	18

a. All items were scaled from 1 (Not at all Likely) to 5 (Extremely Likely).

b. To facilitate interpretation, the scoring of this item was reversed when computing its scale.

ing "slightly agree," "agree," or "strongly agree" for each statement is presented in the two tables. Table 6.6 contains the respondent attitudes toward five statements. The first four statements concern various changes equalizing the earnings of employees on the low- and high-wage tiers and the potential related outcomes. The fifth statement measures employee attitudes toward the establishment of a fringe benefit tier in order to help obtain the outcome of larger raises. Table 6.7 contains statements about the establishment of a third wage tier and the potential related outcomes.

Of the changes and potential outcomes shown in table 6.6, the respondents were most favorable toward raising the low-wage tier rates to the high-wage tier level, even though the high-wage tier employees would obtain a smaller increase than those on the low-wage tier. This was the only change endorsed by a majority of the respondents. It is not surprising that a greater percentage of low- than high-wage tier respondents favored this option. What is surprising is that nearly 40 percent of the high-wage tier respondents agreed with the statement. This suggests that equalization of the wage tiers may be a politically feasible goal for the union representing Mayway's employees to pursue. Similar to the pattern of responses for the first item, the responses of the low-tier employees toward lowering the high-tier rates to the low-tier rates for the purpose of preventing store closings appear in line with the statements of Balliet (1984). He argued that the low-tier employees would have little interest in protecting the higher rates "of those who originally negotiated their inferior status" (p. 7).

Establishing a fringe benefit tier in order to help obtain larger raises for the current employees received the least overall support of any of the items in the table. When combined with the results shown in table 6.7, the overall results show very little support for the concept of extending tiers (instituting a third level of a wage tier or a fringe benefit tier) when the purpose was to facilitate the company's expansion or to get raises for current employees. The strongest support for the development of a third wage tier was found if it was related to keeping stores from closing. Not surprisingly, there was more support from the low- than the high-wage tier employees for the development of a third wage tier if it would assist in equalizing the low- and high-wage tier rates.

Data for the sixth research question regarding the respondents' perceptions of selected statements with respect to two-tier wage structures is presented in table 6.8. The statements focused on issues such as the expectations of the company and union officers, the political problems and tension resulting from the existing wage structure, and the duty of fair representation. These statements are similar to those included in Jacoby and Mitchell's (1986) survey regarding managerial attitudes toward two-tier wage plans. Employee responses to each item were based on the same seven-point response format as in tables 6.6 and 6.7 and are displayed in the same manner as in those two tables. As seen in the table, 49 percent of the respondents believed that the company intended to equalize the wage tiers by lowering the high-tier rates in future negotiations, while a slightly smaller percentage believed that the union would pursue equalization by raising the low-tier rates. The responses to these two items indicate that more of the respondents in the high-tier groups anticipate the equalization of the wage tiers to be an issue in future negotiations.

The high-tier groups generally were in greater agreement with the items suggesting that wage tiers had led to the development of internal political problems for the union and tensions between employees on the two wage tier levels. Overall, 34 percent of the respondents agreed that tiers had created political problems for the union while only 19 percent disagreed. Also, 42 percent agreed that pay rate differences of wage tiers had created employee tension while 31 percent disagreed. The high-wage tier employees' responses to both items are likely related to the fact that they were employed before the plan was negotiated and had the opportunity to view more of the impact of the two-tier plan. Their perceptions of the impact on union political problems and employees tensions may be attributable to their belief that they will be relatively disadvantaged vis-a-vis the low-wage tier employees if the existing differences are narrowed or eliminated.

The fewest respondents expressed agreement with item 3 in the table, that a union was still treating its members fairly when it negotiates a two-tier wage structure. The lesser agreement of the low-wage tier respondents is of interest, given the contention that a union has failed

Table 6.6

Attitudes Toward Selected Changes in the Tiered Wage Structure and the Potential Related Outcomes Related to Research Question 5

(Percent of respondents answering "Slightly Agree," "Agree," or "Strongly Agree")

Change and potential outcome[a]	Scale label	Tier form and level								
		Wage		Store-status		Employment-status		Job-duty		Overall percent
		High	Low	Old	New	Full time	Part time	Food	GM	
		n=264	n=807	n=571	n=500	n=217	n=854	n=621	n=450	N=1071
1. The low-wage tier rates should be raised to the high-wage tier level even though the high-wage tier employees would get a much smaller increase than those on the low tier.	EQUALPAY	39	63	57	58	49	60	58	57	57
2. The high-wage tier rates should be lowered to the low-wage tier level if it would prevent the closing of all company-owned stores in the area.	EQUALPAY	19	49	35	49	34	44	41	43	42
3. The high-wage tier rates should be lowered to the low-wage tier level if it would help prevent the closing of the respondent's store.	EQUALPAY	12	44	29	44	26	38	34	38	36

4. If pay rates cannot be equalized, low-wage tier employees should be able to work more hours, making their weekly earnings equal to those of high-wage tier employees.

EQUALPAY	6	43	31	37	19	37	29	41	34

5. The fringe benefits of all new employees should be reduced if it would help get larger raises for current employees.

THIRDTIER	21	27	21	30	25	26	26	25	25

a. All items were scaled from 1 (Strongly Disagree) to 7 (Strongly Agree).

Table 6.7

Attitudes Toward the Establishment of a Third Wage Tier and the Potential Related Outcomes
Related to Research Question 5

(Percent of respondents answering "Slightly Agree," "Agree," or "Strongly Agree")

Change and potential outcome[a]	Scale label	Tier form and level								
		Wage		Store-status		Employment-status		Job-duty		Overall percent
		High	Low	Old	New	Full time	Part time	Food	GM	
		n=264	n=807	n=571	n=500	n=217	n=854	n=621	n=450	N=1071
A third wage tier should be created for all new employees if it would help the company										
1. from closing the respondent's store.	THIRDTIER	32	41	35	43	38	39	39	39	39
2. from closing other stores (not the respondent's).	THIRDTIER	27	30	26	34	33	29	30	29	30
3. to open new stores.	THIRDTIER	13	14	12	15	15	13	14	13	14
4. raise the current low-wage tier rates to the high-wage tier level in the next contract.	THIRDTIER	14	25	18	26	19	23	22	21	22
5. get larger raises for current employees.	THIRDTIER	22	24	20	27	26	22	23	23	23

a. All items were scaled from 1 (Strongly Disagree) to 7 (Strongly Agree).

in its duty of fair representation to its members on the low-wage tier by the negotiation of a permanent tiered agreement. The more technical legal issue of whether the union's treatment of its members when it negotiated tiers was "unfair representation" could not be adequately addressed in the survey of employees. This is the only item included in the survey that approaches measuring the issue of the duty of fair representation.

Overall, some patterns can be seen in the responses to the individual items in the four tables (6.5 through 6.8) and in the scales developed from the second set of research questions and presented in table 6.9. Many of the items included in the second set of research questions, and in three of the four scales developed from them, were related to either the likelihood of or preference for changes to the two-tier wage plan. Thus, most of the following discussion will relate to this matter.

Both sets of analyses on the scale, Likelihood of Narrowing the Distance between the Two Wage Tiers, showed that the high-wage tier respondents perceived such narrowing to be more likely than did the low-wage tier respondents. The percentages shown in table 6.5, however, indicate that neither group perceived equalization to be a highly likely occurrence in future bargaining. The most desired change by respondents on each level of each tier form, equalization of the rates by raising the low-wage tier rates more than the high-wage tier rates (item 1 in table 6.6), was perceived as the least likely to occur of the seven potential bargaining outcomes presented. Nonsignificant correlations were found between that desired change and the items in table 6.5 regarding the likelihood of raising the low-wage tier rates to equal the high-wage tier rates; the desire was not related to the perceptions of the likelihood of that desire being fulfilled. Further, the correlations found between item 4 in table 6.5 concerning the likelihood of lowering the high-wage tier rates to equal the low-wage tier rates with the two items incorporating the desire to lower the high-wage tier in table 6.6 were $-.14$ and $-.13$ ($p < .001$).

Both sets of analyses on the scale, Desire to Create a Third Tier, indicated that the employees in the high-wage and old-store tier groups were significantly less inclined to support the establishment of a third wage tier, given the related outcomes. This follows from the high-wage

Table 6.8
Attitudes Toward Selected Statements Concerning Two-Tier Wage Structures
Related to Research Question 6
(Percent of respondents answering "Slightly Agree," "Agree," or "Strongly Agree")

Statement[a]	Scale label	Tier form and level								
		Wage		Store-status		Employment-status		Job-duty		Overall percent
		High	Low	Old	New	Full time	Part time	Food	GM	
		n=264	n=807	n=571	n=500	n=217	n=854	n=621	n=450	N=1071
1. The company probably expects to lower the high-wage tier pay rates to the low-wage tier level in some future negotiations.	NARROWRATES	66	44	50	48	60	46	54	43	49
2. The union officers probably expect to raise the low-wage tier rates to the high-wage tier level in some future negotiations.	NARROWRATES	53	37	42	40	50	39	43	38	41
3. When a union negotiates two-tier rate differences, it is still treating its members fairly.	UNIONPBS[b]	31	22	24	25	30	23	26	23	25

4. The two-tier rate differences have created internal political problems for the union.	UNIONPBS	41	31	37	30	37	33	35	32	34
5. Pay rate differences between the high- and low-wage tiers have created tensions between employees on the two tiers.	UNIONPBS	48	39	46	36	43	41	39	44	42

a. All items were scaled from 1 (Strongly Disagree) to 7 (Strongly Agree).
b. To facilitate interpretation, the scoring of this item was reversed when computing its scale.

Table 6.9
Analyses of Scales Related to the Second Set of Research Questions

Scale label and title	Scale reliability	Wage		Store-status		Employment-status		Job-duty		Overall mean
		High	Low	Old	New	Full time	Part time	Food	GM	
		n=264	n=807	n=571	n=500	n=217	n=854	n=621	n=450	N=1071
NARROWRATES: Likelihood of Narrowing the Distance Between the Two Wage Tiers	.50	.26***	-.08***	.02	-.03	.09***	-.03***	.05***	-.08***	0.00
THIRDTIER: Desire to Create a Third Tier	.89	2.87**	3.29**	3.01***	3.39***	3.16	3.19	3.17	3.21	3.18
EQUALPAY: Desire to Equalize the Earnings of the Two Wage Tiers	.77	2.45***	4.29***	3.57***	4.14***	3.22***	3.99***	3.67***	4.06***	3.84
UNIONPBS: Union Problems	.57	4.40	4.36	4.47**	4.25**	4.36	4.37	4.33	4.41	4.37

NOTES: Scale NARROWRATES is formed from standardized items (mean=0, standard deviation =1). The remaining scales used 7-point formats, with higher scores indicating agreement (4 is the scale midpoint). Asterisks indicate the significance level of the difference between the two tier levels in the total sample analyses. Underline indicates a significant difference (p < .05) when that portion of the sample paid at the top rate of its pay progression is examined.

*p < .05
**p < .01
***p < .001

and old-store employees' greater concerns about the adverse effect of wage tiers on both opportunities and on the high-wage tier employees (as reflected in the scales presented in table 6.4). Also, these findings support the statements of Seaberry (1985), who noted that some low-tier employees would rather protect their positions by agreeing to a third tier of even lower wages for future new hires, thus passing concessions along to those who had not yet been hired.

The responses on this scale also reflect different interests between employees on the high- and low-wage tier and in old and new stores regarding potential changes to tiers and job security. Two of the six items in this scale related to store closings (items 1 and 2 in table 6.7). Any store closing would place low-wage tier employee positions at risk, as the high-wage tier employees with their greater seniority could exercise greater job rights in a store that remained open. Further, the greater seniority of old-store employees, when compared to new-store employees, meant that if an old store were closed, much of the workforce would be able to displace the new-store employees. Thus, the higher scores of the low-wage tier employees on this scale likely reflect their desire to protect their positions. In contrast, the high-wage tier and old-store employees wanted to protect their status by avoiding a third wage tier altogether.

The relationship between attitudes concerning the likelihood of changes to the existing compensation system and the scale, Desire to Create a Third Tier, was also examined. Correlational results suggested that the respondents who believed the institution of a third tier was a likely outcome in future bargaining (item 1 in table 6.5) were not those who supported the creation of a third wage tier. When combined with the results concerning raising the low-wage tier and lowering the high-wage tier discussed previously, it appears that in no instance were the respondents' perceptions of the likelihood of a specific change significantly positively related to the desire for such a change.

There were several significant differences between the high- and low-tier groups for the scale, Desire to Equalize the Earnings of the Two Wage Tiers. The scale scores in both sets of analyses revealed significant differences between the high- and low-wage tier employees; the high wage-tier employees opposed equalization while low-wage tier employees favored the change. The responses of the employees is understood, given that if the earnings of those on the two wage tiers were equalized, the high-wage tier employees would benefit less or be disadvantaged more than the low-wage tier employees. Similarly, Wessel (1985) noted that because the low-tier employees are becoming the majority in some UFCW locals, closing the gap usually means smaller raises for high-tier workers while giving larger raises to the low-tier employees to get them closer to the high tier.

Focusing on specific items in this scale, the high-wage tier employee opposition was considerable and the low-wage tier employee support strong when equalization of the earnings would take place through the lowering of the high-wage tier rates to the low-wage tier rates to prevent store closings (items 2 and 3 in table 6.6).[4] As stated previously, if the high-wage tier rates were lowered, the high-wage tier employees would be disadvantaged. On the other hand, if the store(s) were closed, the low-wage tier employees would suffer job losses.[5] The responses to item 4 in table 6.6 reveal the strongest (90 percent) opposition by the high-wage tier employees, in contrast to the strong (43 percent) support of the low-wage tier employees. This item suggested that if the pay rates could not be equalized, low-wage tier employees should be able to work more hours for the purpose of equalizing earnings. Given that the number of hours scheduled in a store is generally invariable in the short run, any increase in hours by one group would necessarily mean a decrease in hours by another. Thus, if the hours of the low-wage tier employees were increased, the high-wage tier employees would lose income.

In the last scale in table 6.9, Union Problems, more favorable responses were found in both sets of analyses for only the new-store employees. This difference may be attributed to the fact that while most employees in the new stores were and always had been on the low-wage tier, the old stores were much more heterogeneous in relation to the wage tier. In other words, while most of the new-store employees had never worked in a store with a majority of employees on the high-wage tier, most of the old-store employees had worked in stores where the majority of employees were on the high-wage tier. It had only been within the previous two years when, due to turnover and the increase of employees in the Mayway stores, low-wage tier employees became a majority in the old stores. Thus the high- and low-wage tier employees in old stores would be more likely to perceive that the plan had created political problems for the union and had created tensions between employees on the separate tiers.

Taken altogether, the results for several items in the scales shown in table 6.9 support the suggestion that employee group divisiveness is a major potential problem in tiered employment settings. As such, the maintenance of tiers leads to different and conflicting interests among employees. The moderately low disagreement with item 4, table 6.8, that tiers have created tensions between employees, is perhaps the most direct support. The conflicting interests and divisions between wage tier groups are seen in the responses to most items in the scales, Desire to Create a Third Tier and Desire to Equalize the Earnings of the Two Wage Tiers. Rather than supporting the objective best interests of the workforce as a whole, i.e., keeping more stores open, the employee responses were consistently more favorable toward supporting each group's own interests to the disadvantage of the other group.

Attitude Differences by Geographic Area

Analyses of the scales derived from the first two sets of research questions revealed more statistically significant differences between the urban and rural areas than within those areas. Thus, table 6.10, pertaining to the seventh research question includes only those scales that showed significant differences between the urban and rural areas.[6]

For both sets of analyses, the table shows that for each significant difference, the urban area had a more positive or favorable response to the scales than the rural area. Urban employees were more likely to believe that the tiers were originally negotiated to protect the employees; they had less negative perceptions concerning the effects of tiers on compensation, on the high-wage tier employees, on the other groups who might have benefited, and on any problems the plan might have caused the union. Those in the urban area also believed that the

Table 6.10
Significant Scale Differences by Area
Related to Research Question 7

| | Area | |
| | Urban | Rural |
Scale label and title	n=604	n=468
OTHERSBENF: Other Groups Benefiting	2.07	1.97
EARNINGS: Effects on Compensation	2.31	2.23
HTEFFECT: Effects on High-Wage Tier Employees	3.16**	2.94**
PROTECT: Negotiation for Protection	3.37**	3.21**
NUMSTORES: Effects on Number of Stores	3.71**	3.60**
THIRDTIER: Desire to Create a Third Tier	3.31**	3.02**
EQUALPAY: Desire to Equalize the Earnings of the Two Wage Tiers	3.96**	3.66**
UNIONPBS: Union Problems	4.32	4.43

NOTES: Asterisks indicate the significance level of the difference between the two areas in the total sample analyses. Underline indicates a significant difference ($p < .05$) when that portion of the sample paid at the top rate of its pay progression is examined.
**$p < .01$

negotiation of wage tiers had resulted in more stores being open. They also had more favorable attitudes toward the concepts of creating a third tier and equalizing the earnings of the two wage tiers.

The direction of these differences appears related to the dissimilarities in the economic conditions, the nature of the retail food industry, and the different wage rates paid in the two areas. For example, urban employees were more sensitized to the problem of store closings, given the extensive number of recent closings by the unionized competition in the urban area. This divergence could explain the differences on four scales (Negotiation for Protection, Effects on Number of Stores, Desire to Equalize the Earnings of the Two Wage Tiers, and Desire to Create a Third Tier), which include items pertaining to opening stores or keeping them from closing. Logically, the urban employees would be more inclined to ascertain a positive relationship between the negotiation of tiers at Mayway and the number of stores in operation. In contrast, the altogether stronger economy with generally lower unemployment rates during the 1980-1983 recession likely led to less concern for store closings and job loss among rural area employees.

The differences in perceptions by area for the scales, Other Groups Benefiting, Effects on Compensation, and Effects on High-Wage Tier Employees, may be partially attributed to the generally higher wage rates paid in the urban area.[7] When the wage tiers were first implemented at Mayway, the urban low-tier rates were set at a higher level than those in the rural area. In the first contract extending tiers, the high-tier rates in the urban area were also set at a higher level than those in the rural area. By the time of the survey, some of the urban low-tier rates were almost as high as the highest rates of the competition. The results in the table suggest that the urban employees perceived that high-wage tier employees had been less negatively affected by the implementation of tiers, and for those with greater seniority (at the top rate of their rate progression), that other groups had benefited more and that compensation had been less negatively affected. Thus, the area differences on these three scales is not surprising.

Finally, the finding that urban employees at the top rate were significantly less likely to perceive that wage rate differences had led to union problems may be in part attributed to the greater proportion of new stores in the urban area. With a greater proportion of new stores, there would be less diversity and decreased contact between the high- and low-wage tier employees in the urban area, resulting in a perception there that rate differences between tiers had led to fewer problems for the union.

Equal Employment Opportunity

The data presented in table 6.11 pertain to the eighth research question and are the percentages of employees in two EEO-protected classes—female and minority group members. For each set of analyses, significant differences indicate disproportionate employment of a protected class within a tier form. The concern expressed in the literature (e.g., Bowers and Roderick 1987; Jacoby and Mitchell 1986) is the disproportional employment of protected classes on the low level of the tier forms, particularly the wage tier form. As can be seen in table 6.11, the data for the wage-tier form suggest that women and minorities are not disproportionately employed on the low-wage tier at Mayway. In fact, both sets of analyses indicate that significantly more women were employed on the high-wage tier than on the low-wage tier. Members of the minority classes, while not a large percentage of the workforce, were equally employed on both levels of the wage-tier form.

The results concerning the other tier forms are unequivocal for both sets of analyses in relation to minority group members. Approximately equal percentages of minority group respondents were employed on the high and low level of each of those tier forms. A disproportionate percentage of females, however, was employed on the low level of three tier forms in the total sample analyses. Further examination of the results of both sets of analyses, in combination with additional survey data, suggests that the protected classes are not disproportionately employed involuntarily on the low level of any tier form. Although both sets of analyses indicate that females are disproportionately employed in part-time positions, the responses to a survey item used to determine whether

Table 6.11
Equal Employment Opportunity Items
Related to Research Question 8

	Tier form and level									
	Wage		Store-status		Employment-status		Job-duty		Overall
Variables	High	Low	Old	New	Full time	Part time	Food	GM	average
	n=369	n=1230	n=949	n=650	n=322	n=1277	n=927	n=672	N=1599
1. Sex (% female)[a]	77***	62***	62*	66*	60***	70***	60**	71**	64
2. Race (% minority)	8	8	9	6	8	8	7	8	8

NOTES: Asterisks indicate the significance level of the difference between the two tier levels in the total sample analyses. Underline indicates a significant difference (p<.05) when that portion of the sample paid at the top rate of its pay progression is examined.

a. Variable 1 is based on a test of population differences, rather than the sample.

*p<.05
**p<.01
***p<.001

employees were working part-time voluntarily or involuntarily suggest that significantly fewer female than male top-rated employees were employed involuntarily in part-time positions.[8] In addition, the data indicate that as women increase in seniority, they are promoted from GM to food department positions and are proportionately employed in both old and new stores.

Concluding Comments

This chapter has focused on the development and subsequent examination of eight research questions related to tiers. Most of the research questions focused specifically on general employee views about the two-tier wage structure at Mayway. As the first empirical study of employee perceptions of their tiered compensation structure, our findings go beyond the largely anecdotal reports and news articles reviewed in chapter 2. Of particular interest is the consistent finding that high-wage tier employees perceived that the tiered wage structure had less beneficial effects than did the low-wage tier employees. Another finding of note is that new-store employees generally had more positive attitudes toward wage tiers and their effects than old-store employees. Overall, many of our findings support the conventional understanding regarding employee perceptions of tiers and their effects. In chapter 8, conclusions drawn from this chapter will be integrated with the findings from chapter 7 to build testable and generalizable propositions.

NOTES

1. Overall, for tables 6.4 and 6.9, it was not unexpected that the most significant differences found within any tier form were within the wage tier form, given that three of the research questions focused specifically on the wage tiers. Also, given the very close relationship between the negotiation of wage tiers and the establishment of new stores, it was expected that the store-status tier form would also have a moderate number of significant differences; this was indeed the case. There were fewer significant differences found within the remaining two tier forms, and only one significant difference found for each of those two tier forms in the top-rate analyses. If a significant difference was found within the employment-status and job-duty tier forms, there was also a significant difference within the wage-tier form for that scale. Further, the differences within the employment-status and job-duty tier forms, given their significant correlation with the wage-tier form, appear at least partially attributable to the differences within the wage-tier form. Thus, there is little separate discussion of results for the employment-status or job-duty tier forms for either set of research questions.

2. The table also presents the scale reliability. This was determined by means of Cronbach's alpha (Cronbach 1951), which depends on the average inter-item correlation and the number of items in the scale. Scale reliabilities of .50 or greater are generally considered adequate for exploratory research.

3. The figure, 20 percent, is derived from averaging the 36 percent of high-wage tier employees who responded to the two lowest response choices on item 10 in table 6.1 ("not at all important" and "not too important") with the two other items in the scale, Effects on High-wage Tier Employees. In computing the scale, the 36 percent figure does not appear in the table because the former item is reversed. Note that this percentage and the percentage shown in the table do not total 100 percent because responses at the scale midpoint, "somewhat important," were excluded. A similar process was used to calculate the 46 percent for the low-wage tier employees. Other percentage figures presented in the text will be calculated in the same manner.

4. About 80 percent of the high-wage tier employees opposed instituting each of those two options (i.e., answered "strongly disagree," "disagree," or "slightly disagree").

5. It might be argued that the choices presented in the items in this scale pit the two wage tier groups against each other in an artificial manner. The pattern of results (but not the magnitude of percentages), however, is the same for all four items in the scale. Implementing the changes in the first item would not lower the income of the high-wage tier employees in an absolute sense. Yet, as for every other item in the scale, a greater percentage (44 percent) of the high-wage tier employees opposed that change than favored it, and a greater percentage of the low-wage tier employees favored such a change than opposed it. Further, several retail food companies in the state where Mayway operated had asked employees for reductions in wage rates in order to avoid closing stores. Thus, the options presented do not appear artificial and, even if they were, would not likely have distorted the results and therefore the conclusions.

6. Four of the scales in table 6.10 showed significant wage tier effects. Because the percentage of high-wage tier respondents (and employees) was significantly ($p < .001$) lower in the urban than in the rural area (19 versus 32 percent), it was possible that the significant area effects were really tier effects. To check for this possibility, separate analyses were performed examining urban and rural differences within both the low- and high-wage tiers. Those analyses showed that all but one of the eight scales in the table had significant area differences independent of a wage tier effect.

7. This can be clearly seen in the top wage rate for cashiers, one of the largest job classes. That rate for urban high-wage tier cashiers was $10.95 an hour; for urban low-wage tier cashiers, it was $10.25 an hour. The top rate for rural high-wage tier cashiers was $10.15 an hour; for rural low-wage tier cashiers, it was $8.70 an hour.

8. The sex difference for employment-status is not restricted to tiered employment situations, as Deutermann and Brown (1978) note that women have traditionally been far more likely than men to work part time. They state, similar to the situation at Mayway, that women are more than twice as likely as men to be working part time. Using the Current Population Survey as their primary data source, they note that in May 1977, one in three women employees were working part time, compared with one in seven men. Also, about half of all men who worked part time did so regularly and by choice versus 70 percent for women.

Treiman and Hartmann (1981) contend that, while it is clear that women are concentrated in jobs that pay less, it is unclear to what extent this is because women select jobs with low pay, to what extent women are restricted to such jobs, and to what extent some jobs pay less than others because they are disproportionately held by women. At Mayway, while the sample data indicate that men were paid significantly ($p < .001$) more per hour than women, the overall average difference was only a little over $.11 per hour.

7
Hypotheses Concerning Tiers

Theory, research, and experience clearly indicate that employees view their compensation as a principal reward or outcome in the employment relationship (Heneman 1985). Because of this, employees naturally have many behavioral and attitudinal reactions to compensation, and thus to tiered employment situations which affect compensation. This chapter focuses on the development and subsequent testing of five hypotheses concerning the relationship of tiers to employee behaviors and attitudes. All of the hypotheses contain directional predictions of differences between the tier levels. As with the research question scales, the analyses involve both the total sample and the top-rate sample. In addition, there will be discussion of some *post hoc* tests within certain tier forms.

The chapter begins by presenting a framework based on equity theory. In the sections that follow, equity theory is used extensively in the development of the hypotheses and in the interpretation of results.

Hypothesis Framework Based on Equity Theory

The concepts of equity invariably are involved in any discussion of pay or compensation satisfaction. It has been proposed that employees are guided by notions of justice and equity in the evaluation of their pay (Adams 1965; Homans 1961; Patchen 1961). Certainly, the process of establishing fair and equitable compensation practices is one of the more important activities carried out by an organization (Hills 1980; Milkovich and Newman 1987). The justness of actual pay and actual pay distribution becomes more salient for employees in a setting where there is "built-in" inequity, such as a tiered employment situation (Martin and Lee 1989; Martin and Peterson 1987).

Equity theory suggests that a person formulates a ratio of outcomes (e.g., pay, job security) to inputs or investments (e.g., effort, attendance). A critical premise of equity theory is that employees compare and attempt to equate their ratios of work outcomes to work inputs with the ratios of other relevant individuals or their own experiences, based on the standards they select, called referents (Adams 1965; Dittrich and Carrell 1979; Mowday 1983; Pritchard, Dunnette, and Jorgenson 1972; Vecchio 1984).[1] If the two perceived ratios correspond, the employees experience feelings of equity and satisfaction. Divergence in the ratios of individuals and their standard of comparison, however, leads to feelings of pay inequity and dissatisfaction. If an employee's ratio is less than the referent's ratio, the employee feels inequitably undercompensated.

If the employees's ratio exceeds the referent's ratio, the employee feels inequitably overcompensated.[2] Note that inequity does not necessarily exist if an employee has high inputs and low outcomes as long as the referent used for comparison has similar outcome/input ratios.

Knowing how individuals choose a standard of comparison against which to evaluate inputs and outcomes will help to better understand the different behaviors and attitudes of employees in different tier groups. Goodman (1974) examined the types of referents or actual comparison standards used in evaluation and differentiated between three classes: (1) others, (2) self, and (3) system referents. He notes that the most common class of referents discussed in the literature is other individuals. These could be persons internal or external to the individual's organization. For example, within the same organization, comparisons may be made with persons holding equivalent or different positions in the same or other tier groups—internal referents. Comparisons may also be made with persons similarly employed in other organizations, with persons employed in specific industries, or with family and friends—external referents—(Martin and Lee 1989).

Self referents or standards are unique to the individual but different from the current ratio of outcomes to inputs, i.e., comparing the current ratio against the ratio associated with an earlier job. Thus, past ratios can be compared to current ratios, or an expected ratio can be compared with a current ratio.

The third class of referent, system referents, refers to an employee's implicit or explicit contractual expectations of the organization's compensation plan. At the time of hire, for example, an employee may be promised rewards in the future, and this can become a foundation for evaluating the employment relationship.

Equity theory research has found that individuals may choose from one or more referents in determining the equitableness of their compensation and other employment conditions, and that they often use multiple referents (Goodman 1974; Hills 1980; Martin 1981; Mowday 1983; Oldham, Kulik, Stepina, and Ambrose 1986; Ronen 1986). Goodman (1977) and Mowday (1983) have suggested that the selection of a referent is a function of both the availability of information about the referent and the relevance or attractiveness of a referent in relation to its ability to satisfy the comparer's needs.

Feelings of inequity (dissatisfaction) will likely cause the employee to attempt to reduce the inequity (Adams 1965). Weick (1966) notes that the most common methods for employees of reestablishing equity involve reducing their inputs (such as effort) in ways that impose costs on the organization. Overall, equity theory emphasizes that pay satisfaction is affected by feelings regarding the equity of the compensation received. These feelings of equity or fairness are the result of an employee's perceptual and multiple comparison processes (Goodman 1977). These processes are rather complex, suggesting that satisfaction with compensation may be influenced in many different ways.

Equity Theory and Tiers

Other researchers have used equity theory in empirical examinations of the attitudes and behaviors of employees in work settings with tiers.[3] Cappelli and Sherer (1988) applied equity theory to a tiered employment setting examining differences in attitudes between employees on different levels of a wage tier. They cite economists' arguments that job satisfaction comparisons, including pay comparisons, use the labor market and, in unionized companies, use other contract settlements (Dunlop 1957; Livernash 1957; Ross 1948). Cappelli and Sherer conclude that the behavioral arguments closest to those of the economists were the ones associated with equity theory. Martin and Peterson (1987) generated hypotheses based on equity theory to analyze data from workers employed on several tier forms at Mayway in 1983. They found that the vast majority of their significant results were consistent with predictions derived from equity theory. Martin and Peterson further argue that in unionized companies, labor agreements and union newspapers provide relevant information, both about the internal pay structure and what the competition is paying, which readily enables comparisons to be made and referents to be selected.

Descriptions of tiered employment situations suggest that low-tier employees resent their lower pay, considering it less fair than the pay of the high-tier employees (Ross 1985; Seaberry 1985). Low-tier employees receive the lowest pay, the least favorable work schedules, and the fewest allotted hours per week. Although we believe that both the high- and low-tier group members perceive inequity associated with tiers, this inequity might best be viewed along a continuum, with the low-tier groups discerning greater inequity. A greater understanding of these differences requires some identification of the relevant referents that may be used by these tier groups.

The existence of tiers would likely result in the selection of different referents by employees in the different tier groups against which their outcome/input ratios are evaluated (Cappelli and Sherer 1987; 1988; Martin and Lee 1989; Martin and Peterson 1987). In such situations, it appears that two factors impact greatly on the selection of referents: first, the length of time the individual has been employed in a particular tiered employment setting (i.e., seniority, which is closely related to one's position on a tier or a wage progression within a tier), and second, whether a second or successive contract maintaining tiers has been implemented. Further, the literature reviewed in the second chapter linked these two factors to the problems and concerns associated with tiers (Bernstein and Schiller 1985; Ross 1985).

Regarding the first factor, both Martin and Peterson (1987) and Cappelli and Sherer (1987; 1988) found significant attitudinal differences among employees in different tier groups related to such outcome variables as pay equity, pay satisfaction, job satisfaction, and commitment. Both studies argued that those differences were likely related to both the tier level employees were on and their position on the wage progression within a tier level. Therefore, it appears that the selection of referents in a tiered employment setting is based on both the employee's tier level and position on the wage progression.

In relation to the second factor, employees would likely perceive the plan as a more permanent part of the employment situation after a second contract extending tiers has been negotiated. The low-tier employees as a group (or at least a large portion of them) would no longer be as new[4] to the company as under the first contract, and thus the employees in that group would likely have different referents than they did prior to the second contract. The relative permanency of tiers is also important because, during the negotiation of succeeding contracts that maintain tiers, the employer may pressure the union to lower the compensation of the high-tier groups to a level equal to or closer to that of the low-tier groups (Wessel 1985). At this point, the pay that the high-tier groups had expected prior to the negotiation of a succeeding contract becomes relevant as a referent.

Selection of Referents by Tier Form

Table 7.1 lists three major types of pay referents that are likely to be used by employees in the different tier groups. They are: (1) internal referents, i.e., other high- and low-wage tier employees; (2) external referents, i.e., employees at other companies; and (3) self referents, i.e., work history, and pay expectations or perceived entitlements. Based on the previous research on pay referents and on their use within tiered settings, specific predictions are made regarding which referents are most relevant for each tier group.

Martin's (1981) work is useful in understanding referent selection in a tiered employment situation, as she found that the two most commonly used referents were upward similar and upward dissimilar ones. The work of Festinger (1954) and Suls and Miller (1977) similarly suggests that when the outcomes being compared are valued, individuals prefer to make upward, rather than downward, comparisons. Martin further notes that downward comparisons were very unlikely.

In table 7.1, which is a cross-tabulation of the tier groups with possible referents, X denotes possible referents that are likely to be used by

Table 7.1

Relevant Referents for Employees in Each Tier Group

| | Tier Form and Level | | | | | | | |
| | Wage | | Employment-Status | | Job-Duty | | Store-Status | |
Possible referents	High	Low	Full time	Part time	Food	GM	Old store	New store
Internal referents								
1. High-wage tier	X		X		X		X	X
2. Low-wage tier		X						
3. Full time			X	X				
4. Part time				X				
5. Food department					X			
6. General merchandise department						X		
7. Old store							X	X
8. New store								X
External referents								
9. High paid	X		X		X		X	
10. Low paid		X		X		X		X
Self-referents								
11. Past		X						
12. Expectations	X		X		X		X	

NOTE: The "X" indicates the most likely relevant referents for employees in each tier group.

those in a particular tier group at Mayway. For example, for the wage-tier group columns, high-wage tier employees would use high-wage tier employees as referents (which would include some upward similar and some upward dissimilar comparisons), and low-wage tier employees would use both high-wage tier referents (upward comparisons) and low-wage tier referents (which would include some upward similar and some upward dissimilar comparisons). A similar pattern of referent selection for high- and low-tier employees in the other three tier forms is shown in the table.

Dornstein (1988) argues that employees will compare themselves with those similar in skills and productive contributions. Her work suggests that high-tier groups would find high-paid external referents relevant, and that the low-tier groups would find low-paid (yet possibly better paid) external referents relevant. Thus, each high-tier column has an X for a high-paid external referent, and each low-tier column has an X for a low-paid external referent. The following discussion focuses primarily on the additional referents that likely would be used by employees at Mayway.

Wage-Tier Referents

High-wage tier employees have greater information than employees on the low-wage tier about the existing tiered compensation structure and the concessions that occurred following its implementation.[5] Thus, it appears that an additional relevant referent for high-wage tier employees would be an expected pay referent, that is, the pay schedule that they believe would have existed for them in the absence of the two-tier wage structure. The work of Cappelli and Sherer (1987; 1988) suggests that the referents used by the high-wage tier groups would likely include other high-wage tier employees[6] and their expectations about future pay. Martin and Lee (1989), in a study of referents used at Mayway,[7] found that the most salient referent for the high-wage tier group was an expected pay referent, which was negatively related to an evaluation of their work situation.

Employees on the low-wage tier who have been with the organization long enough to reach the top rate of their wage progression, would likely find their position of being between the high-wage tier group and the remaining low-wage tier employees to be most salient in selecting referents. At Mayway, top-rate, low-tier employees are paid (mean = $8.23 per hour) significantly (p < .001) less than those in the high-wage tier (mean = $9.53), but significantly (p < .001) more than the more recently hired low-tier employees (mean = $4.70). At this time, further increases for the top-rate, low-tier employees would be difficult to obtain without changing the contract. Thus, for these employees, relevant upward internal comparisons would be associated with a negative evaluation of their work situation. Martin and Lee (1989) found that the use of internal referents by this group was negatively related to attitudes about pay.

An important determinant of the referents selected by the low-wage tier employees not at the top rate relates to their relative newness to the organization and their relative lack of information about the existing tiered employment setting.[8] The most recent hires are likely to focus their attention on the peculiar norms and practices of their organization which maintains a novel compensation system even though they may generally understand it (Louis 1980). It is likely that these employees are not as aware of all of the psychological, economic, and political ramifications of tiers as those in the other groups. Cappelli and Sherer (1987; 1988) argue that because the low-wage tier employees would be "new" to the company and not identify with it as strongly (and perhaps not have as much information about its pay structure) as the remaining employees, such employees would be less likely to make pay comparisons within the company than with their former jobs (self‚past) or other jobs that they could have had (low-paid external).

The next three sections discuss the potential referents employees in the other three tier forms might use. Unlike the permanent wage-tier form, remember that these three forms are temporary, with employees able to move to the higher level as openings occur. It is argued here that, for those on the high levels of these three tier forms (who are limited in their ability to increase their pay outcomes), the referents selected would be essentially the same as those used by the high-wage tier group. Thus, the following discussion will focus primarily on the potential relevant referents used by employees in the low-tier groups.

Job-Duty Tier Referents

There appear to be two predominant situational factors that may impact on the selection of referents by employees working in the general merchandise departments. The first factor affecting the selection of referents by general merchandise employees is the wage disparity between GM and food department employees. The average food department employee on either wage tier earned approximately $3.50 more per hour than the GM department employees. The second factor was a clearly defined career path from the GM positions to the food positions. The career path was highly salient, given that most GM employees aspired to work in the food departments. Thus, an important relevant referent for them would be the food department employees, likely leading to a negative evaluation of their work situation. Additionally, it appears that the GM employees would use other GM employees as standards of comparison.

Employment-Status Tier Referents

The findings of Logan, O'Reilly, and Roberts (1973) and Martin and Peterson (1987) and the discussion in Miller and Terborg (1979) support the argument that the most relevant referents for full-time employees would be other full-timers and for part-time employees, other part-timers. Also, a salient situational factor for the Mayway part-timers is the career line which exists from part- to full-time positions (although not as strong as the one from GM positions to food positions). Those who aspire to full-time positions would likely perceive full-timers as a relevant standard of comparison, which would subsequently lead to a negative evaluation of the part-time employee's situation.

In addition to the internal referents at Mayway, other possible referents for the part- and full-time employees would be the low-paid and high-paid external referents respectively. While there are few unionized part-timers, they typically receive a much greater wage premium over their nonunion counterparts than full-timers do (Martin and Peterson, 1987; Mellor and Stamas 1982; Nollen and Martin 1978). To the extent that the two groups rely on the use of their external counterparts as referents, the part-time employees may actually perceive greater pay equity than the full-time employees.

Store-Status Referents

There are two situational factors which likely affect the selection of referents by new-store employees. First, the new-store, high-wage tier employees, as voluntary transferees, would have likely improved their work situation over their old-store positions in some manner. The use of their previous old-store positions as a referent would likely lead to a favorable evaluation of their work situation. A second situational factor is that high-wage tier employees are not a large proportion of the new-store employees (only 8 percent of the new-store employees would be on the high-wage tier versus 32 percent for the old stores). This means that most interactions in new stores take place among low-wage tier employees. It also means that for the new-store, low-wage tier employees, there are few employees above them in the job hierarchy. Thus, they would likely perceive greater promotion opportunity than similarly situated old-store employees. To the extent that new-store, low-wage tier employees see more opportunity for promotion, they will evaluate the pay and work situation more positively (Patchen 1961).

As new-store, low-wage tier employees reach the top rate, they would become more knowledgeable about the permanent pay rate differences associated with wage tiers.[9] At that time, the high-wage tier employees (or at least their rates) would likely become more relevant as a referent. Given the career lines to full-time and food positions, it is unlikely that the high-wage tier rates would be as important to the part-time and GM employees. Thus, the new-store employees will evaluate their pay and work situation less favorably if the high-wage tier employees or rates are perceived as the most relevant referent. If, however, promotional opportunity is seen as more important, these employees will select referents resulting in a more positive evaluation of their pay and work situation.

Hypothesis Development

Similar to the method used with the research questions, the five hypotheses predict differences in employee behaviors and attitudes between the high and low levels within each of the four tier forms. Analyses of both the entire sample and that portion of the sample at the top rate will be used to test the hypotheses. As was indicated in chapter 5, some of the effects of seniority on the tests of the hypotheses are eliminated when the top-rate sample is used. Further, analyzing and comparing both the total sample and that portion at the top rate has two important implications relative to equity theory.

First, employees on the low-wage tier not at the top of their pay progression are able to increase their pay outcomes at a more rapid rate than employees in the other two groups. Since employees in the latter groups are already at the top rate, they have fewer opportunities to increase their pay outcomes; the contract in effect at the time of the survey contained no increases for employees at the top rate of their pay progression on both wage tiers over the three years from 1984 to 1987. Thus, such employees could no longer increase their outcomes simply by remaining longer in their job classification but instead would need promotions, as their pay outcomes were generally constant. In contrast, low-wage tier employees not at the top rate of their wage progression could improve their pay outcomes both in relation to their own work history and relative to those of the remaining employees until they reached the top rate. The second implication, as indicated in the research discussed previously, is that employees on the low-wage tier not at the top rate likely use different referents than employees who have reached the top rate. Thus, use of the two sets of analyses permits a comparison of findings where the change in pay outcomes and referents varies widely within the low-wage tier with findings where they are more constant.

Employment-Related Behaviors

The first two hypotheses concern behaviors used to restore equity for the high- and low-tier employees at Mayway. The predictions are based on two factors: (1) the literature reviewed previously concerning the selection of referents and the differential perceptions of inequity by those on different tier levels; and (2) the discussion of the potential problems of tiers in the second chapter. Equity theory states that employees who perceive inequity can balance the inequality by reducing their work inputs (Adams 1965; Mowday 1983).

Carrell and Dittrich (1976) found that perceived equity of employees within a service organization was a significant predictor of absenteeism within departments. Dittrich and Carrell (1979) stated that absenteeism, as a form of withdrawal behavior, could represent a reduction in effort or "leaving the field," two forms of inequity resolution. They demonstrated that employees are most likely to be absent and permanently withdrawn from an organization when they perceive their pay as unfair.

An additional means of behaviorally restoring equity is through increasing or decreasing the effort expended on the job. Mowday's (1983) review of research on employee behavioral reactions to compensation, suggests support for equity theory predictions related to effort. Schuster and Clark (1970) found that employees attempt to "balance pay with performance." Both Ross (1985) and Salpukas (1987) report the belief that low-tier employees put less effort into their work than high-tier employees. Ross also concludes that they are less productive than high-tier employees. A way to examine whether low-tier groups are less productive is to examine the data on an aggregated storewide level. For example, the proportion of employees in the low-tier groups could be associated with store productivity. A discussion of this method appears in appendix C, along with the results of such an examination.

Another means of behaviorally restoring equity is to reduce the amount of political support provided for a union. Summers, Betton and DeCotiis (1986) state that equity theory may contribute to our understanding of the relationship between job satisfaction and union voting behavior. They suggest that perceptions of inequity trigger search behavior for a leveling mechanism (i.e., a union) that serves to increase outcomes while holding inputs constant. Kochan (1979) found indirect support for this suggestion. Employees who find their unions ineffective in improving comparative ratios of outcomes to inputs may vote against the union in a decertification election.

Reducing political support for the union can serve as withdrawal for those perceiving inequity in their employment situation. The literature suggests that low-tier employees will be less politically supportive of the union because they perceive that the union did not support them, both when it first negotiated the two-tier plan, resulting in their lower class status, and when it continued the plan (Balliet 1984; Ploscowe 1986). Both Balliet and Ploscowe offer anecdotal evidence to suggest that the low-tier groups might not be active in the union. Further, Ploscowe cites union sources who believe that the low-tier employees would oppose the union leadership that maintained tiers. Opposition by the low-tier employees could involve both withdrawal behavior and, by voting against incumbent union officers who maintained tiers or voting against ratifying contracts containing tiers, they may be able to restore equity through the elimination of tiers. By voting against ratifying contracts containing tiers, the low-tier employees are taking direct actions to change the outcomes of both the high- and low-tier employees.

The preceding discussion leads to the first two hypotheses. The specific hypotheses are as follows.

(1) The employees in the low-tier groups will have a higher absenteeism rate and report less effort expended on the job than will the employees in high-tier groups.

(2) The employees in the low-tier groups will participate less in union activities, and be more likely to (a) vote against ratifying union contracts that maintain tiers, and (b) vote against incumbent union officers, than will the employees in the high-tier groups.

Employment-Related Attitudes

The next three hypotheses concern employment-related attitudes related to the inequity of tiers for employees at Mayway. It is predicted that the low-tier employees will perceive specific inequities and low union instrumentality where tiers have maintained apparently discrepant ratios between those on different tier levels. Specifically, it is expected that the employees in the low-tier groups would have less favorable attitudes on issues directly related to tiers or outcomes, such as their pay, the actual two-tier wage plan, and the number of hours they work.

This leads to the third hypothesis. The specific hypothesis is as follows.

(3) Compared to the employees in the high-tier groups, the employees in the low-tier groups will have: (a) perceptions of less pay fairness and

lower union instrumentality in obtaining fair pay; and (b) lower satisfaction with their pay, the two-tier plan, and the number of hours they work.

Two important predictors of such employment-related attitudes as commitment and job satisfaction are the employees' perceptions of internal promotion opportunity and perceived external employment mobility (Hall 1979; Mowday, Porter, and Steers 1982). Both of these predictors, but particularly the latter, are closely related to employee turnover (Mowday, Porter, and Steers 1982) and would be relevant to include in a study of tiers given that employee turnover on the low-tier levels has been identified as a potential problem (Ross 1985; Wessel 1985). A study of Telly, French, and Scott (1971) further suggests that turnover may be one method used by employees to remove feelings of inequity. While absence and turnover may originate from the same feelings (Dittrich and Carrell 1979), withdrawal from an organization may be more directly influenced by the perceived possibility of intra-organizational work transfer and by the perceived number of extra-organizational alternatives (March and Simon 1958).

Regarding promotion opportunity, all the high-tier employees have reached the top of their wage progressions and many have moved to food and full-time positions or reached the highest classification possible given their training and abilities. In contrast, a large proportion of the low-tier employees began in part-time positions, at lower level job classifications (e.g., bagger), lower paid departments (e.g., GM), and would not have reached the top of the wage progression. Thus, it is predicted that the low-tier employees will perceive more opportunity for promotion than the high-tier employees.

The high- and low-tier groups may differ in the perceived opportunity for external employment based on their determination of employment stake; that is, by their estimates of the benefits of working for a new employer minus the personal costs to them of leaving their current employer. Relative to the low-tier groups, the high-tier employees would likely be older, more dependent on their employer for support of themselves and their family, and higher in seniority. This dependency is reinforced by the heavy personal investments (economic and psychological) that they have made as a result of their tenure with the company (Homans 1961).

Additionally, the high-wage tier employees are generally paid higher wages than the competitors' employees and would likely believe that no other employer would pay the same rates and benefits they currently receive. Further, if these employees moved to another employer, they would not likely be placed at the top of the wage progression. They would tend to see themselves as being "locked in" to their employment situation and feel compelled to stay regardless of their attitudes toward their employer and union. The low-tier employees, in contrast, are less dependent on their employer, with some intending to stay at their current jobs for only a short period of time. It is believed that many of them would consider leaving if better opportunities became available. Thus, it is predicted that the low-tier employees will perceive external employment opportunities that would enable them to increase their outcomes to a greater degree.

The preceding discussion leads to the fourth hypothesis. The specific hypothesis is as follows.

(4) The employees in the low-tier groups will perceive greater promotional opportunity and greater opportunity for external employment than will the employees in the high-tier groups.

A critical concern raised by the existence of a two-tier structure relates to its effect on the employment-related attitudes of workers toward both the company and union. Commitment, whether to the employer or union, is important both as an attitude and as a predictor of turnover and job satisfaction (Gordon, et al. 1980; Mowday, Porter, and Steers 1982). Cappelli and Sherer (1987) state that anecdotal manifestations of a lack of company and union commitment on the part of low-tier workers have frequently been reported in news analyses. Given that perceived pay equity (Rhodes and Steers 1981) and such personal characteristics as age and tenure (Angle and Perry 1981; Hall 1979) have been found to be related to commitment, it would appear that high-tier employees would have higher commitment. However, the development of a hypothesis concerning company and union commitment and job satisfaction requires the consideration of specific events surrounding the negotiation and implementation of tiers at Mayway that appear to have had a significant enduring impact on both commitment and job satisfaction.

For example, the two-tier plan was negotiated immediately after the 1978 affiliation of Mayway's independent union with the Retail Clerks. Many of those employed at the time of the affiliation subsequently became more negative in their perceptions of the union, partially because the union attempted to improve relations with the company. Clearly, many members, all of whom would have been on the high-wage tier at the time of the survey, did not have their goals met after the independent union affiliated with the Retail Clerks, i.e., the outcomes anticipated by these employees prior to the affiliation were not realized.

On the other hand, many of the low-tier employees could perceive the creation of their jobs as having resulted from the negotiated exchange between the union and management. Viewing the union and management leaders as having created the low-tier jobs, the low-tier employees would likely have higher commitment to the union and employer than they would have had in the absence of such nonpay outcomes. These contextual factors suggest that high-tier employees, many of whose objectives were not fulfilled after the independent union affiliated with the Retail Clerks and who perceived lower levels of job security,[10] would have lower attitudinal commitment toward both the union and employer. While such a prediction may appear situational, Cappelli and Sherer (1987) also found that low-tier employees had higher union and employer commitment (and higher job satisfaction and job security) than the high-tier employees in their study.

Given the relationships suggested between job satisfaction and other variables examined in this study, it is of interest to examine how this affective reaction relates to tiers. Wiener and Vardi (1980) noted that, while the overall dynamics of the commitment/satisfaction relationship appear quite complex, job satisfaction has been found to be associated with organizational commitment. Although the relationship between commitment and satisfaction is not fully understood, their conclusion that organizational commitment was an antecedent to job satisfaction assists in predicting differences in job satisfaction between the high- and low-tier employees. Also, considering that the unmet expected outcomes of the affiliation of their union with the Retail Clerks led to rather enduring dissatisfaction for many high tier employees, it is predicted they would have lower job satisfaction than would the low-tier employees.

The preceding discussion leads to the fifth hypothesis. The specific hypothesis is as follows.

(5) The low-tier groups will have higher union and employer commitment and higher job satisfaction than will the high-tier groups.

Results and Discussion

Results of tests of the hypotheses are presented in tables 7.2 through 7.6.[11] Significant differences are shown only where a significant total sample multivariate tier effect existed, with all variables testing a hypothesis entered as a block.[12] Each table displays the variable scores in essentially the same manner that the scale scores were displayed in the previous chapter. One exception is that for any significant difference found for a variable within the top-rate analyses where there was no difference within the total sample analyses, the higher group mean is marked by a footnote. Where significant differences were found for variables within both sets of analyses, the direction of the top-rate difference is the same as that for the total sample difference.

A brief examination of the results reveals that the first two hypotheses generally were not supported in either set of analyses, while the third, fourth, and fifth hypotheses received considerable support. As can be seen in table 7.4 for both sets of analyses, the majority of items testing hypothesis 3 indicate that the high-tier employees in the wage and job-duty tier forms had significantly more positive attitudes. Mixed results were found for the store-status and employment-status tier forms. Tables 7.5 and 7.6, which present the results for hypotheses 4 and 5, generally indicate higher scores and more favorable perceptions for the low-tier employees. This trend holds for all tier forms in both sets of analyses

Table 7.2
Behaviors to Restore Equity
Variables Testing Hypothesis 1

Variable[a]	Scale reliability	Tier Form and Level								Overall mean
		Wage		Store-Status		Employment-Status		Job-Duty		
		High	Low	Old	New	Full time	Part time	Food	GM	
		n=369	n=1230	n=949	n=650	n=322	n=1277	n=927	n=672	N=1599
1. Self-reported effort	.77	5.35	5.29	5.27	5.35	5.59***	5.23***	5.25*	5.38*	5.30
		(1.19)	(1.06)	(1.14)	(1.01)	(1.12)	(1.07)	(1.06)	(1.12)	(1.09)
2. Days absent during 1985		4.37	3.74	4.19*	3.59*	4.28*	3.82*	4.25**	3.36**	3.29
		(5.08)	(4.43)	(4.95)	(4.21)	(5.14)	(4.48)	(4.78)	(4.42)	(4.32)

NOTES: Standard deviations are in parentheses below the group means. Asterisks indicate the significance level of the difference between the two tier levels in the total sample analyses. Underline indicates a significant difference ($p < .05$) when that portion of the sample paid at the top rate of its pay progression is examined.

a. Variable 1 used 7-point formats with higher values representing higher effort. The total sample size for variable 2 is 1004.

*$p < .05$
**$p < .01$
***$p < .001$

Table 7.3
Behaviors to Restore Equity
Variables Testing Hypothesis 2

Variable[a]	Scale reliability	Tier Form and Level								
		Wage		Store-Status		Employment-Status		Job-Duty		Overall mean
		High	Low	Old	New	Full time	Part time	Food	GM	
		n=353	n=687	n=633	n=407	n=294	n=746	n=687	n=353	N=1040
1. Union activities	.70	1.94***	-1.03***	.29**	-.51**	1.37***	-.57***	.38***	-.82***	-.02
		(6.10)	(2.91)	(5.03)	(3.45)	(5.99)	(3.59)	(4.50)	(4.36)	(4.49)
2. Voted against ratifying the current contract (%)		57*	43*	51*	44*	53*	46*	53***	37***	48
		(.50)	(.50)	(.50)	(.50)	(.50)	(.50)	(.50)	(.48)	(.50)
3. Voted against an incumbent union officer (%)		13***	4***	9*	5*	10	7	8	7	8
		(.33)	(.21)	(.29)	(.23)	(.30)	(.26)	(.27)	(.26)	(.27)

NOTES: Standard deviations are in parentheses below the group means. Asterisks indicate the significance level of the difference between the two tier levels in the total sample analyses. Underline indicates a significant difference (p < .05) when that portion of the sample paid at the top rate of its pay progression is examined.

a. The items making up the "Union Activities" scale can be found in appendix B. The overall sample size for variable 2 was 1007, and for variable 3 was 846.

*p < .05
**p < .01
***p < .001

Table 7.4
Work-Related Outcome
Variables Testing Hypothesis 3

Variable[a]	Scale reliability	Tier Form and Level								Overall mean
		Wage		Store-Status		Employment-Status		Job-Duty		
		High	Low	Old	New	Full time	Part time	Food	GM	
		n=369	n=1230	n=949	n=650	n=322	n=1277	n=927	n=672	N=1599
1. Satisfaction with two-tier pay plan		3.20***	2.63***	2.72	2.83	2.87[b]	2.74	2.90***	2.58***	2.76
		(1.79)	(1.54)	(1.64)	(1.58)	(1.76)	(1.58)	(1.67)	(1.52)	(1.62)
2. Pay fairness	.78	4.43***	3.64***	3.81	3.83	3.92*	3.79*	4.14***	3.38***	3.82
		(1.35)	(1.39)	(1.43)	(1.40)	(1.50)	(1.40)	(1.36)	(1.38)	(1.42)
3. Pay satisfaction	.93	4.05***	3.28***	3.47	3.44	3.36	3.48	4.04***	2.66***	3.45
		(1.73)	(1.74)	(1.76)	(1.77)	(1.70)	(1.78)	(1.68)	(1.56)	(1.77)
4. Union instrumentality	.81	3.69[b]	3.69	3.61**	3.81**	3.55	3.37	3.90***	3.41***	3.69
		(1.63)	(1.52)	(1.55)	(1.53)	(1.55)	(1.55)	(1.53)	(1.53)	(1.55)
5. Satisfaction with number of hours	.71	.34***	-.10***	.01	-.01	.63***	-.16***	-.05*	.11*	.00
		(.85)	(.87)	(.89)	(.89)	(.64)	(.87)	(.89)	(.88)	(.89)

NOTES: Standard deviations are in parentheses below the group means. Asterisks indicate the significance level of the difference between the two tier levels in the total sample analyses. Underline indicates a significant difference (p < .05) when that portion of the sample paid at the top rate of its pay progression is examined.

a. All scales except "Satisfaction with number of hours" used 7-point formats with higher values being more favorable. That scale is formed from standardized variables (mean=0, standard deviation=1) with higher scores representing more satisfaction.

b. This group mean is significantly higher than the mean of the other tier level when that portion of the sample at the top of the pay progression is examined.

*p < .05
**p < .01
***p < .001

Table 7.5
Perceived Promotion and Employment Opportunity Variables Testing Hypothesis 4

Variable[a]	Scale reliability	Tier Form and Level								Overall mean
		Wage		Store-Status		Employment-Status		Job-Duty		
		High	Low	Old	New	Full time	Part time	Food	GM	
		n=369	n=1230	n=949	n=650	n=322	n=1277	n=927	n=672	N=1599
1. Perceived promotion opportunity		2.51***	3.61***	3.17***	3.62***	3.05***	3.43***	3.26*	3.49*	3.36
		(1.54)	(1.82)	(1.78)	(1.83)	(1.86)	(1.80)	(1.80)	(1.84)	(1.82)
2. Perceived employment mobility	.76	-.76***	.15***	-.04	-.10	-.44***	.03***	-.47***	.49***	-.07
		(2.04)	(1.94)	(2.01)	(1.97)	(1.97)	(1.99)	(1.97)	(1.89)	(2.00)

NOTES: Standard deviations are in parentheses below the group means. Asterisks indicate the significance level of the difference between the two tier levels in the total sample analyses. Underline dicates a significant difference ($p < .05$) when that portion of the sample paid at the top rate of its pay progression is examined.

a. Variable 1 used a 7-point format with a higher value representing high opportunity. Variable 2 is formed from standardized variables (mean=0, standard deviation=1) with higher scores representing more perceived employment mobility.

*p < .05
**p < .01
***p < .001

Table 7.6
Commitment and Job Satisfaction
Variables Testing Hypothesis 5

Variable[a]	Scale reliability	Wage		Store-Status		Employment-Status		Job-Duty		Overall mean
		High	Low	Old	New	Full time	Part time	Food	GM	
		n=369	n=1230	n=949	n=650	n=322	n=1277	n=927	n=672	N=1599
1. Company commitment	.85	3.51***	4.14***	3.80***	4.28***	3.78**	4.05**	3.93	4.09	4.00
		(1.59)	(1.44)	(1.54)	(1.40)	(1.54)	(1.48)	(1.52)	(1.47)	(1.50)
2. Union commitment	.93	3.12***	3.52***	3.31***	3.60***	3.35[b]	3.45	3.42	3.44	3.43
		(1.58)	(1.50)	(1.52)	(1.51)	(1.54)	(1.52)	(1.55)	(1.49)	(1.52)
3. Job satisfaction	.82	4.49***	4.91***	4.66***	5.03***	4.78	4.82	4.80	4.83	4.81
		(1.56)	(1.42)	(1.51)	(1.37)	(1.43)	(1.47)	(1.47)	(1.46)	(1.47)

NOTES: Standard deviations are in parentheses below the group means. Asterisks indicate the significance level of the difference between the two tier levels in the total sample analyses. Underline indicates a significant difference (p < .05) when that portion of the sample paid at the top rate of its pay progression is examined.

a. All variables are scaled 1 (Strongly disagree) to 7 (Strongly agree).

b. This group mean is significantly higher than the mean of the other tier level when that portion of the sample at the top of the pay progression is examined.

*p < .05
**p < .01
***p < .001

for hypothesis 4, while a more complex pattern of findings is evident for hypothesis 5. The remainder of the chapter will examine in detail the results related to each of the hypotheses.

Behaviors to Restore Equity

The two variables of self-reported work effort and absenteeism relate to the first hypothesis concerning behavioral means of restoring equity and are shown in table 7.2. The significance levels and the direction of the overall mean differences shown in the table suggest that the hypothesis was not supported for any tier form.

For the variable of self-reported effort, only within the employment-status tier form was a significant difference found that was consistent with the predictions. In each of the analyses, the part-time employees reported expending less effort on the job. Discussions with informed individuals revealed that it was commonplace for employers in retail trade to assign tasks with more difficult components (some of which required more physical or mental effort) to full-time employees so that fewer employees would need to be trained in such tasks. Thus, this difference is likely attributable to the greater proportion of full- than part-time employees involved in assignments requiring more effort. The job-duty tier form differences in self-reported effort were not in the predicted direction. One can only speculate on the cause (i.e., situational factors, referent selection, job content); post-survey interviews did not lead to any explicit conclusions.

The first hypothesis also considered employee absenteeism as a means of behaviorally restoring equity. The results for each set of analyses indicate that in no instance were the number of days absent during 1985 significantly higher in the low-tier groups. No difference was found within the wage-tier form, with employees on the low levels of the other three tier forms generally absent significantly fewer days. Although these results clearly run counter to our prediction and counter to the findings of Dittrich and Carrell (1979), it appears that these results may be situational, given Mayway's policies concerning absences.

As discussed in chapter 4, employees with eight years seniority at Mayway were allotted eight paid absences per year. Nearly all such employees would be on the high-wage tier and most would be on the high level of the other tier forms. For the employees with less than eight years experience but hired before April 1, 1983, six paid absences were allotted per year. Employees hired after this date received four paid absences per year. All employees receiving the four paid absences would by definition be on the low-wage tier, and most would be on the low-levels of the other tier forms. Naturally, because employees in the high-tier groups received more paid absences, it follows that they would have higher absenteeism rates than employees in the low-tier groups.[13] Overall, the two variables examined in the first hypothesis had such a low proportion of predicted significant differences that the first hypothesis was not supported.

As shown in table 7.3, the second hypothesis examining behaviors to restore equity included three variables relating to union activities and different forms of union political support. This hypothesis states that the low-tier groups will participate less in union activities and will be less supportive of the union. Examination of the direction of the group mean differences suggests that the hypothesis was not supported within any tier form. In both analyses, the only differences found consistent with the hypothesis were for the union activities variable. The members of each low-tier group reported that they participated significantly less in union activities. Contrary to the second hypothesis, however, in the total sample analyses a higher percentage of each high-tier group reported that they voted against ratifying the current contract. In the top-rate sample analyses, only the job-duty tier form difference remained significant. Also in opposition to the hypothesis in both analyses, the high-wage tier employees were more likely to report that they had voted against an incumbent union officer. Overall, just under one-half of all respondents stated that they voted against ratification of the current contract, while a much lower percentage of all respondents reported voting against an incumbent officer.

The results for the first two hypotheses indicate that the low-tier respondents did not use the behaviors measured in the survey to restore equity, i.e., changing either the outcomes (the contract or the union officers) or the inputs (absences or effort) of the outcome/input ratios. There appear to be two factors, however, that qualify the results relative to the second hypothesis. As discussed in chapter 4, the last contract negotiations prior to the administration of the survey had eliminated double-time pay on Sundays and frozen the top wage rate for both wage tiers. These changes had a more negative effect on the high-wage tier employees because Sunday shift scheduling was based on seniority and because all of the high-wage tier employees were paid at the top rate (compared to about one-fourth of those on the low-wage tier). Thus, the high-tier employees were more likely to vote against ratifying the current contract and perhaps to vote against the incumbent officers.[14]

Further, numerous studies (Anderson 1979; Hoyman and Stallworth 1987) have found that seniority is significantly positively correlated with participation in union activities. The lesser participation in union activities among the low-tier employees is logical, given the relationship between the different tier levels and seniority at Mayway. Although some literature has suggested that low-tier employees would be less inclined to support the union, the results in this study did not support that suggestion.

Employment-Related Attitudes

The five tier- or work-related outcome variables shown in table 7.4 relate to the third hypothesis, which states that the low-tier groups have lower satisfaction with their pay, the two-tier plan, and the number of hours they work. The hypothesis also predicts that the low-tier groups will perceive less pay fairness and lower union instrumentality in obtaining fair pay. The group means for the first item in the table, "satisfaction with the two-tier pay plan," are of interest because they are all below the scale midpoint of 4 (neutral). This suggests that no tier group was satisfied with the pay plan. In both sets of analyses, the high-tier groups in the wage and job-duty tier forms had more favorable attitudes on this item, as predicted. The next two items showed a similar pattern of significant differences as the high-wage tier and food department employees also had more favorable attitudes toward their pay.

Within the other two tier forms, however, only one significant difference was found in both sets of analyses for the first three items. The part-time employees perceived their pay as significantly less fair. Those who aspired to full-time positions likely viewed full-timers as a relevant standard of comparison and subsequently evaluated their pay as unfair. The difference in satisfaction with the plan, seen only in the top-rate analyses between part- and full-time employees, suggests that many part-time employees who only desired short-term, part-time employment had left the organization. Many of the remaining top-rate, part-time employees, who likely aspired to full-time positions, were dissatisfied with the plan as a result of the inability to increase their pay rate upon promotion to full-time status.

A different pattern of significant differences can be seen for the remaining two variables testing hypothesis 3. In the total sample analyses, there were differences within the store-status and job-duty tier forms regarding the union's instrumentality in obtaining fair pay and benefits. In the top-rate analyses, significant differences were found for the wage and department tier forms for this item.

The direction of the difference for the store-status form, however, was opposite to the stated hypothesis. Employees not at the top rate constituted two-thirds of all new-store employees, and likely used an external referent, leading to a favorable evaluation of the union's instrumentality. It is likely that old-store employees with relatively low seniority would have been actively socialized by the more senior employees to be more negative toward the union, and thus they would tend to see the union as less instrumental. As new-store employees interact primarily with low seniority employees, they would remain more favorable in regard to the union and its instrumentality. In the top-rate analyses, employees in both old and new stores faced a three-year wage freeze, and thus their perceptions of union instrumentality would likely converge. Finally, the lack of differences within the store-status form for the other variables suggests that the employees were not likely to make comparisons between old and new stores.

Additionally, the "union instrumentality" variable differs significantly within the wage-tier form for the top-rate analyses, but not for the total sample analyses. The newer employees, those not at the top rate, likely using an external or past pay referent in comparisons, perceived that the union had been more instrumental in gaining valued economic outcomes such as fair pay and benefits than did the low-wage tier employees at the top rate.[15] Apart from changes in group mean differences which are caused merely by excluding the newer employees, a logical explanation for the difference rests in the different selection of referents by the top-rate, low-wage tier employees, i.e., high-wage tier employees. This would result in less favorable perceptions regarding union instrumentality than either the high-wage tier group or the remaining low-wage tier employees.

For the final variable shown in table 7.4, "satisfaction with number of hours," the analyses found significant differences that were consistent with the hypothesis within the wage and employment-status tier forms. The significant difference within the job-duty tier form was not consistent with the predictions. The results appear attributable to the fact that the high-wage tier and GM departments had a significantly higher proportion of full-timers than did the low-wage tier and food departments. Thus, in reference to satisfaction with number of hours worked, the use of full-time employees as a comparison may lead to a negative evaluation. For the store-status form, there was an approximately equal percentage of part-time employees in both the old and new stores.

The fourth hypothesis examined the two variables of "perceived promotion opportunity" and "perceived employment mobility" shown in table 7.5. This hypothesis, which states that the low-tier groups will perceive greater promotional opportunity and greater opportunity for external employment, was generally supported in each of the analyses for each tier form.

For the "perceived promotion opportunity" variable in the total sample analyses, each of the low-tier groups perceived significantly greater opportunity. The cross-tabulation of various tier forms (see table 5.7) suggests that many employees are indeed promoted by the time they reach the top rate. For example, often by the time that many employees who began in part-time or GM positions reach the top rate, they have progressed to full-time and/or food department positions. Given that most of the promotions would have taken place, the lack of significant differences in the top-rate analyses for the employment-status and job-duty tier forms is understandable.

For the wage-tier form, it is not surprising that the high-tier employees perceived significantly less promotion opportunity given that they had a minimum of seven and one-half years of seniority. The significantly higher scores among the new-store employees in both sets of analyses are probably related to the high proportion of low-wage tier employees in new stores (Martin and Peterson 1987).

The results also indicate that the low-tier employees perceived external opportunities that would enable them to increase their outcomes to a greater extent than employees in the respective high-tier groups. The higher perception of external employment mobility among the low-tier employees may be one factor contributing to higher low-tier employee turnover rates reported by Ross (1985) and Wessel (1985).

The three employment-related attitudinal variables of "company commitment," "union commitment," and "job satisfaction" are shown in table 7.6 and pertain to the fifth hypothesis. This hypothesis states that the low-tier groups will have higher union and company commitment, and job satisfaction. The significant differences for the three variables within the wage and store-status forms supported the hypothesis for the total sample analyses. The significant difference for company commitment within the employment-status tier form also was consistent with the hypothesis.

In the top-rate analyses, the predictions were supported only in the store-status tier form. Note that the differences found in the total sample analyses for the wage and employment-status tier forms were no longer significant in the top-rate analyses. Also, the significant difference in the top-rate analyses for "union commitment" between part- and full-time employees was opposite to the predictions.

The changes in the significant differences between the two analyses for the employment-status tier form may be explained by seniority and the use of different referents. The new part-time employees (not at the top rate) likely use external part-time positions as referents (Cappelli and Sherer 1988). As discussed previously, the wage premium that Mayway's unionized part-timers earn in comparison to most other part-time positions is much greater than it is for Mayway's full-timers. Thus, irrespective of the referent used by the full-timers, their employer commitment would likely not be as high as that of the part-timers. In the top-rate analyses, however, the part-time employees would have greater knowledge of the pay and working conditions of Mayway's full-time employees. Further, as many of them aspired to full-time positions, they would likely use those full-timers as a referent (Martin 1981), resulting in no significant difference in employer commitment between the two groups.

The results concerning union commitment within the employment-status form showed a different pattern. The new part-time employees would not likely know much about the union and thus would not differ from the full-timers on union commitment. The part-timers at the top rate would have been employed long enough to be socialized by the senior employees to acquire some negative attitudes toward the union. These part-timers would also find that most of the promotions to full-time positions had taken place, with further promotions more difficult. If they blamed this fact on the union, they would tend to have lower union commitment than the full-timers.

The complex pattern of results for this hypothesis resulted in several additional analyses. As can be seen for the wage tier form, significant differences were found for each variable only in the total sample analyses. For the three variables, the additional analyses revealed that the low-wage tier employees who were not at the top rate had significantly more favorable attitudes than the top-rate, low-wage tier employees and high-wage tier employees. This relationship held irrespective of whether the employees were in old or new stores. Thus, it appears that the large proportion of low-wage tier employees not at the top of their rate progression accounted for the higher scores for company commitment, union commitment, and job satisfaction of the entire low-wage tier group in the total sample analyses.

For the store-status form, the results show significant differences for all three variables in each set of analyses. The lack of difference between the two analyses indicate that there were not major seniority or socialization effects working to change the referents and employee attitudes for this tier form. The results suggest that the new-store employees used referents that resulted in a more favorable evaluation of their "company commitment," "union commitment," and "job satisfaction." As the new-store employees interact primarily with the less senior low-wage tier employees, they remain more favorable toward the company, union, and job than their counterparts at the old stores. These findings support the research of Martin and Peterson (1987), who found that each attitude they measured among low-wage tier employees was significantly more favorable in new stores than in old stores.

Further analyses focused specifically on low-tier groups in old and new stores for the eight items testing the third and fifth hypotheses. Of the 24 tests between old- and new-store employees, 14 indicated that the new-store employees had significantly more favorable attitudes toward the employment situation. In no case did the old-store employees have more favorable attitudes. These results indicate that new-store employees who were in the low level of the other tier forms generally had more favorable work-related attitudes. Overall, these results, in combination with the results from chapter 6, strongly suggest that the new-store employees do not consider themselves as disadvantaged due to their store status.

Summary

This chapter has centered on the development and subsequent testing of five hypotheses which focus on the relationship between tiers and employee behaviors and attitudes. Of the five hypotheses developed from equity theory, the first two, which related to behaviors to restore equity, were generally not supported. In retrospect, it appears that the large proportion of nonsupportive results were a function of the nature of the variables used to test the hypotheses. Moderately strong support was found for the remaining three hypotheses relating to employment attitudes. Excluding the tests of the store-status tier form, for each set of analyses there would be a total of 30 separate tests spread equally across the three tier forms. Support was found in 20 of the 30 tests in the total sample analyses, with the results of one test opposite in direction to the prediction. In the top-rate analyses, support was found in 16 of the tests, with the results of two tests opposite in direction to the prediction.

Chapters 6 and 7 have gone beyond the largely anecdotal literature concerning tiers and their relationship to employee attitudes, behaviors, and characteristics; they provide a systematic empirical examination of these relationships at one tiered employment setting. Chapter 8 will further discuss some of the results presented in the last two chapters and generalize from them to other settings. The final chapter will include the author's overall conclusions.

NOTES

1. While pay appears to be the most common basis for comparison (Mowday 1983), other job facets, such as hours, job security, and benefits may be related to the selection of referents (Oldham et al. 1986).

2. Martin and Peterson (1987) argue that high-tier employees would not perceive themselves as overcompensated because they would view their pay rate as the historical standard rate and make equity comparisons with their own pay history rather than with the low-tier employees.

3. Other theoretical frameworks that may be useful in explaining the effects of tiered compensation structures include social construction of reality theory (Salancik and Pfeffer 1978), behavioral commitment theory (Salancik 1977; Staw 1974), and relative deprivation theory (Martin 1981).

4. The typical labor contract is in effect for about three years. It is likely that employees would base their perceptions of the permanency of tiers and thus their selection of referents on the length of contracts normally in effect at their employer.

5. At Mayway, the perceived knowledge of the collective bargaining contract as measured by a five-point scale was significantly ($p < .001$) less among the low-wage tier employees. The results also indicated that they had read significantly ($p < .001$) fewer issues of the union newspaper in the prior year. Both of these results support the suggestion that low-wage tier employees have less knowledge about tiers and concessions.

6. Cappelli and Sherer (1987; 1988) suggest that high-wage tier employees used other employees in their industry as referents. Their discussions indicate that respondents were using individuals in comparable positions and on the high-wage tier of the competition.

7. Martin and Lee (1989) used a different data set; that data collection was funded by an ANR Pipeline Company Business Administration Fellowship.

8. Using the same items discussed in note 5, low-wage tier employees not at the top rate knew significantly (p < .001) less about the contract and read significantly (p < .001) fewer issues of the union newspaper than the top-rate, low-wage tier employees.

9. Using the same items discussed in notes 5 and 8, new-store employees not at the top rate knew significantly (p < .001) less about the contract and read significantly (p < .001) fewer issues of the union newspaper than those at the top rate.

10. The first three items in table 6.3 support the suggestion that low-tier employees perceive greater job security than high-tier employees.

11. The hypothesis tests are based on the sample size of 1599, although for some of the analyses the sample size was smaller. For example, to vote in the union officer election, an employee had to be employed by November 1983. Similarly, a meaningful analysis of the number of absences taken during 1985 meant that the respondent had to be employed prior to 1985. The sample size shown in the tables for some of the other items may represent a larger number than was actually analyzed due to missing data on a particular item or set of items.

12. In no case where the total sample effect for a tier form was not significant was a significant top-rate multivariate effect found. Also, in only one instance where the multivariate effect was not significant was a significant difference found for a variable within a tier form. See chapter 5 for further discussion of the methodology.

13. Another method of examining days absent during 1985 focuses on the number of unpaid absences taken by employees. In both sets of analyses, significantly (p < .001) more unpaid absences were taken by high-tier employees only for the wage tier form. This change does not alter the conclusion that the hypothesis was not supported.

14. Voting is often considered a union activity (Anderson 1979). In this study, the two union voting items are separated from the union activities variable because, unlike the concepts included in the general union activities variable, the union voting items incorporate the notion of being against the union goals or officers.

15. A one-way ANOVA found that the low-wage tier employees not at the top rate had significantly (p < .01) more favorable perceptions of "union instrumentality" than the top-rate, low-wage tier employees.

8
Summary and Conclusions

This book is the first to examine in detail the impact of tiered compensation structures on unions, employers, and employees. Chapters 1 and 2 introduced tiers and described their role in the United States industrial relations system. Chapter 1 defined tiers and examined their types (permanent and temporary) and forms (wage, benefit, job-duty, employment-status, among others). Also, two predominant views of tiers expressed in the literature were discussed. Overall, in contrast to other discussions (Cappelli and Sherer 1987; 1988; Jacoby and Mitchell 1986), tiers have been presented here as a more complex and broad phenomena. Chapter 2 examined the industries and conditions under which tiers are most likely to be found, how they function, potential benefits and problems, and trends in the incidence of tiers. Chapter 3 included a detailed discussion of labor-management relations in the retail food industry and the competitive pressures that led to the implementation of tiers. The first three chapters together provide the groundwork for the remainder of the book.

Chapter 4 discussed the historical and environmental factors that led to the implementation and maintenance of tiers at Mayway Food Market Company, the company whose employees were surveyed. Chapter 5 described the sample and the methodology used in the survey. Both chapter 6 (which examined the research questions) and chapter 7 (which examined the hypotheses) concerned the perceptions of rank-and-file employees at Mayway and built upon the previous research and literature on tiers. The hypotheses were developed and the results were interpreted within the framework of equity theory.

This chapter begins with the advancement of five propositions which appear generalizable to other mature tiered employment settings. The chapter also examines the relative costs and benefits of maintaining tiers at Mayway and the generalizability of the Mayway experience. It also discusses the limitations of this study and presents some additional areas for research. The chapter concludes with the author's perspective on the future of tiers.

Propositions

Five testable propositions appear to be generalizable to settings where tiers have been in effect through more than one contract (referred to as mature tiers), and where there is at least a large minority of low-tier employees. These propositions integrate findings from throughout the book. The five propositions either support the current conventional understandings or add to our understanding of the impact of tiered compensation structures.

Proposition 1: Employee groups on each level of each tier form will perceive few, if any, benefits from a two-tier compensation plan. Further, all employee groups will express dissatisfaction with the existence of such a plan and will oppose the establishment of new, lower tier levels for new cohorts of employees.

Much of the literature reviewed in chapter 2 that examines the dissatisfaction of tiered employees focuses on low-tier employees. Less attention has been given to the disenchantment of the high-tier employees or, in nontiered situations, to the potential high-tier employees. The results of this study indicate overall dissatisfaction with the effects of tiers among the high-wage tier employees, which in some cases was significantly greater than among the low-wage tier employees. This surprising finding can be explained in terms of the perceived disparity between their actual compensation (and other actual work-related outcomes) and the higher compensation (and other more favorable work-related outcomes) high-tier employees believe they would have obtained in the absence of tiers.

All of the tier groups expressed dissatisfaction with the two-tier plan and perceived that the plan had negative effects on compensation, job security, and promotion opportunities. Although more than 70 percent of the employees perceived that the existence of the plan had increased the opening of new stores (a stated goal of management in negotiating the plan and one which objectively led to increased promotion opportunities and job security), less than one-eighth and one-fourth of the respondents perceived that their promotion opportunities and job security, respectively, had been increased by the negotiation of the plan. Also, the results indicated moderate to strong opposition to the notion of new lower levels for the wage or benefit tier, even if such changes would lead to larger raises for the current employees.

Proposition 2: The implementation of wage tiers will result in divisiveness between the employee groups on the two wage-tier levels.

Some of the literature reviewed in chapter 2 suggests that the maintenance of disparate wage rates through tiers leads to different and conflicting interests among the employees and results in friction between those on each wage tier level. The findings of this study were consistent with that suggestion. First, each wage tier group preferred changes to tiers given the related outcomes that would benefit their own tier group and disadvantage employees on the other tier level. Second, each group perceived that the other group had benefited more in terms of some specific work-related outcomes, i.e., job security. Third, over 40 percent of all respondents perceived that pay rate differences had created tensions between employees on the two tier levels. Although not directly addressed by the survey, it appears that the implementation of tiers may eventually lead to friction and hostility among employee groups and/or poor union-member relations. These employee perceptions make clear the need for improved communication to the workforce regarding the plan and its effects on work-related outcomes.

Proposition 3: When employees on the low-wage tier become a sizeable minority, it may be politically feasible for the union to seek to raise the low-wage tier rates up to the high-wage tier level.

This study's findings indicated that a majority of all respondents and a large minority of those on the high-wage tier supported raising the low-wage tier rates up to the high-wage tier level. Although such a change is potentially volatile, given the larger percentage and dollar increases of the low-wage tier group, equalization may limit the divisiveness and friction among employees in the long run. Through equalization, a union may be able to limit political losses and increase the solidarity among the membership over the long term. Salpukas (1987) gives an example of where tiers were eliminated by providing the high-wage tier employees with lump-sum payments and by raising the low-wage tier rates to the high-tier level over a six-year period. When the wage disparities resulting from tiers are eliminated, the new rate is usually below what the rate would have been had wage tiers or other concessions not been negotiated (BNA 1988; Wessel 1985).

At Mayway, in both 1984 and 1987, the union eliminated wage differentials for some job classes, while instituting a new, lower wage tier level for those same classes. The union also narrowed the differences between the tiers for many of the other job classes. Those changes, along with the survey results, suggest that equalization can be carried out without the union incurring too great a political cost. The institution of a new, lower tier would likely increase the employer's willingness to raise the low-wage tier, despite possible employee resistance to that option.[1]

Proposition 4: Companies with tiered compensation structures that expand to new geographically separate locations (from the previous work locations) will find less negative attitudes concerning tiers and their effects than companies with tiers that do not expand.

While there has been some work that examined tiers as part of a business strategy for expansion (see chapters 1 and 2), little is known about the effects of expansion on employee attitudes. Although proposition 1 suggested that employee groups on all levels of each tier form will perceive few benefits from a two-tier plan, it appears that companies with tiers that expand will find employees in new locations, i.e., those established after tiers were implemented, will have more favorable attitudes than employees in previously established locations. Also, companies with tiers that expand will find more favorable attitudes among employees in general relative to companies with tiers that do not expand.

As stated previously, a concomitant of expansion with its creation of new jobs is that both high- and low-tier employees benefit from increased promotion opportunities. They also benefit from increased job security, as previously-hired employees have rights to the new jobs in the event of layoffs. To test proposition 4, it is necessary to compare the attitudes of employees in similar companies with wage tiers, one that has expanded geographically and one that has not. While the relative impact of the objective benefits from expansion on high- and low-tier employee attitudes remains an empirical question, both the literature and our findings suggest that employees in companies that expand will have more favorable attitudes.

As noted in chapter 7, Martin and Peterson (1987) found that new-store employees had significantly more favorable attitudes than old-store employees. They attributed these findings to the much greater proportion of low-tier employees in new stores and the much greater perceived promotion opportunity in such stores. They argued, therefore, that the referents selected by new-store employees would result in a more favorable evaluation of their work situation. The findings of this study indicate that the new-store employees had more favorable perceptions concerning the effects of tiers on their opportunities and on the high-wage tier employees. New-store employees also perceived that the negotiation of wage tiers had caused the union fewer problems. Further, greater job satisfaction and union and employer commitment were found among new-store employees. These findings may be attributed largely to differences between low-wage tier employees in new and old stores. Such store-status differences include the socialization of the low-wage tier employees, their knowledge of the tiered pay plan, their selection of referents, and the amount of contact and thus the degree of "friction" with employees on the high-wage tier.

Proposition 5: Disproportionate employment of women and minority groups on the low-tier levels is not a necessary outcome of tiers.

The discussion in chapter 2 identified the EEO public policy concern associated with the implementation and maintenance of tiers. The belief was that, due in part to changes in the labor market, the low-tier groups would consist of a disproportionate number of protected class members, such as women and minorities. The results of the current study suggest that disproportionate employment of protected class members on the low tier levels is not a necessary outcome of tier implementation and maintenance. At Mayway, minority group members were employed proportionately on each level of the tier forms. Further, there was actually a higher percentage of women on the high-wage tier rather than the low-wage tier. Where there existed a disproportionate number of women on the low level of a tier form, the data indicate that as they gained seniority the women progressed to the high level, or in the case of part-time employment, a significantly greater percentage were voluntarily employed part-time. The violation of the tenet of equal pay for equal work is inherent to most tier forms, discrimination on the basis of race and sex is not.

Costs and Benefits of Tiers at Mayway

This section discusses the costs and benefits of tiers at Mayway for the three principal participants in the labor relations process as identified by Holley and Jennings (1988) framework: management, union leaders, and employees.

Tiered compensation allows management to reduce direct employment costs over the long term. In this study, we did not assess the indirect employment costs of recruitment, selection, training, and turnover that may have increased as a result of the implementation of tiers. What could be determined was that in 1987 the use of wage tiers alone saved Mayway over 13 percent of its retail store employee payroll, or more than 27 million dollars a year. This was determined by comparing the existing situation with the identical employment situation with all employees paid as though they were on a unitary wage scale that used only the high-tier wage rates. The use of tiers had also greatly facilitated both the building of new stores and the expansion of jobs within the new stores and the previously built stores. Sixteen new stores had been built and a minimum of 6,000 new employees had been added.

A critical potential problem for management, as suggested by the literature on tiers and equity theory, is that the marked wage disparity between high- and low-wage tier workers performing essentially the same jobs would result in decreased productivity and low morale. The data examined in this study were inconclusive as to the effects of wage disparities on Mayway productivity. Low morale, however, is suggested by the finding that all of the tier groups expressed dissatisfaction with the two-tier plan and perceived that the plan had negative effects on compensation, job security, and promotion opportunities. While not assessed, the employees' negative attitudes about the work and the work setting may have been associated with increased turnover (or turnover intention), increased absenteeism and tardiness, and decreased quality of customer service (and possibly, customer decisions to shop elsewhere), all of which may increase costs to the employer.

Of particular concern to the union is the effect of different and conflicting interests, e.g., goals for the union to pursue in bargaining, among the various employee groups and the resulting friction between those on each wage tier level on the membership solidarity. As stated in the discussion of proposition 2, the results of this study suggest that the maintenance of disparate wage rates through tiers leads to different and conflicting interests between the employee groups. The research question results indicate that many respondents perceived that pay rate differences had created tensions between employees and agreed that rate differences had created internal political problems for the union. At Mayway, the conflicting interests and tensions have not led to such potential problems as decertification drives and campaigns to remove incumbent union leaders. Last, the movement toward the elimination of tiers had become an area of contention in negotiations between union and management and may be seen as a cost for both union and management.

The union benefited from a substantial increase in membership as the new jobs were filled by new union members. The local union, unlike many local unions during the 1980s, did not lose members but instead showed a substantial increase in membership. Further, new-store employees had more favorable attitudes toward the union than their counterparts in old stores. An often cited benefit of tiered compensation structures is that the union can preserve the current pay levels and increase employment without harming the current employees. The union representing Mayway's employees, which did not want to negotiate concessions for members already on the job, did not decrease the wage levels of the previously employed members.

The actual benefits of tiers for Mayway's employees were the greater promotion opportunities and job security resulting from the increased number of new stores and the increased number of jobs within each store. In addition, many of the jobs held by Mayway's low-wage tier employees were a direct result of the organization's expansion. Even though the high-wage tier employees indicated disfavor with tiers, a benefit to them was that their wages had not decreased as would have occurred with some other labor cost containment methods, i.e., across-the-board cuts. All employee groups at Mayway, as stated in the first proposition, however, expressed dissatisfaction with the two-tier plan and perceived that the tiers had several major negative employment-related effects.

Generalizability of the Mayway Experience with Tiers

This section examines the generalizability of Mayway's experience with tiers. Chapter 4 outlined in detail the company expansion that accompanied the implementation and maintenance of tiers at Mayway. Given the benefits derived at this company, one must ask whether the functioning of tiers and their effects at Mayway are an anomaly.

The author believes that the functioning of tiers and their impact are clearly generalizable to those organizations marked by a continuing increase in the proportion of new employees on the low-wage tier, such as expanding companies or those with a high rate of turnover. Additionally, generalizations may be made to organizations possessing high opportunities for employee advancement. At Mayway, with the development of the job-duty tier and the establishment of the employment-status tier, the low-tier employees would be able to progress from the lower to higher paid positions as openings occurred. Finally, the permanent wage tiers at Mayway never included the most skilled positions or department heads (equivalent to leadmen or leadwomen in other industries) in the bargaining unit. Thus, the experience at Mayway may be generalized to organizations with a core of skilled workers who supervise and train new employees, who know most of the jobs in the workplace, and who are able to react to environmental changes fairly rapidly. The company expansion created such positions and also the need to have them filled.

The Mayway experience with tiers is also clearly generalizable to other organizations using a proactive business strategy of expansion while operating under strong exogenous forces and constraints. Thus, the company's experience appears generalizable to those organizations with tiers that exist in environments where restraints or conditions limit some behaviors or outcomes yet permit latitude and choice in others, e.g., organizations with tiers in highly competitive environments that nonetheless maintain high individual choice of strategy. Mayway's experience with tiers would be less generalizable to situations where organizations have minimum choice or where tiers have been introduced as part of a business strategy for economic survival.

The characteristics of the union and its approach to negotiating tiers were critical to the Mayway experience and thus should be noted here. The union leaders, who were secure in their positions, continually worked to convince the members of the benefits of tiers over the shorter run. In the most recent bargaining rounds, in 1984 and 1987, they convinced management to reduce the distance between the wage tiers for most job classes, and eliminated them for a few large job classes. They also raised a large number of employees in two highly paid low-tier job classes to the high-tier rates by equalizing rates over a four-year period. Further, the union leaders created a third wage tier level that would eventually become the low-wage tier. These changes to the tiered employment structure, as well as the existence of the promotional opportunities discussed previously, probably provided the low-wage employees with some hope that they would not be on the low-wage tier permanently.

Overall, the generalizability of this company's experience is enhanced because the major common goals of the participants in the labor relations process at Mayway were standard participant goals (see discussion of framework in chapter 1). The standard goal for management was to increase profits, which was done at Mayway through the moderation of labor costs and company expansion. The principal objective of the union leaders, protecting their political positions, was accomplished by obtaining increases in employee wages and job security. The standard employee goals of increased wages and job security may be viewed as either sufficiently satisfied or as not thwarted to the extent that the union leaders suffered significant political damage.

Limitations of the Study and Additional Areas for Research

There are several limitations of the study that may potentially restrict the generalizations and predictions as they apply to other sites and industries. First, the survey data were obtained from one company in a single industry at one point in time. While some information was obtained through interviews and technical reports, the data did not allow the making of any causal inferences. Second, the resources allowed for the surveying of employees in only 17 of the 39 stores covered by the union-management agreement. These stores were selected in geographic areas with differing economic conditions so as to be widely representative, although in each subarea the number of stores surveyed was very small. Further, store- and individual-level data that would have permitted the assessment of the nature of the relationship between tiers and productivity or other economic performance measures with a higher degree of confidence could not be obtained.

A third limitation of this study relates to the nature of the survey instrument. Prior research has focused almost exclusively on the wage tier form (Cappelli and Sherer 1987; 1988; Jacoby and Mitchell 1986); thus this study began with that focus. The considerable impact of the other tier forms was not recognized until after the survey was administered. Fourth, regarding equity theory, alternative explanations for the study results are possible given that many factors were uncontrolled for and the actual referents selected were not determined. Interpretation of these results becomes equivocal to the extent that respondents used different referents in evaluating facets of their work situation than we predicted.

Despite the limitations of the current study, the findings should be of interest to other researchers and practitioners interested in tiers. Clearly, additional research in this area is necessary if we are to more adequately understand the effects of such structures. Often, research efforts focusing on tiered compensation structures have been limited because union leaders and management were unwilling to cooperate. Unions and management may be concerned that the results of such research will be used by their counterparts in collective bargaining. In addition, many factors (i.e., the highly competitive nature of American industry) may increase the reluctance of management to participate in such a study or to permit surveying and/or access to hard data, such as that related to productivity.

Additional research is necessary on the relationship between productivity and a marked wage disparity among workers performing essentially the same jobs. This may be assessed by comparing the performance/productivity of individuals in similar positions but who are on different tier levels within the same company, statistically controlling for employee background variables which may differ systematically by tier level, i.e., age. Five additional areas requiring attention include the following: (1) longitudinal investigations of multiple sites in both the manufacturing and service sectors; (2) analyses of sites where tiers have been terminated; (3) comparisons of unionized and nonunion tiered settings; (4) comparisons of the costs and benefits of different tier forms; and (5) assessments of the costs/benefits of tiers versus other methods of controlling labor costs. Such research would provide unions and management with additional information upon which to make informed decisions regarding tiers.

The Future for Tiers

A wide range of opinion currently exists as to the appropriateness of tiers as a response to the changes in the competitiveness of the economic environment. Thus, it is not surprising to find a lack of consensus among prognosticators concerning the future prevalence of tiers in the United States. Predictions based on data collected prior to 1986 or based on a predominantly managerial perspective (e.g., Essick 1987; Jacoby and Mitchell 1986; Ploscowe 1986) are relatively positive with regard to the suitability of tiers as a means of responding to environmental pressures. Predictions based on data collected after 1986 or based predominantly on union views (e.g., Bernstein and Schiller 1985; BNA 1988; BNA March 2, 1988) tend to be less favorable. These latter predictions suggest that union leaders now are heightening their efforts to eliminate or avoid such structures, and they have suggested that there is evidence that tiers are falling from repute with management as well.

Overall, based on the literature, technical data, several in-depth interviews, and changes in the economy and workforce demographics since the early 1980s, it is believed there will be an increase in the rate of elimination of the existing two-tier structures, along with a more rapid decrease in the negotiation of new plans. Thus, during the early and mid-1990s, the proportion of contracts containing tiers will peak and then decline. Where mature tiers exist in a contract, unions will continue in their efforts to eliminate or lessen existing wage disparities and to convert permanent tiers to temporary tiers. Therefore, it is believed that permanent tiers will become less common as they are phased out or replaced by temporary tiers.

Tiers, while still a potential human resource strategy option, will likely be seen as just one of several newer and alternative compensation strategies available for adoption by management to lower or control labor costs. These include such pay policies as lump-sum payments, knowledge-based pay, gain sharing, employee stock ownership plans, profit sharing, pay for performance, and work rule changes, among others, to help control labor costs (BNA 1988; Katz and Milkovich 1986; O'Dell and McAdams 1986). These other newer strategies will be more attractive to unions and their members because they have much less potential to adversely affect union solidarity. Further, tiers are the only alternative compensation option that cannot enhance the use of participative human resource strategies. If these other compensation strategies are not seen as viable options for the employer, however, unions will likely opt for tiers when the alternative is incurring across-the-board wage cuts.

Finally, it is also believed that tiers will become even more concentrated in the service sector relative to the manufacturing sector of the economy. Tiered compensation structures, in the context of proactive business plans, will continue to facilitate the expansion of many service sector companies into new markets. Tiers in the manufacturing sector will have a shorter life span (in any particular company there), as they may be terminated when the need for immediate contract concessions passes.

NOTE

1. As tiers and changes to them are the result of bilateral negotiations, management agreement would be needed to achieve such equalization. Chapter 2 suggested that management would likely take into consideration such factors as the state of the labor market, comparisons of both the low- and high-wage tier rates with alternative jobs, comparisons of the company's rates to those of the competition, the company's competitive position, and the company's profit picture. Clearly, neither party would want changes to result in job loss or a decrease in the rate of job expansion (based on speculations of the rate of job expansion that would occur without alterations).

Appendix A
Survey Items and Response Formats

Section 1

THIS FIRST SET OF STATEMENTS CONCERNS YOUR FEELINGS TOWARD YOUR WORK SITUATION, PAY, AND RELATED ISSUES. Please indicate how strongly you AGREE or DISAGREE with each by *circling the number* representing the most appropriate response to each statement.

1. I am satisfied with the number of hours I normally work in a week.
2. All in all, I am satisfied with my job.
3. It would be very difficult for me to find another job that is as good as the one I have now.
4. Local [X] has obtained fair pay for me.
5. During the past year, the effort I put into my job was much more than my typical co-worker.
6. I put more effort into my job beyond what is necessary to do satisfactory work.
7. I am very happy with the amount of money I make.
8. Considering my skills and the effort I put into my work, I am very satisfied with my pay.
9. During the past year, my job performance was much better than that of my typical co-worker.
10. I would probably refuse a promotion if one were offered.
11. I am likely to receive a promotion within the next two years.
12. It would be very hard for me to leave my job even if I wanted to.
13. Local [X] has obtained fair benefits for its members.
14. I talk up my employer to my friends as a great employer to work for.
15. I find that my values and my employer's values are very similar.
16. I am proud to tell others that I am part of my employer's organization.
17. In general, I like working here.
18. I talk up Local [X] to my friends as a great organization to be a member of.
19. My values and the Union's values are very similar.
20. I feel a sense of pride being a part of Local [X].
21. Local [X] has helped the membership in general obtain fair pay.
22. In general, I *don't* like my job.
23. My pay is fair compared to the pay of people doing the same kind of work for other employers.

24. My pay is fair compared to that of onboard employees in general in my store.
    REMINDER: **Onboard** employees (entering their job title prior to November 1978) receive a higher top pay rate than **hereafter** employees (entering the same job title after that date).
25. My pay is fair compared to that of hereafter employees in general in my store.
26. My pay is fair compared to the pay of other people doing the same job in my store.

The response format for Section 1 and Section 8 was as follows:

1. Strongly Disagree
2. Disagree
3. Slightly Disagree
4. Neither Agree nor Disagree
5. Slightly Agree
6. Agree
7. Strongly Agree

Section 2

THIS SET OF QUESTIONS CONCERNS MORE *GENERAL* FEELINGS ABOUT YOUR WORK SITUATION. Please answer each question by *circling the number in front* of the appropriate response to each question.

1. If you really look for another job in the near future, what do you think are your chances of finding one as good or better than your present job?
   1. No chance of finding such a job
   2. Some chance of finding such a job
   3. Probably would find such a job
   4. Certain to find such a job

2. Choose the *one* statement which best tells how well you *presently* like the hereafter-onboard pay plan.
   1. Very dissatisfied
   2. Dissatisfied
   3. Slightly dissatisfied
   4. Neither satisfied nor dissatisfied
   5. Slightly satisfied
   6. Satisfied
   7. Very satisfied

3. How satisfied are you with the amount of pay you get?
    1. Very dissatisfied
    2. Dissatisfied
    3. Slightly dissatisfied
    4. Neither satisfied nor dissatisfied
    5. Slightly satisfied
    6. Satisfied
    7. Very satisfied

4. In general, which *one* of the following best reflects how you feel about your pay?
    1. I am very much overpaid
    2. I am moderately overpaid
    3. I am slightly overpaid
    4. I am paid about right
    5. I am slightly underpaid
    6. I am moderately underpaid
    7. I am very much underpaid

Section 3

LISTED BELOW ARE A NUMBER OF POSSIBLE REASONS WHY EMPLOYERS AND UNIONS NEGOTIATE DIFFERENT RATES FOR HEREAFTER AND ONBOARD EMPLOYEES WITH THE SAME JOB TITLE. Please examine each of them and then *circle the number* in the appropriate column which represents your best estimate of how important you think each might have been as a reason for your employer and union to negotiate the hereafter-onboard rate differences in the first place.

1. To help [the company] compete with nonunion competitors
2. To help [the company] get a new contract ratified
3. To help Local [X] get a new contract ratified
4. To allow [the company] to open new stores
5. To help [the company] compete with other unionized competitors
6. To protect the wages of the onboard employees at [the company]
7. To keep stores from closing
8. To save the company money
9. To protect the jobs of Local [X] members in general
10. To give management an incentive to get rid of onboard employees

The response format for section 3 was as follows:

1. Not At All Important
2. Not Too Important
3. Somewhat Important
4. Important
5. Extremely Important

Section 4

HOW DO YOU THINK THE FOLLOWING HAVE BEEN AFFECTED BY THE EXISTENCE OF THE HEREAFTER-ONBOARD RATE DIFFERENCES AT [THE COMPANY]? Please *circle the number which represents* your best personal estimate of the effect on each of the following:

1. The closing of stores by [the company]
2. The opening of new stores by [the company]
3. The job security of onboard employees in general at your store
4. The job security of hereafter employees in general at your store
5. Your personal job security
6. The number of hours you are able to work in a week
7. Your promotion opportunities
8. Your current hourly pay rate
9. The dollar amount of your raises in the future at [the company]
10. Your current weekly earnings
11. Your current fringe benefits

The response format for section 4 was as follows:

1. Definitely Increased
2. Probably Increased
3. Probably No Effect
4. Probably Decreased
5. Definitely Decreased

Section 5

ABOUT HOW MUCH HAVE EACH OF THE FOLLOWING GROUPS BENEFITED *OVERALL* FROM THE EXISTENCE OF THE HEREAFTER ONBOARD RATE DIFFERENCES? Please *circle the number* in the appropriate column which best represents your estimate of how much each group listed below has benefited, if at all, from these rate differences.

1. The Company ([name])
2. The Union
3. Onboard employees in general
4. Hereafter employees in general
5. Customers
6. Employees in general at your store

The response format for section 5 was as follows:

    1. Not At All
    2. Somewhat
    3. A Moderate Amount
    4. Pretty Much
    5. Very Much

Section 6

Now think about what *might* happen in the future. HERE ARE SOME POSSIBLE RESULTS FROM BARGAINING OVER THE HEREAFTER-ONBOARD PAY RATES DURING THE NEXT TWO (2) CONTRACT NEGOTIATIONS. Please *predict* the likelihood you think each possibility listed below has of occurring by *circling the number* in the appropriate column.

1. Lowering the onboard rates down to equal those of the hereafter rates
2. Freezing the onboard rates until the hereafter rates rise up to equal the onboard rates
3. New lower pay scales will be negotiated for employees hired after the date of the next contract
4. There will be no change in the dollar differential between the hereafter and onboard rates

5. Raising *both* hereafter rates and onboard rates so that after a period of time, both will be equal
6. Onboard employees will receive greater percentage increases than hereafter employees
7. Hereafter employees will receive greater dollar increases than onboard employees, but the rates will not be equalized

The response format for section 6 was as follows:

1. Not At All Likely
2. Not Too Likely
3. Somewhat Likely
4. Likely
5. Extremely Likely

Section 7

This next set of questions relates to *your own* activities. Please *circle the number* which represents the most appropriate answer for you.

1. About how many issues of *the Local [X] newspaper* have you read *in the last year*?

   None at all.................................... 0
   1 or 2 issues.................................. 1
   3 or 4 issues.................................. 2
   5 to 7 issues.................................. 3
   8 or 9 issues.................................. 4
   All of them.................................... 5

2. About how many issues of *the company newsletter ([name])* have you read *in the last year*?

   None at all.................................... 0
   1 or 2 issues.................................. 1
   3 or 4 issues.................................. 2
   5 to 7 issues.................................. 3
   8 to 10 issues................................. 4
   11 to 15 issues................................ 5
   16 to 20 issues................................ 6
   All of them.................................... 7

3. From the list below, please put a check mark next to *each* experience you have had since 1978 as a member of Local [X].

   ____ 1. I served as a steward
   ____ 2. I served as a union officer or business representative
   ____ 3. I served on a bargaining committee
   ____ 4. I served on another union committee
   ____ 5. I attended a new member meeting
   ____ 6. I ran for a union office
   ____ 7. I filed one or more grievances *on my behalf*
   ____ 8. I worked on a union election campaign
   ____ 9. I worked on a union organizing drive
   ____10. I voted *against* ratifying our current contract
   ____11. I voted *against* an incumbent union officer
   ____12. NONE OF THE ABOVE

4. Approximately how many days on which you were scheduled to work were you absent *for any reason* during 1985?

None	0
1 or 2	1
3 to 5	2
6 to 8	3
9 to 12	4
13 to 16	5
17 to 21	6
22 to 25	7
More than 25	8

5. About how often do you go to regional Union meetings?

I never go to the meeting–(0%)	1
I sometimes go to the meetings–(about 25%)	2
I go to about half the meetings–(about 50%)	3
I usually go to more than half the meetings–(about 75%)	4
I go to almost all the meetings–(about 90–100%)	5

6. How knowledgeable are you about your collective bargaining contract?

> I don't know anything at all about what is in the
> collective bargaining contract.................... 1
> I know a little about what is in the contract......... 2
> I know some of what is in the contract............. 3
> I know quite a bit of what is in the contract......... 4
> I know a lot about what is in the contract........... 5

Section 8

In this section, please indicate your personal FEELINGS about the hereafter-onboard rate differences.

1. If the pay rates cannot be equalized, hereafter employees should be able to get more hours than onboard employees so they can earn as much in a week as onboard employees do.
2. If it would help me get a larger raise in the next contract, I would personally favor creating *additional lower pay scales* for all new employees hired.
3. If it would help the company open new stores, I would personally favor creating *additional lower pay scales* for all new employees hired.
4. If it would help keep my store from closing, I would personally favor creating *additional lower pay scales* for all new employees hired.
5. If it would help keep the company from closing other stores (not my store), I would personally favor creating *additional lower pay scales* for all new employees hired.
6. If it would help keep my store from closing, I would personally favor lowering the onboard rates down to those of the hereafter rates.
7. If it would help keep the company from closing all its stores in this area, I would personally favor lowering the onboard rates down to those of the hereafter rates.
8. I would personally favor raising the hereafter rates up to those of the onboard employees even though the onboards would get a much smaller increase than the hereafter employees.
9. If it would help me get a larger raise in the next contract, I would personally favor reducing the fringe benefits for all new employees hired.
10. If it would help raise the current hereafter rates up to the onboard rates in the next contract, I would personally favor creating lower pay scales for all new employees hired.

11. The hereafter-onboard rate differences have created tensions between the hereafter and onboard employees.

12. Our company probably expects to LOWER the pay of the onboard employees to hereafter pay rates in some future negotiation.

13. Our union officers probably expect to RAISE the pay of the hereafter employees to the onboard pay rates in some future negotiation.

14. Hereafter pay rates should only be implemented when the employer's current level of pay is high relative to the competition.

15. When a union negotiates hereafter-onboard rate differences, it is still treating all its members fairly.

16. The hereafter-onboard rate differences have created internal membership political problems for Local [X].

Appendix B
Scales

The first four scales were adapted from the work of Martin and Peterson (1987). All item references are to appendix A.

1. Pay Fairness, items 23 to 26, section 1.
2. Union Instrumentality, items 4, 13, and 21, section 1.
3. Company Commitment, items 14, 15, and 16, section 1.
4. Union Commitment, items 18, 19, and 20, section 1.

The following three scales were adapted from the *Michigan Organizational Assessment Package* (Institute for Social Research, 1975).

5. Pay Satisfaction, items 7 and 8, section 1, and item 3, section 2.
6. Job Satisfaction, items 2, 17, and 22 (reverse scored).
7. Perceived Employment Mobility (all items were reverse scored) items 3 and 12, section 1, item 1, section 2. The last item is from Danserau, Cashman, and Graen (1973).

8. The "Self-Reported Effort" scale was adapted from the work of Allen and Keaveny (1985), and consisted of items 8, 9, and 11, section 1.
9. The "Union Activities" scale was adapted from the work of Magenau, Martin, and Peterson (1988), and consisted of items 1, 3-1, 3-6, 3-7, 3-8, 3-9, 5, and 6, section 7.
10. The scale, "Satisfaction with Number of Hours," was developed specifically for this study and consisted of item 1, section 1 and the following item taken from the demographic and background variables section. If you had a choice, would you work:
    More scheduled hours each week . . . 1
    Less scheduled hours each week . . . 2
    The same number of scheduled hours each week . . . 3
    (Choice 1 was recoded to 2.)

Appendix C
Tiers and Store Productivity

Wage bill savings resulting from the implementation and maintenance of a tiered compensation structure may not translate directly into cost savings if the reduced cooperation of labor leads to decreased productivity, and the unit labor costs (defined as payroll costs per dollar of output) increase.

The discussion in chapter 4 indicated that the implementation of tiers at Mayway led to labor cost savings and facilitated the company's expansion plans. Yet a critical question which needs to be addressed concerns the relationship of a tiered compensation structure to store productivity at Mayway. A predominant perception found in the literature reviewed in chapter 2 is that low-tier employees are less productive than high-tier employees (e.g., Ross 1985; Salpukas 1987). This perception is in accordance with predictions derived from equity theory (see chapter 7), which suggests that the greater perceived pay inequity of low-tier employees may be negatively associated with work-related behaviors. The studies reviewed in chapter 2, however, do not adequately answer the question at hand; these studies suggest that the impact may vary depending on the situation. Likewise, no relationship was reported in chapter 7 between employee tier level and the productivity-related measures of self-reported effort and absenteeism.

Given the concerns about the potentially negative impact of permanent wage tiers and other tier forms on employee productivity, we attempted to examine this relationship. Although other methods, such as cohort analyses, may more adequately address the proposition that low-tier employees are less productive than high-tier employees, with the data available we examined the relationship between the proportion of employees on the low levels of each of the tier forms and productivity across stores. We believe other factors being equal, that if low-tier employees were less productive than high-tier employees, it would follow that the greater the proportion of employees on a low-tier form within a store, the lower that store's productivity would be.

Productivity Measurement

Simply and broadly defined, productivity is the ratio between the inputs that go into producing a particular product or service and the outputs, the actual product or service itself (Barocci and Wever 1985). Barocci and Wever note that the inputs may include capital, labor, intermediates (purchased goods and services), and energy. Outputs would be the quantity or dollar value produced. Partial measures can be used to determine the productivity of specific in-

229

puts. Thus the formula used to measure labor productivity is simply outputs divided by labor inputs.

Greenberg (1975), in a review of productivity definitions and concepts, notes that the most common type of productivity ratio is labor productivity, usually expressed as output per man-hour. He contends that the most appropriate productivity index, conceptually, "would be one in which the output component is obtained by combining the different products or services with weights equal to the hourly earnings assignable to each product or service" (p. 7). Such an index would take into account the disparities in compensation present in a tiered-employment situation. The use of labor costs as opposed to labor hours as an input, however, is not completely accepted by economists because earnings generally rise over time (Greenberg 1975; Siegel 1983). The use of labor hours as an input (with the outputs stated in terms of quantity of units produced) is a more useful index for determining changes in productivity over time. Determining changes in productivity is less reliable when unit labor costs are used. Because of its simplicity, however, Siegel states that, "In business circles, unit labor cost, which is of interest in its own right, is frequently commended as a better measure of productivity than productivity itself!" (p. 31). In fact, Hochner, Granrose, Goode, Simon, and Applebaum (1988), in their discussion of retail food store economic outcomes, argue that unit labor costs are conceptually very closely related to productivity.

Store Productivity Indices

The number of hours worked should be included in an input quantity (denominator), given that hours can be increased or varied according to store sales volume. Also, any determination of store productivity must recognize that the hours worked can be expanded as store interior is redesigned to increase or vary the mix of products. Further, the dollar costs of the hours worked must be included in the input to incorporate the differences in compensation due to tiers. The average hourly wage, as defined in note 2 of chapter 5, incorporates both the individual employee hours worked and pay rates. Multiplying the average hourly wage by the number of employees in a store gives the total average hourly payroll used in this study as the input for the store productivity index. This input incorporates the rates of employees in high- and low-paid job classifications and on the high and low levels of the different tier forms and incorporates individual differences in the hours worked.[1]

The output quantity (numerator) included in this study's productivity index for retail stores is dollar sales. Due to the highly competitive nature of the retail food industry, Mayway's sales figures on a store by store basis were not available for analysis. Thus, a reasonable sales estimate had to be determined from a proxy. That sales proxy was lottery ticket sales as obtained from the state lottery bureau. The lottery tickets were sold along with groceries and other merchandise at Mayway's checkout lanes.[2] Analyses of sales data for eight stores from a competitor[3] revealed a significant positive correlation ($r = .84$, $p < .01$) between the lottery ticket sales and total store sales.[4]

Further examination of unpublished data from the state lottery bureau indicated that lottery tickets were sold differentially to various population segments and differentially between urban and rural areas. Since the surveyed stores in the urban and rural areas served differing socioeconomic groups, it is possible that lottery ticket sales represented different proportions of total store sales. To check for that possibility, store lottery ticket sales were first divided by the total weekly hours worked in each store to adjust ticket sales, at least in part, for store sales volume. A two-way ANOVA was then carried out on (1) area (urban or rural) and (2) store status ("old" or "new") with the result of the previous division as the dependent variable.[5]

That analysis revealed no significant effects, suggesting that lottery ticket sales at Mayway did not represent significantly different proportions of total store sales by area and store status. Further, there were significant ($p < .001$) correlations between lottery ticket sales and two other factors closely related to potential store sales volume (Food Marketing Institute 1986): the number of employees in a store ($r = .82$) and the sales floor space ($r = .79$). The high correlation between lottery ticket sales and total store sales for the competitor, as well as the other characteristics of lottery ticket sales at Mayway discussed above, suggested that the two sales figures would be significantly correlated at Mayway.

Therefore, the productivity index used in this study is the lottery ticket sales divided by the total average hourly payroll.[6] Due to the potential unknown character of lottery ticket sales as a measure of total store sales, we recognize that the productivity index used in the analyses is a rough estimate that may not have captured systematic differences in store productivity.

Tiers and the Productivity Index

Table C.1 repeats some of the most relevant store characteristics from the tables in chapter 5, as well as adding the following: total average hourly payroll (the number of employees multiplied by the average hourly wage), sales proxy figure, and productivity index (sales proxy figure divided by total average hourly payroll). Using the store as the unit of analysis, we can now look at the relationship between tiers and productivity and examine whether a greater

Table C.1
Summary of Mayway Store Characteristics

Subarea and store number	Number of employees (1)	Percent of low-wage tier (2)	Average hourly wage (3)	Total average hourly payroll (4)=1x3	Sales proxy (5)	Productivity index (6)=5/4
Cyclical industrial[a]						
1*	475	71.2	7.06	3353.50	63,694	18.99
2*	451	72.7	7.10	3202.10	58,500	18.27
3	266	86.2	6.33	1683.78	38,500	22.87
4	321	94.4	6.64	2131.44	33,000	15.48
5	338	89.1	6.61	2234.18	31,000	13.88
Outer suburban[a]						
6*	515	78.1	6.65	3424.75	52,000	15.18
7	397	94.2	5.95	2362.15	28,500	12.07
Suburban[a]						
8*	614	77.7	6.37	3911.18	63,752	16.30
9*	594	82.3	6.82	4051.08	52,500	12.96
10	439	95.0	6.29	2761.31	51,809	18.76
Rural center						
11*	231	71.0	6.08	1404.48	32,500	23.14
12	275	90.9	5.97	1641.75	37,000	22.54
Balanced						
13*	339	70.8	6.37	2159.43	30,000	13.89
14*	453	72.8	6.14	2781.42	41,500	14.92
15	289	93.4	5.74	1658.86	30,500	18.39
Stable industrial						
16*	156	62.8	6.61	1031.16	16,000	15.52
17	337	85.2	5.34	1799.58	25,000	13.89

a. These subareas are all urban, the remainder are rural.

*Represents an "Old Store" opened before the two-tier wage structure was negotiated.

proportion of low-tier employees is related to lower store productivity. To test this proposition, correlations were computed between the proportion of store employees on the low levels of three tier forms (wage, employment-status, and job-duty) and the store productivity index. A statistically significant negative correlation would mean that the higher the proportion of low-tier employees on the particular tier form, the lower the store productivity as measured by the index used here.[7]

Due to the significant differences among the stores as discussed in chapter 5,[8] the following five sets of correlations between the proportion of employees on the low level of three tier forms and the productivity index were computed: (1) the 10 urban stores; (2) the 7 rural stores; (3) the 9 old stores; (4) the 8 new stores; and (5) all of the 17 stores together. Analyses using all Mayway stores, while providing a larger sample size and thus more statistical power could be confounded by combining stores from different areas and old and new stores. Separate analyses by area and by store status were thus carried out to control partially for possible differences in store ticket sales and the input components of the productivity index. The results of these analyses indicated that only one of 15 correlation coefficients (five sets of three correlations) was significant; the significant correlation was opposite in direction to the stated proposition. Thus, the stated proposition was not supported.

Another method of testing the proposition was to examine the store sales and productivity data for each of the six subareas, i.e., county groupings (see chapter 5). Greenberg (1975) notes that the characteristics of store workforces, which vary according to labor market differences, could affect productivity. This examination reduced some of the confounding effects of subarea and socioeconomic differences; however, the method was only possible for the wage-tier form.[9] As shown in table C.1, every new store had a higher proportion of employees on the low-wage tier than every old store. Thus, a comparison was made between the productivity of old and new stores within each subarea.

When the data presented in table C.1 are examined by subarea, three different types of relationships emerged between store status and the productivity index. Within three of the subareas, Rural Center, Stable Industrial and Outer Suburban, the old store had a slightly higher productivity index. Within the Suburban and Balanced subareas, the new store had a higher productivity index. Finally, no clear relationship emerged between old and new stores among the five stores in the Cyclical Industrial subarea. Overall, examining the store data in this manner showed no consistent pattern. Thus, the results of the above analyses do not support the predominant perception that employees on low-tier levels are less productive.

Discussion

Given the presence of several limitations, any conclusions concerning the relationship between tiers and productivity must be considered tenuous. One must question whether the proxy measure used was a valid indicator of store sales at Mayway. Also, the conclusions are limited because the data assessed were from a single time period. Certainly, if the resources had allowed, using actual productivity data in a cohort analysis design would provide a more adequate examination of the proposition. Further, the very small sample size of stores from which data were collected and the division of stores by subarea suggest that extreme caution must be exercised in making any generalizations.

A final limitation is that the entire concept of productivity is different in the service and manufacturing sectors. Daft and Steers (1986) have identified two principal differences related to the concept of productivity between these sectors. First, the output of a service firm is intangible and cannot be stored in an inventory. Second, in the service sector, customers are involved in the production process; the customers and employees interact to deliver the service. Others have noted that these characteristics, particularly the customer contact, affect productivity in the service and manufacturing sectors differently (Greenberg 1975).[10]

It is likely that a closer relationship would be found, if one exists, between tiers and productivity in the manufacturing sector. Since most manufacturing sector industries only increase the number of hours worked, e.g., by adding a shift to increase production (i.e., the amount of product manufactured), it is likely that the number of employee hours worked is more directly related to production. Also, if the identical product were manufactured at multiple plants, plant location by itself should not be a cause of variability in labor productivity.[11] In contrast, for the service sector industries, labor productivity is dependent on the location served, and thus on the number of customers, their scheduling, and the amount and types of their purchases. As a result, a service sector company with geographically separated units likely would have varying productivity by location. Thus, where the distribution of employees on low-tier levels varies among manufacturing plants producing an identical product, it is likely that the relationship between tiers and productivity would be more directly evident than for a similar distribution of employees on the low-tier levels among firms offering the same service in the service sector.

Conclusion

This appendix has presented two different types of analyses which examined the relationship of tiers to a proxy measure of store productivity. The analyses indicate no consistent patterns to suggest that low-tier employees were more or less productive than high-tier employees. Any conclusions drawn from these analyses must be tenuous given the limitations in the design, and differences in the concept of productivity between service and manufacturing sectors.

NOTES

1. Analyses using the total weekly hours worked as the input of the productivity measure were also carried out. With one exception, the magnitude of the findings from these analyses were identical to those reported in this appendix. That exception was that within the Stable Industrial subarea, the new store had a much lower productivity index than the old store.

2. If an individual desired to purchase lottery tickets only, they were available at other more easily accessible licensed lottery outlets such as drug stores, newsstands, and liquor stores.

3. The eight stores of the competitor were in both urban and rural areas and geographically close to and in direct competition with the surveyed stores.

4. Lottery ticket sales were relatively stable between the first quarters of 1985 and 1986 for both Mayway and the competitor (for both companies, $r = .90$, $p < .001$).

5. Such an ANOVA was not carried out on the competitor stores' data given no "old" and "new" store classification and only two rural area stores.

6. All of the Mayway stores across the state were open the same number of hours, thus simplifying the calculations used.

7. The store-status tier form was not analyzed in this manner given no variance within the two types of stores, i.e., old or new. An analysis of variance on store status using area as the covariate (with the productivity index as the dependent variable) found no significant store status or covariate effect.

8. Analyses in chapter 5 indicated that urban stores compared to rural stores had significantly more employees ($p < .001$), a significantly higher average hourly wage ($p < .05$), and a significantly greater proportion of employees on the low-wage tier ($p < .001$). The same data also indicate that new stores compared to old stores had significantly fewer employees ($p < .05$), a significantly lower average hourly wage ($p < .05$), and a significantly greater proportion of employees on the low-wage tier ($p < .001$). The proportion of employees on the low level of the other tier forms did not differ significantly between either urban or rural stores or old or new stores.

9. The data presented in chapter 5 indicate that the proportion of employees on the low level of the employment-status and job-duty tier forms did not vary systematically by store status within all subareas.

10. Other service industries which have implemented tiered compensation structures, such as the airline industry, share many of the characteristics that differentiate the retail food industry from industries in the manufacturing sector. The number of customers both for a particular retail food store and for a route of a specific airline is dependent on the competition, the type of market served, and the services offered.

11. There may be some variability in productivity by plant location related to the characteristics of the different labor markets from which the plants hire their workforces.

REFERENCES

Adams, Edward F., Dennis R. Laker, and Charles L. Hulin. "An Investigation of the Influence of Job Level and Functional Specialty on Job Attitudes and Perceptions," *Journal of Applied Psychology* 62 (1977): 335-343.

Adams, J. Stacy. "Inequity in Social Exchange," in *Advances in Experimental Social Psychology,* edited by Leonard Berkowitz (New York: Academic Press, 1965).

_____. "Toward an Understanding of Inequity," *Journal of Abnormal and Social Psychology* 67 (1963): 422-436.

Allen, Robert E. and Timothy J. Keaveny. "Some Implications of Having Wages Red-Circled," *Proceedings of the Thirty-Seventh Annual Meeting,* Industrial Relations Research Association, Madison, WI, 1985.

Anderson, John C. "Local Union Participation: A Re-examination," *Industrial Relations* 18 (1979): 18-31.

Angle, Harold L. and James L. Perry. "An Empirical Assessment of Organizational Commitment and Organizational Effectiveness," *Administrative Science Quarterly* 26 (1981): 1-14.

Apcar, Leonard M. "Railroads, Big Union Tentatively Agree on New Pact That Includes Concessions," *Wall Street Journal* (June 24, 1985): 19.

Arouca, Dennis A. "Railroad Collective Bargaining—Anatomy or Pathology?" *Proceedings of the Thirty-Seventh Annual Meeting,* Industrial Relations Research Association, Madison, WI, 1985.

Ballagh, James H. "An Overview of the Problem and Forecast for 1985," in *Employee Relations Outlook: Impact of Foreign and Domestic Competition,* edited by James H. Ballagh (Los Angeles: UCLA Institute of Industrial Relations, 1985).

Balliet, Lee. "Labor Solidarity and the Two-Tier Collective Bargaining Agreement," Paper presented at the Thirty-Seventh Annual Meeting, Industrial Relations Research Association, Dallas, Texas, December 1984.

Barocci, Thomas A. and Kirsten R. Wever. "A Primer on Productivity Measurement," in *Human Resource Management and Industrial Relations: Text, Readings, and Cases,* edited by Thomas A. Kochan and Thomas A. Barocci (Boston: Little, Brown, 1985).

Bell, Daniel. *The Coming of the Post-Industrial Society* (New York: Basic Books, 1973).

Bernstein, Aaron and Zachary Schiller. "The Double Standard That's Setting Worker Against Worker," *Business Week* (April 8, 1985): 70-71.

Block, Richard N., Morris M. Kleiner, Myron Roomkin, and Sidney W. Salsburg. "Industrial Relations and the Performance of the Firm: An Overview," in *Human Resources and the Performance of the Firm*, edited by Morris M. Kleiner, Richard N. Block, Myron Roomkin, and Sidney W. Salsburg (Madison, WI: Industrial Relations Research Association, 1987).

Borum, Joan, James Conley and Edward Wasilewski. "Collective Bargaining in 1987: Local, Regional Issues to Set Tone," *Monthly Labor Review* 111 (January 1987): 23-36.

Bowers, Mollie H. and Roger D. Roderick. "Two-Tier Pay Systems: The Good, the Bad and the Debatable," *Personnel Administrator* 34 (June 1987): 101-102, 104, 106-108, 112.

Brophy, Beth and Maureen Walsh. "Thanks for the Bonus, But Where's My Raise?" *U.S. News and World Report* (July 20, 1987): 43-44.

Brown, Francis C., III and Teri Agins. "AMR Won't Bid to Take Over Pan American," *Wall Street Journal* (February 24, 1987): 2.

Bureau of Labor Statistics. *Employment and Earnings* 35 (March 1988).

Bureau of National Affairs, Inc. "Agreements with Two-Tier Wage Plans Continue to Decline in 1987, Study Says," *Daily Labor Report* (March 1, 1988): B1-B3.

_____ . "Agreements with Two-Tier Wage Plans Continue to Decline in 1987, Study Says," *Labor Relations Week* (March 2, 1988): 201-202.

_____ . *Changing Pay Practices: New Developments in Employee Compensation, A BNA Special Report* (Washington, DC: Bureau of National Affairs, Inc., 1988).

_____ . "Economic Trends," *Labor Relations Week* (January 25, 1989): 82-83.

_____ . "Economic Trends," *Labor Relations Week* (March 15, 1989): 253-254.

_____ . "Employer Bargaining Objectives, 1989," *Collective Bargaining Negotiations and Contracts* 1131 (October 6, 1988): 951-958.

_____ . "First-Year Wage Increase Slides to Five-Year Low: Lump-Sums Spread," *Daily Labor Report* (January 20, 1987): B1-B5.

_____ . "IRRA Panelists Address Two-Tier Implications for Fair Representation and Equal Opportunity," *Daily Labor Report* (January 10, 1985): A5-A7.

_____ . "Lump-Sum Pay Provisions," *Collective Bargaining Negotiations and Contracts* 1091 (March 26, 1987): 17-18.

_____ . "Machinists at Northwest Airlines Considering 10 Percent Pay Hike, Two-Tier Pay in New Pact," *Daily Labor Report* (June 17, 1985): A12-A13.

_____ . "Northwest Flight Attendants' Committee Puts Tentative Pact to Vote of Membership," *Daily Labor Report* (March 29, 1988): A10-A11.

————. "Two-Tier Wage Systems Still on Rise, Reported in 11 Percent of 1985 Pacts," *Retail/Services Labor Report* (February 24, 1986): 216-219.

————. "Two-Tier Wage Plans—1988," *What's New in Collective Bargaining Negotiations and Contracts,* 1141, Part 2 (February 23, 1989).

————. "Two-Tier Wage Plans," *What's New in Collective Bargaining Negotiations and Contracts* 1089, Part 2 (February 26, 1987): 461-462.

————. "Two-Tier Wage Systems Found More Common in Nonmanufacturing Sector," *Daily Labor Report* (February 20, 1985): B1-B4.

————. "Wages and Benefits: First-Three-Quarters 1987," *Collective Bargaining Negotiations and Contracts* 1105 (October 8, 1987): 1001-1004.

Business Week. "Greyhound Collides Head On with its Union." (November 21, 1983): 47.

————. "How Low Inflation Stings the Supermarkets." (March 19, 1984): 34.

————. "Slim Pickings for Supermarket Workers." (August 27, 1984): 26.

————. "Supermarket Workers Are Facing Leaner Years." (December 28, 1981): 54-55.

Cappelli, Peter. "Concession Bargaining and the National Economy," *Proceedings of the Thirty-Fifth Annual Meeting,* Industrial Relations Research Association, Madison, WI, 1983.

————. "Competitive Pressures and Labor Relations in the Airline Industry," *Industrial Relations* 24 (1985a): 316-338.

————. "Plant-Level Concession Bargaining," *Industrial and Labor Relations Review* 39 (1985b): 90-104.

Cappelli, Peter and Timothy A. Harris. "The Changing System of Airline Industrial Relations," *Proceedings of the Thirty-Seventh Annual Meeting,* Industrial Relations Research Association, Madison, WI, 1985.

Cappelli, Peter and Peter D. Sherer. "Assessing Worker Attitudes Under a Two-Tier Wage Plan." Working paper #726, Wharton School of the University of Pennsylvania, November 1987.

————. "Satisfaction, Market Wages, and Labor Relations: An Airline Study," *Industrial Relations* 27 (1988): 56-73.

Carrell, Michael R. and John E. Dittrich. "Employee Perceptions of Fair Treatment," *Personnel Journal* 55 (1976): 523-524.

Craft, James A., Suhail Abboushi, and Trudy Labovitz. "Concession Bargaining and Unions: Impacts and Implications," *Journal of Labor Research* 6 (1985): 167-180.

Crawley, Nancy. "Two-Tiered Pay Scales on the Decline," *Grand Rapids Press* (March 27, 1988): D1-D2.

Cronbach, Lee J. "Coefficient Alpha and the Internal Structure of Tests," *Psychometrics* 6 (1951): 297-334.

Daft, Richard L. and Richard M. Steers. *Organizations: A Micro/Macro Approach* (Glenview, IL: Scott, Foresman, 1986).

Dalton, Dan R. and Idalene F. Kesner. "The Windfall Account of Employee Turnover Extended: Implications for Two-Tiered Salary Structures," *Journal of Business Research* 14 (1986): 269-278.

Dansereau, Fred Jr., James Cashman, and George Graen. "Expectancy as a Moderator of the Relationship Between Job Attitudes and Turnover," *Journal of Applied Psychology* 59 (1974): 228-229.

Detailed Tabulations from the Food Marketing Institute Speaks (Washington, DC: Food Marketing Institute, 1986).

Deutermann, William V., Jr. and Scott Campbell Brown. "Voluntary Part-Time Workers: A Growing Part of the Labor Force," *Monthly Labor Review* 101 (June 1978): 3-10.

Dittrich, John E. and Michael R. Carrell. "Organizational Equity Perceptions, Employee Job Satisfaction, and Departmental Absence and Turnover Rates," *Organizational Behavior and Human Performance* 24 (1979): 29-40.

Dornstein, Miriam. "Wage Reference Groups and Their Determinants: A Study of Blue-Collar and White-Collar Employees in Israel," *Journal of Occupational Psychology* 61 (1988): 221-235.

Dunlop, John T. "The Task of Contemporary Wage Theory," in *New Concepts in Wage Determination,* edited by George W. Taylor and Frank C. Pierson (New York: McGraw-Hill, 1957).

Essick, Charles E. "A Survey of Two-Tier Wage Systems," *Compensation and Benefits Management* 3 (1987): 229-232.

Estey, Marten S. "The Grocery Clerks: Center of Retail Unionism," *Industrial Relations* 7 (1968): 249-261.

Festinger, Leon. "A Theory of Social Comparison Processes," *Human Relations* 7 (1954): 117-140.

Flax, Steven. "Pay Cuts Before the Job Even Starts," *Fortune* (January 9, 1984): 75-77.

Fogel, Helen. "A 'Hot Issue' with Negotiators: Companies Push 2-Tier Wage Pacts," *Detroit Free Press* (November 24, 1985): 1D, 9D.

Fortune. "I Didn't Try to Break the Union." (January 9, 1984): 76-77.

Goodman, Paul S. "An Examination of Referents Used in the Evaluation of Pay," *Organizational Behavior and Human Performance* 12 (1974): 170-195.

————. "Social Comparison Processes in Organizations," in *New Directions in Organizational Behavior,* edited by Barry M. Staw and Gerald R. Salancik (Chicago: St. Clair Press, 1977).

241

Gordon, Michael E., John W. Philpot. Robert E. Burt, Cynthia A. Thompson, and William E. Spiller. "Commitment to the Union: Development of a Measure and an Examination of Its Correlates," *Journal of Applied Psychology* 65 (1980): 479-499.

Granrose, Cheryln S., Eileen Appelbaum, and Virendra Singh. "Saving Jobs Through Worker Buyouts: Economic and Qualitative Outcomes for Workers in Worker-Owned, QWL, and Non-QWL Supermarkets," *Proceedings of the Thirty-Eighth Annual Meeting,* Industrial Relations Research Association, Madison, WI, 1986.

Greenberg, Leon. "Definitions and Concepts," in *Collective Bargaining and Productivity,* edited by Gerald Somers, Arvid Anderson, Malcolm Denise, and Leonard Sayles (Madison, WI: Industrial Relations Research Association, 1975).

Hall, Douglas T. "Organizational Commitment: Theory, Research and Measurement." Working paper, Northwestern University, April 1979.

Hall, William K. "Survival Strategies for a Hostile Environment," *Harvard Business Review* 58 (1980): 75-85.

Harris, Roy J. Jr. "Boeing Accord Attacks Narrowing Pay Gap Between Skilled and Less-Skilled Workers," *Wall Street Journal* (October 11, 1983a): 33.

_____ . "Cost-Cutting Stance Seems Avoided In Wage Talks of Three Aerospace Firms," *Wall Street Journal* (September 9, 1983b): 8.

_____ . "More Concerns Set Two-Tier Pacts With Unions, Penalizing New Hires," *Wall Street Journal* (December 15, 1983c): 33.

Harvard Law Review. "Two-Tier Wage Discrimination and Duty of Fair Representation." (January 1985): 631-649.

Heneman, Herbert G., III. "Pay Satisfaction," in *Research in Personnel and Human Resources Management,* Vol. 3, edited by Kendrith M. Rowland and Gerald R. Ferris (Greenwich, CT: JAI Press, 1985).

Hills, Frederick S. "The Relevant Other in Pay Comparisons," *Industrial Relations* 19 (1980): 345-351.

Hochner, Arthur, Cherlyn S. Granrose, Judith Goode, Elaine Simon and Eileen Applebaum. *Job-Saving Strategies: Worker Buyouts and QWL* (Kalamazoo, MI: W.E. Upjohn Institute for Employment Research, 1988).

Hoerr, John and Dan Cook. "A Pioneering Pact Promises Jobs for Life," *Business Week* (December 31, 1984): 48-49.

Hofer, Charles W. and Dan Schendel. *Strategy Formulation: Analytical Concepts* (St. Paul, MN: West, 1978).

Holley, William H. and Kenneth M. Jennings. *The Labor Relations Process,* 3rd edition (New York: Dryden Press, 1988).

Homans, George. *Social Behavior: Its Elementary Forms* (New York: Harcourt, Brace and World, 1961).

Hoyman, Michele M. and Lamont Stallworth. "Participation in Local Unions: A Comparison of Black and White Members," *Industrial and Labor Relations Review* 40 (1987): 323-335.

Hulin, Charles L. and Milton R. Blood. "Job Enlargement, Individual Differences and Worker Responses," *Psychological Bulletin* 69 (1968): 41-55.

Institute for Social Research. *Michigan Organizational Assessment Package: Project Report II* (Ann Arbor, MI: Survey Research Center, 1975).

Jacoby, Sanford M. and Daniel J.B. Mitchell. "Management Attitudes Toward Two-Tier Pay Plans," *Journal of Labor Research* 7 (1986): 221-237.

Kassalow, Everett M. "Concession Bargaining—Something Old, But Also Something Quite New," *Proceedings of the Thirty-Fifth Annual Meeting,* Industrial Relations Research Association, Madison WI, 1983.

Katz, Harry C. and George T. Milkovich. "Introduction" to special report on flexible pay systems, *ILR Report* 24 (1986): 4-6.

Katz, Harry C., Thomas A. Kochan and Kenneth R. Gobeille. "Industrial Relations Performance, Economic Performance, and QWL Programs: An Interplant Analysis," *Industrial and Labor Relations Review* 37 (1983): 3-17.

Kochan, Thomas A., "How American Workers View Labor Unions," *Monthly Labor Review* 102 (January 1979): 23-31.

Kochan, Thomas A., Harry C. Katz and Robert B. McKersie. *The Transformation of American Industrial Relations* (New York, Basic Books, 1986).

Lengnick-Hall, Cynthia A. and Mark L. Lengnick-Hall. "Strategic Human Resources Management: A Review of the Literature and a Proposed Typology," *Academy of Management Review* 13 (1988): 454-470.

Lewis, Robert. "Many Companies Abandoning Once-Popular 2-Tier Pay Scales," *Ann Arbor News* (March 12, 1989).

Liggett, Malcolm H. "The Two-Tiered Labor-Management Agreement and the Duty of Fair Representation," Paper presented at the Thirty-Seventh Annual Meeting, Industrial Relations Research Association, Dallas, Texas, 1984.

Livernash, Robert E. "The Internal Wage Structure," in *New Concepts in Wage Determination,* edited by George W. Taylor and Frank C. Pierson (New York: McGraw-Hill, 1957).

Logan, Nancy, Charles A. O'Reilly, III and Karlene H. Roberts. "Job Satisfaction Among Part-Time and Full-Time Employees," *Journal of Vocational Behavior* 3 (1973): 33-41.

Lopatka, Kenneth T. "Developing Concepts in Title VII Law," in *Equal Rights and Industrial Relations*, edited by Leonard J. Hausman, Orley Ashenfelter, Bayard Rustin, Richard F. Schubert, and Donald Slaiman (Madison, WI: Industrial Relations Research Association, 1977).

Louis, Meryl Reis. "Surprise and Sense Making: What Newcomers Experience in Entering Unfamiliar Organizational Settings," *Administrative Science Quarterly* 25 (1980): 226-251.

Lublin, Joann S. "Teamster Rejection of Wage Concessions Seen as Setback for Union's Chief, Presser," *Wall Street Journal* (September 19, 1983): 5.

Magenau, John M., James E. Martin, and Melanie M. Peterson. "Dual and Unilateral Commitment Among Stewards and Rank-and-File Union Members," *Academy of Management Journal* 31 (1988): 359-376.

March, James G. and Herbert A. Simon. *Organizations* (New York: Wiley, 1958.)

Martin, James E. and Raymond T. Lee. "Use of Referents in the Evaluation of Pay in a Tiered-Wage Setting." Working paper, Department of Management and Organization Sciences, Wayne State University, 1989.

Martin, James E. and Melanie M. Peterson. "Two-Tier Wage Structures: Implications for Equity Theory," *Academy of Management Journal* 30 (1987): 297-315.

Martin, Joanne. "Relative Deprivation: A Theory of Distributive Justice for an Era of Shrinking Resources," in *Research in Organizational Behavior*, Vol. 3, edited by Barry M. Staw and Larry L. Cummings (Greenwich, CT: JAI Press, 1981).

Mellor, Earl F. and George D. Stamas. "Usual Weekly Earnings: Another Look at Intergroup Differences and Basic Trends," *Monthly Labor Review* 105 (April 1982): 15-24.

Merwin, John. "A Piece of the Action," *Forbes* (September 24, 1984) 146-148, 152, 156.

Miles, Raymond E., Charles C. Snow, Alan D. Meyer and Henry J. Coleman, Jr. "Organizational Strategy, Structure and Process," *Academy of Management Review* 3 (1978): 546-562.

Milkovich, George T. and Jerry M. Newman. *Compensation*, 2nd edition (Plano, TX: Business Publications, 1987).

Miller, Howard E. and James R. Terborg. "Job Attitudes of Part-Time and Full-Time Employees," *Journal of Applied Psychology* 64 (1979): 380-386.

Mitchell, Daniel J.B. "The 1982 Union Wage Concessions: A Turning Point for Collective Bargaining?" *California Management Review* 25 (1983): 78-92.

Mowday, Richard T. "Equity Theory Predictions of Behavior in Organizations," in *Motivation and Work Behavior*, 3rd edition, edited by Lyman W. Porter and Richard M. Steers (New York: McGraw-Hill, 1983).

244

Mowday, Richard T., Lyman W. Porter, and Richard M. Steers. *Employee-Organization Linkages: The Psychology of Commitment, Absenteeism, and Turnover* (New York: Academic Press, 1982).

National Commission on Food Marketing. *Organization and Competition in Food Retailing*, Technical Study No. 7 (Washington, DC: Government Printing Office, 1966).

Nollen, Stanley D. and Virginia H. Martin. *Alternative Work Schedules*, Parts 2 and 3. An AMA Survey Report (New York: AMACOM, 1978).

Northrup, Herbert R. and Gordon R. Storholm. *Restrictive Labor Practices in the Supermarket Industry* (Philadelphia: University of Pennsylvania Press, 1967).

O'Dell, Carla and Jerry McAdams. *A Full Report on the American Productivity Center/American Compensation Association National Survey of Nontraditional Reward and Human Resource Practices* (Houston, TX: American Productivity Center, 1986).

Oldham, Greg R., Carol T. Kulik, Lee P. Stepina, and Maureen L. Ambrose. "Relations Between Situational Factors and the Comparative Referents Used by Employees," *Academy of Management Journal* 29 (1986): 599-608.

Patchen, Martin. *The Choice of Wage Comparisons* (Englewood Cliffs, NJ: Prentice-Hall, 1961).

Ploscowe, Stephen A. "Two-Tier Compensation Plans," *ILR Report* 24 (1986): 23-28.

Pritchard, Robert D., Marvin D. Dunnette, and Dale W. Jorgenson. "Effects of Perceptions of Equity and Inequity on Worker Performance and Satisfaction," *Journal of Applied Psychology* 56 (1972): 75-94.

Ray, Philip E. "The Labor Relations Impact of Store Closings in the Retail Food Industry," *Labor Law Journal* 31 (1980): 482-486.

Retail/Services Labor Report (RSLR) published by the Bureau of National Affairs, various issues.

Rhodes, Susan R. and Richard M. Steers. "Conventional vs. Worker-Owned Organizations," *Human Relations* 34 (1981): 1013-1035.

Ronen, Simcha. "Equity Perception in Multiple Comparisons: A Field Study," *Human Relations* 39 (1986): 333-346.

Rosenblum, Marc J. "The EEO Implications of the Two-Tiered Agreement," Paper presented at the Thirty-Seventh Annual Meeting, Industrial Relations Research Association, Dallas, Texas, December 1984.

Ross, Arthur. *Trade Union Wage Policy* (Berkeley, CA: University of California Press, 1948).

Ross, Irwin. "Employers Win Big In the Move to Two-Tier Contracts," *Fortune* (April 29, 1985): 82, 84, 88, 92.

Ruben, George. "Labor-Management Scene in 1986 Reflects Continuing Difficulties," *Monthly Labor Review* 110 (1987): 37-48.

Salancik, Gerald R. "Commitment and the Control of Organizational Behavior and Belief," in *New Directions in Organizational Behavior,* edited by Barry M. Staw and Gerald R. Salancik (Chicago: St. Clair Press, 1977).

Salancik, Gerald R. and Jeffrey Pfeffer. "A Social Information Processing Approach to Job Attitudes and Task Design," *Administrative Science Quarterly* 23 (1978): 224-253.

Salpukas, Agis. "Cutting Airline Labor Costs," *New York Times* (January 25, 1984): 23, 26.

_____ . "The Two-Tier Wage Impact," *New York Times* (October 30, 1985): D1, D6.

_____ . "The 2-Tier Wage System Is Found To Be 2-Edged Sword by Industry," *New York Times* (July 21, 1987): 1, 47.

Seaberry, Jane. 'Two-Tiered Wages: More Jobs vs. More Worker Alienation," *Washington Post* (April 7, 1985): G1, G3.

Sichenze, Celeste M. "An Exploratory Study of Two-Tier Labor Contracts in the Retail Food Industry," *Proceedings of the Forty-First Annual Meeting,* Industrial Relations Research Association, Madison, WI, 1989.

_____ . "An Exploratory Study of Two-Tier Labor Contracts in the Retail Food Industry." Unpublished doctoral dissertation. George Washington University, Washington, DC, 1988.

Siegel, Irving H. "Work Ethic and Productivity," in *The Work Ethic—A Critical Analysis,* edited by Jack Barbash, Robert J. Lampman, Sar A. Levitan, and Gus Tyler (Madison, WI: Industrial Relations Research Association, 1983).

Schuster, Jay R. and Barbara Clark. "Individual Differences Related to Feelings Toward Pay," *Personnel Psychology* 23 (1970): 591-604.

Staw, Barry M. "Attitudinal and Behavioral Consequences of Changing a Major Organizational Reward: A Natural Field Experiment," *Journal of Personality and Social Psychology* 29 (1974): 741-751.

Suls, Jerry M. and Richard L. Miller. *Social Comparison Processes* (Washington, DC: Hemisphere, 1977).

Summers, Clyde. "Individual Rights in Arbitration," in *Arbitration in Practice,* edited by Arnold M. Zack (Ithaca, NY: ILR Press, 1984).

Summers, Timothy P., John H. Betton, and Thomas A. DeCotiis. "Voting For and Against Unions: A Decision Model," *Academy of Management Review* 11 (1986): 643-655.

Telly, Charles S., Wendell L. French and William G. Scott. "The Relationship of Inequity to Turnover Among Hourly Workers," *Administrative Science Quarterly* 16 (1971): 164-171.

246

Thomas, Steven L. "Some Observations on the Impact of Two-Tier Collective Bargaining on Firm Performance." Paper presented at the Midwest Academy of Management Meetings, Toledo, OH, April 1988.

Treiman, Donald J. and Heidi I. Hartmann, editors. *Women, Work, and Wages: Equal Pay for Jobs of Equal Worth* (Washington: National Academy Press, 1981).

Uchitelle, Louis. "Bonuses Replace Wage Rises and Workers are the Losers," *New York Times* (June 26, 1987): A-1, D-3.

Vecchio, Robert P. "Models of Psychological Inequity," *Organizational Behavior and Human Performance* 34 (1984): 266-282.

Wall Street Journal. "The Two-Tier System Is Working Well at GM's Delco Plant in Rochester, N.Y." (October 14, 1985): 9.

Walsh, David J. "Accounting for the Proliferation of Two-Tier Wage Settlements in the U.S. Airline Industry, 1983-1986," *Industrial and Labor Relations Review* 42 (1988): 50-62.

Walsh, John P. "Technological Change and the Division of Labor in Retail Trade: The Supermarket Industry from WWII to the Present." Unpublished doctoral dissertation, Northwestern University, Evanston, IL, 1988.

Weick, Karl E. "The Concept of Equity in the Perception of Pay," *Administrative Science Quarterly* 11 (1967): 414-439.

Wessel, David. "Split Personality: Two-Tier Pay Spreads but the Pioneer Firms Encounter Problems," *Wall Street Journal* (October 14, 1985): 1, 9.

Wiener, Yoash and Yoav Vardi. "Relationships between Job, Organization, and Career Commitments and Work Outcomes—An Integrative Approach," *Organizational Behavior and Human Performance* 26 (1980): 81-96.

Winter, Ralph E. "New Givebacks: Even Profitable Firms Press Workers to Take Permanent Pay Cuts," *Wall Street Journal* (March 6, 1984): 1, 24.

INDEX

Abboushi, Suhail, 15, 45
Absenteeism, 49
Adams, Edward F., 133
Adams, J Stacy, 17, 171, 172, 173, 181
Aerospace industry, 34-35
Agins, Teri, 36-37
Airline Deregulation Act of 1978, 36
Airline industry, 36-38
Allen, Robert E., 227
Amalgamated Meat Cutters and Butcher Workmen of North America. *See* Meat Cutters union
Amalgamated Transit Union, 37
Ambrose, Maureen L., 173
American Airlines, 36-37, 41, 47
American Federation of Labor-Congress of Industrial Organization (AFL-CIO), 81
Anderson, John C., 195, 202n14
Angle, Harold L., 185
A&P. *See* Great Atlantic and Pacific Tea Company (A&P)
Apcar, Leonard M., 38
Applebaum, Eileen, 47, 230
Arouca, Dennis A., 38

Ballagh, James H., 29
Balliet, Lee, 15, 43, 44, 45, 55, 152, 183
Bargaining associations, multi-employer, 67-68, 72, 78
Bargaining process: elements creating change in, 72-78; for Mayway at state level, 94-102; Mayway refusal to enter Retail Clerks, 84; tiers in concession, 12, 15 95-96; tier structure under collective, 4-5
Barocci, Thomas A., 229
Bell, Daniel, 26
Benefit tiers, 6, 76-77, 99
Bernstein, Aaron, 40, 43, 44, 45, 47, 56, 57, 78, 145, 174, 214
Betton, John, 182
Block, Richard N., 27
Blood, Milton R., 133
Boeing, 35
Borum, Joan, 57
Bowers, Mollie H., 18n8, 40, 43, 44, 45, 46, 48, 52, 53, 145, 166
Brophy, Beth, 58

Brown, Francis C., III, 36-37
Brown, Scott Campbell, 169n8
Bureau of Labor Statistics, 26
Bureau of National Affairs, Retail/Services Labor Reports (RSLR), 69, 70, 71, 72, 73, 74, 75, 76, 77, 78, 79n2, 206, 214
Bureau of National Affairs (BNA), 12, 13, 18nn3,4, 21, 26, 29, 32, 42, 47, 48, 51-52, 55-58, 61n5, 62n13, 79n9
Business Week, 37, 73, 74, 79n5

Cappelli, Peter, 2, 3, 10, 13, 14, 19nn11,14, 27, 32, 36, 37, 40, 61nn7,8, 173, 174, 177, 178, 185, 186, 201n6, 203, 212
Carrell, Michael R., 172, 182, 184, 193
Cashman, James, 227
Chain stores: conflict in multi-employer bargaining of, 68; definition of, 63; development of, 64-65; labor costs for, 67-68; unionization of, 66-67, 88, 90-91
Civil Rights Act of 1964, Title VII, 52-53
Clark, Barbara, 182
Compensation policies, 2, 13
Competition in retail food industry, 69-72, 78-79
Competitive advantage, 12-15
Concession bargaining, 12, 15, 95-96
Conley, James, 57
Consolidated Rail Corporation, 38
Cook, Dan, 34
Craft, James A., 15, 45
Crawley, Nancy, 56
Cronbach, Lee J., 169n2

Dalton, Dan R., 41, 47
Danserau, Fred, Jr., 227
Data analysis, 126-28
DeCotiis, Thomas A., 182
Deregulation effects, 35-38
Deutermann, William V., Jr., 169n8
DFR. *See* Duty of fair representation (DFR) doctrine
Dittrich, John E., 172, 182, 184, 193
Dornstein, Miriam, 177
Dunlop, John T., 173
Dunnette, Marvin D., 172
Duty of fair representation (DFR) doctrine, 50-52

247

EEO. *See* Equal Employment Opportunity (EEO)

Electrical components, automotive, 33-34

Employees, full- and part-time. *See* Full-time employees; Part-time employees

Employees, low- and high-tier. *See* High-tier employees; Low-tier employees

Employers. *See* Managers/employers

Employment-status tier, 7, 76; at Mayway stores, 100, 122-23, 210; referents for, 179

Equal Employment Opportunity (EEO): interpretation of tiered structure under, 52-53

Equity restoration, 181-83, 193-95

Equity theory, 171-73, 181, 212-13; *See also* Referents

Essick, Charles E., 5, 18n2, 22, 43, 44, 47, 48, 49, 52, 55, 59, 61nn1,8, 214

Estey, Marten S., 65-66, 67

Festinger, Leon, 175

Flax, Steven, 40, 43, 53, 55, 107

Fogel, Helen, 42

Food Employer's Council (FEC), 78

Food Marketing Institute (FMI), 63, 67, 231

Ford Motor Co. v. *Huffman*, 50, 51

Fortune, 37

Foxworth v. *Airline Pilots Association*, 51

French, Wendell L., 184

Full-time employees, 7-9, 122-23; in Mayway case, 101-2

Gain sharing, 13

General merchandise (GM) employees: wage disparity with food department employees, 179; wage rates for, 82, 86, 91, 98-99

General Motors Delco Products, 33-34, 41

General Motors Packard Electric Division, 34

Geographic areas, 88, 107-8, 111

Giant Food, 47

GM. *See* General merchandise (GM) employees

Gobeille, Kenneth R., 49

Goode, Judith, 230

Goodman, Paul S., 172, 173

Gordon, Michael E., 185

Graen, George, 227

Granrose, Cherlyn S., 47

Gray v. *Asbestos Workers Local 51*, 50

Great Atlantic and Pacific Tea Company (A&P), 64, 75-76; store closing of, 70

Greenberg, Leon, 49, 230, 233, 234

Greyhound Lines, Inc., 37

Hall, Douglas T., 32, 185

Harris, Roy J., Jr., 14, 27, 34-35, 36, 44, 45, 107

Hartmann, Heidi I., 169n8

Harvard Law Review, 50

Heneman, Herbert G., III, 171

High-tier employees: benefit tiers for, 6; difference in wage rates from low-tier, 5, 22; equity perception of, 174-75; in Mayway labor agreements, 94-102; at Mayway stores, 121-23, 126; merge of low-tiered with, 22, 42; under permanent and temporary compensation structure, 2-5; potential benefits of tiers for, 39-40; potential problems for, 43-45; in retail food industry, 75; tiered wage rates for, 7-9; in union structure, 45-46, 50-52

High-wage employees: tiered wage rate referents for, 177-78

Hills, Frederick S., 171, 173

Hochner, Arthur, 230

Hoerr, John, 34

Hofer, Charles W., 19n9

Holley, William H., 9, 10, 11, 103, 208

Homans, George, 171, 185

Hoyman, Michele M., 195

Hughes Aircraft Company, 47, 48, 49

Hulin, Charles L., 133

Hypotheses related to low-tier employees, 183

Independent stores, 66, 95; definition of, 63; labor costs for, 67

Independent union, Mayway Company, 82-84

Industry sector, 32-39; *See also* Manufacturing sector; Railroad industry; Retail food industry; Transportation industries

Influences, external, 9, 11

Institute for Social Research, 227

Intercity bus transportation industry, 37

Intercity trucking industry, 37-38

International Brotherhood of Teamsters, 38, 64, 66, 69, 73, 78

International Union of Electrical Workers (IUE), 33

Jacoby, Sanford N., 2, 4, 5, 6, 15, 18n8, 19n11, 22, 38, 42, 44, 48, 49, 52, 53, 55, 60, 129n3, 153, 166, 203, 212, 214
Jennings, Kenneth M., 9, 10, 11, 103, 208
Job-duty tier, 6, 77, 82; at Mayway stores, 96, 99, 123, 210; referents for, 179
Job site friction, 44-45
Jorgenson, Dale W., 172

Kassalow, Everett M., 14, 26
Katz, Harry C., 11-12, 13, 14, 19nn11,12, 49, 54, 214
Keaveny, Timothy J., 227
Kesner, Idalene, 41, 47
Kleiner, Morris M., 27
Kochan, Thomas A., 11-12, 13, 19nn11,12, 49, 54, 182
Kroger stores, 71-72, 75-76
Kulik, Carol T., 173

Labor costs: effect of increased competition on, 69-70; introduction of tiers to reduce, 74-77; in retail food industry, 67-69, 73, 212
Labor-management relations, 9; benefits for groups in, 40-42; climate for, 48; external influences on, 9, 11; in retail food industry, 67-69
Labovitz, Trudy, 15, 45
Laker, Dennis R., 133
Lee, Raymond T., 121, 171, 172, 174, 177, 178, 201n7
Lengnick-Hall, Cynthia A., 12, 13
Lengnick-Hall, Mark L., 12, 13
Lewis, Robert, 56
Liggett, Malcolm H., 43, 51-52
Livernash, Robert, 173
Location tier, 6-7, 75-76
Lockheed Aircraft, 35, 41, 47
Logan, Nancy, 179
Lopatka, Kenneth T., 52
Louis, Meryl Reis, 178
Low-tier employees: benefits tier for, 6; difference in wage rates from high-tier, 5, 22; under equal opportunity rules, 52-53;

equity perception of, 174-75; hypotheses related to attitudes of, 183-87, 193-200; hypotheses related to behavior of, 181-83; incidence in industry sectors of, 32-39; in Mayway labor agreements, 94-102; at Mayway stores, 121-23, 126; merge with high-tiered, 22, 42; under permanent and temporary compensation structure, 2-5; potential benefits for, 39-40; potential benefits of tier contract for, 40; potential problems for, 43-45; tiered wage rates for, 7-9; in union structure, 45-46, 50-52
Low-wage employees: tiered wage rate referents for, 177-78
Lublin, Joann S., 38
Lucky stores, 78
Lump-sum payments, 13, 32, 42, 58, 102

McAdams, Jerry, 12, 58, 214
McDonnell-Douglas, 35
McGowan, Peter, 73
McKersie, Robert B., 11-12, 13, 19nn11,12, 54
Magenau, John M., 227
Managers/employers: potential benefit of tier contracts for, 41-42; potential problems for, 46-49; role in labor-management relations of, 10-11
Manufacturing sector: strategies and wage changes in employment in, 26-27; tiers in, 32, 33
March, James G., 184
Martin, James E., 121, 127, 130n11, 171, 172, 173, 174, 177, 178, 179, 198, 200, 201nn2,7, 207, 227
Martin, Joannne, 173, 175, 199, 201n3
Martin, Virginia H., 179
Mayway: costs and benefits of tiered compensation structure at, 208-10
Mayway Company: evolution of wage tiers in, 82-83; generalizing from this experience of, 210-12; high- and low-tier rates in, 86; labor agreements of, 94-102; labor-management relations in, 81-82, 84-85
Meat Cutters Union, 64, 65, 66, 69, 75, 78
Mellor, Earl F., 179
Merwin, John, 67, 69, 70, 71, 72

Miles, Raymond E., 15
Milkovich, George T., 12, 13, 14, 171, 214
Miller, Howard E., 179
Miller, Richard L., 175
Mitchell, Daniel J. B., 2, 4, 5, 6, 14, 15, 18n8, 19n11, 22, 38, 42, 44, 48, 49, 52, 53, 55, 60, 129n3, 153, 166, 203, 212, 214
Morale of employees, 43, 44-45
Mowday, Richard T., 17, 172, 173, 181, 182, 184, 185, 201n1

National Commission on Food Marketing (NCFM), 64-65, 69
National Labor Relations Act (1935), 66
National Labor Relations Board (NLRB), 82-85
Newman, Jerry M., 171
Nixon, Richard, 72
Nollen, Stanley D., 179
Northrop, Herbert R., 64, 65, 66-67, 68, 70, 72, 79n1

O'Dell, Carla, 12, 58, 214
Oldham, Greg R., 173, 201n
O'Reilly, Charles A., 179

Pan American World Airlines, 37
Participants in labor-management relations, 9
Part-time employees, 7-9, 122-23, 184; hypotheses for behavior to restore equity by, 193-95; in Mayway case, 99, 101-2
Patchen, Martin, 171, 180
Pay, knowledge-based, 13
Pay referents. See Referents
Perry, James L., 185
Peterson, Melanie, 127, 130n11, 171, 173, 174, 179, 198, 200, 201n2, 207, 227
Pfeffer, Jeffrey, 201n3
Ploscowe, Stephen A., 15, 40, 41, 42, 44, 46, 48, 51, 52, 56, 57, 59, 77, 145, 183, 214
Porter, Lyman W., 184, 185
Pritchard, Robert D., 172
Productivity, 48-49
Profit sharing, 13
Progression schedule. See Wage progression
Propositions for testing, 204-8
Public policy issues, 43, 49-50

Railroad industry, 37-38
Ray, Philip E., 70, 71
Referents; classes of, 172-73; for employment-status tier, 179; for job-duty tiers, 179; selection of, 174-80; for store-status tier, 180; for tiered wage rates, 177-78
Retail Clerks union (Retail Clerks International Association), 64, 65, 66, 69, 73, 83-85, 97
Retail food industry: characteristics of stores surveyed, 114-18; competition and store closings of, 69-72; effect of two-tier plans in, 38-39, 41, 46-47, 60; job-duty tier in, 6; location tier in, 6-7; nonunion market share in Mayway case, 85; tier introduction in, 74-77; types of stores in, 63; unionization of, 64-67
Retirement plans, early, 42
Rhodes, Susan R., 185
Roberts, Karlene H., 179
Roderick, Roger D., 18n8, 40, 43, 44, 45, 46, 48, 52, 53, 145, 166
Ronen, Simcha, 173
Roomkin, Myron, 27
Rosenblum, Marc J., 53
Ross, Arthur, 173
Ross, Irwin, 2, 5, 6, 18n6, 35, 36, 39, 40, 41, 43, 44, 45, 47, 48, 49, 77, 107, 174, 182, 184, 198, 229
Ruben, George, 18n2, 40

Safeway Stores Company, 73, 78
Salancik, Gerald R., 201n3
Salpukas, Agis, 7, 36, 40, 42, 43, 44, 47, 48, 49, 60, 107, 182, 206, 229
Salsburg, Sidney W., 27
Schendel, Dan, 19n9
Schiller, Zachary, 40, 43, 44, 45, 47, 56, 57, 78, 145, 174, 214
Schuster, Jay R., 182
Scott, William G., 184
Seaberry, Jane, 41, 161, 174
Seniority, 2, 6, 43, 44-45
Service sector: effect of nonunion competition on industry in, 38-39; employment status tier in, 7; strategies and wage changes in employment in, 26-27
Sherer, Peter D., 2, 3, 61n8, 173, 174, 177,

178, 185, 186, 201n6, 203, 212
Sichenze, Celeste M., 18nn4,7, 39, 44, 46-47, 60, 62nn10,11, 75, 76, 77, 79n7
Siegel, Irving H., 49, 230
Simon, Elaine, 230
Simon, Herbert A., 184
Singh, Virendra, 47
Southwest Airlines, 37
Stallworth, Lamont, 195
Stamas, George D., 179
Staw, Barry M., 201n3
Steele v. Louisville and Nashville Railroad, 50-51
Steers, Richard M., 184, 185
Stepina, Lee P., 173
Stock ownership plans, 13
Store-status tier, 122
Storholm, Gordon R., 64, 65, 66-67, 68, 70, 72, 79n1
Strategy: See also Compensation policies; Tiers Strategy, business: in industrial relations theory, 11-12; tiers as, 12-15, 74-75
Strikes in retail food industry, 68, 72-73, 78, 84-85
Suls, Jerry M., 175
Summers, Clyde, 51
Summers, Timothy P., 182
Supermarket: definition of, 63; unionization of, 66

Teamsters' union. See International Brotherhood of Teamsters
Telly, Charles S., 184
Temporary tiers. See Tiered compensation structure
Terborg, James R., 179
Thomas, Steven L., 5, 22, 56
Tiered compensation structure, 13; effect on productivity of, 48-49; forms of, 5-7; incidence of, 53-55; at Mayway Company, 94-103; morale and job-site friction with, 44-45; morale of employees under, 44-45; permanent and temporary, 2-5, 22, 43; potential problems for labor-management groups, 43-49; prediction for future of, 213-15; wage and location tiers for, 75-76; See also Two-tier wage contracts

Tier groups: hypotheses related to attitudes of, 183-87; hypotheses related to behavior of, 181-83
Tiers: as business strategy, 13-15; merge of low- and high-, 22, 42; See also Tiered compensation structure; Wage rates, tiered
Trailways Corporation, 37
Transportation industries deregulation, 35-38
Treiman, Donald J., 169n8
Tunstall v. Brotherhood of Locomotive Firemen and Enginemen, 50-51
Two-tier wage contracts, 21-22, 26; in manufacturing and service sectors, 26-27, 29, 32; trends in implementation of, 55-60; See also Wage rates, tiered

Uchitelle, Louis, 58
UFCW. See United Food and Commercial Workers International Union (UFCW)
Union officials, 10-11
Unions: effect of tiered structure on, 45-46; potential benefits of tier contract for, 40-41; See also Duty of fair representation (DFR) doctrine; High-tier employees; low-tier employees
United Auto Workers (UAW), 33, 35
United Food and Commercial Workers International Union (UFCW), 45, 56, 57, 64, 72, 73-74, 94, 97, 101; position concerning tiers, 77-78, 79
United Steelworkers of America, 72

Vardi, Yoav, 186
Vecchio, Robert P., 172

Wage contracts, 26-27, 29; changes in kinds of
    settlements of, 73-74; two-tier, 21-22, 26-27, 29, 32, 55-60, 85; See also Wage rates, tiered
Wage-price controls, 72
Wage progression, 3-5, 7, 9, 22, 98-99; at Mayway stores, 123; merge time of low-tier with high-tier employee, 22; See also Full-time employees; High-tier employees; Low-tier employees; Part-time employees

Wage rates, tiered, 5, 102, 7-9, 75-76, 78-79; in Mayway stores, 85, 98, 100, 102, 121; referents for, 177-78

Wagner Act. *See* National Labor Relations Act (1935)

Wall Street Journal, 33, 34, 41

Walsh, David J., 35

Walsh, Maureen, 58

Ward's Cove Packing Co., Inc. v. *Atonio*, 62n12

Wasilewski, Edward, 57

Weick, Karl E., 173

Wessel, David, 6, 7, 42, 43, 45, 46, 47, 48, 77, 107, 162, 175, 184, 198, 206

Wever, Kirsten R., 229

Wiener, Yoash, 186

Work rules, 9, 10; *See also* Tiered compensaion structure; Wage contracts

Wynn, William H., 77